HIS SPIRIT IS WITH US

HIS SPIRIT IS WITH US

*A project approach to Christian Nurture
based on the Rite A Communion service*

Leslie Francis

COLLINS

Collins Liturgical Publications
187 Piccadilly, London W1V 9DA

ISBN 0 00 599684 8
First published 1981

Acknowledgements
Thanks are due for permission to reprint extracts from copyright material:
A. M. Allchin, *The World is a Wedding*, published and copyright 1978 Darton,
Longman & Todd, London; M. Quoist, *Prayers of Life*, Gill and Macmillan;
SCM Press Ltd for Alan Richardson, *Genesis 1-11*; and for Alan Richardson
(ed), *Dictionary of Christian Theology*, and *Theological Word Book of the
Bible*; Curtis Brown (Australia) Ltd, for Roger Bush, *Prayers for Pagans*.
Photographs by Mark Woodley.

Typographical design by Colin Reed
Typeset by Rowland Phototypesetting Ltd
Bury St Edmunds, Suffolk
Printed in Great Britain by
MacLehose, Glasgow

Contents

FOREWORD

The idea behind this programme of teaching material began during an after supper conversation between Paul Jenkins and myself. We worked together on the first stage of the programme to produce the picture communion book THE LORD IS HERE and AT THE LORD'S TABLE. Then Paul moved to a new job in another part of England, leaving me to develop our joint concept and to produce the second stage of our work alone.

A number of people have given me encouragement and help in developing this material. I am indebted to all the schools, churches, teachers, clergy and pupils who have tested the teaching units and commented on them. I owe a particular debt of gratitude to Linda Borthwick, Geoffrey Blackwell, Jim Cheeseman, Sue Chapman, Valerie Moore, Nicola Slee, Margaret Turk, Philip Welsh and Margaret Wickham.

A great part of this manuscript passed through the capable and careful hands of my secretary Elsie Pues. Sadly Elsie died on the very morning during which I was making one or two final corrections to the manuscript and when she was sharing my excitement at its completion. It is to her memory that I dedicate the finished work.

Great Wratting Rectory   Leslie Francis
January 1981

INTRODUCTION

The Church and the child

Recent research has highlighted the growing gap between young people and the churches. Nowhere is this gap more apparent than in public worship. Generally the young say that they are bored by church services. They are bored because much of what is happening is so completely different from what happens in the day to day culture of their environment. They are unable to integrate themselves into and to make sense of what is happening in the worship of the church.

Those of us who are familiar with church services easily forget how large the gap is between ourselves and the uninitiated. We tend to believe that the young person is able to drift into our services and immediately to feel at home. This is not the case for three reasons.

First, Christian worship rests upon assumptions which are not any longer common in our society, namely belief in God as Creator, man as creature, and Christ as Saviour. A generation or two ago these assumptions were generally transmitted through secular education and school assemblies, but this is no longer necessarily the case. The basic notion of man standing before God in the attitude of worship may therefore be quite unfamiliar to some young people.

Second, a large part of the content of public worship is strange to the young person. The singing of psalms disappeared from most schools some time ago, and now churches and schools no longer generally share the same hymnody. More fundamentally, the language and imagery of worship are based on scripture. Now that many young people are quite unfamiliar with the content of scripture, the images and themes recurrent in our worship lose their resonance.

Third, the method of instruction generally used in public worship is the form found in the lecture theatre or nineteenth century schoolroom. Current practice in primary schools has moved far away from this model. Young minds are no longer being trained to learn in this way and they find it difficult to adapt to the strange method employed by the church.

Faced with this situation, the churches need to discover new ways of bridging the gap between themselves and young people. It is not sufficient to translate the old form of service into modern language. The gap is not simply a linguistic one. It is a cultural gap. In order to find their place in public worship, the young need to be nurtured into the Christian heritage, and they need to be nurtured in ways which they find acceptable.

Christian nurture

The notion of Christian nurture is something different both from Christian education and religious education. The idea of nurture is to enable the child to grow and develop. The idea of Christian nurture is to enable the child to grow and to develop as a member of the Christian community and in the Christian way of life. Christian nurture is more than education about the Christian faith: it is an introduction to the culture and way of life that makes Christian people different from those who are not Christians.

The aim of this book is to provide material for a programme of Christian nurture within churches and church primary schools. This programme has grown from three basic principles. Theologically, I see the Eucharist as the central act of worship which gives the Christian church its distinctive character. Psychologically, I see the critical period for nurturing the child in the Eucharist to be between the ages of seven and eleven. Educationally, I believe that children learn by doing things, and by enjoying what they do.

My theological argument is that the primary purpose of Christian nurture is not merely that the child should possess a body of knowledge about the bible, about the history of the faith, or about the content of doctrine. Nor is it merely that the child should be familiar with and encouraged to adopt the Christian ethic or code of behaviour. Both knowledge and behaviour are secondary to a sense of belonging to the Christian community, and of feeling part of that community when it is celebrating its distinctive identity. First and foremost, I wish to nurture the child into feeling part of the community that celebrates the Eucharist. Subsequently, the child will want to ask about and to discover the implications of being part of that community in terms of belief and behaviour.

My psychological argument is that attitudes are of central importance in human development. Between the ages of seven and eleven children are beginning to develop the attitudes which will shape their later lives. At this stage attitudes are beginning to determine the areas in which the child will concentrate attention and about which he will learn to think maturely at a later stage. Unless positive attitudes are being developed towards the church at this age, little real learning is likely to take place for some years subsequently.

My educational argument is that the teaching methods and materials employed in the course of Christian nurture must be consistent with the expectations the child forms from his experience of the best secular education. The child needs to discover that what he most enjoys about his secular education has a rightful and respected place within the Christian community. On this account, Christian nurture is not about a different kind of educational activity, but about bringing the familiar aspects of education into contact with the worshipping community and with the Christ who stands at the centre of the worship.

The Child at the Eucharist

The Eucharist stands at the heart of Christian worship. It is the act of worship which is peculiar to the Christian community. Essentially it is the response of the Christian family to the request of their Lord. It is something which the whole Christian family does together, although different members of the family participate in it in different ways. It is a family occasion in which both the communicant and the non-communicant, the child and the adult have different but equally appropriate places. Without the child the eucharistic family is incomplete.

I do not propose to tackle the problem of the admission of children to receive the sacrament of communion. Views and customs vary on this issue from place to place. Whether the child receives the sacrament or not seems to me a secondary issue compared to whether the child is made to feel at home in the eucharistic community and whether he is given the opportunity to explore, to discuss and to come to an understanding of what he is doing as part of the community. If the child is admitted to receive communion at a young age, it is important to assure that this early admission does not detract from the significance of the sacrament at a later age. If the young child is not admitted to receive communion, it is important to assure that this is not interpreted by the child as a sign of rejection. In coming to a decision on this issue, it is also important to recognise the fact that the developing eucharistic community is likely to contain within its membership not only children who have not yet been admitted to receive communion but also adults who have not yet been so admitted.

The Eucharist is a complex phenomenon, rich in meaning and experience. Before the child can be nurtured into the various levels of meaning and experience associated with the Eucharist, he needs to know that he is a valued member of the eucharistic community. He needs to be made to feel welcome and at home. Next, much of what happens in the Eucharist is very different from what happens in the rest of the child's world. The church must begin from an awareness of what these differences are, and then attempt to build bridges across them.

This programme of Christian nurture attempts to build the bridges by beginning from the point where the child himself begins. The starting point is the child's day to day world, and especially the world of school. It is at school that the child is taught to learn. Now the church must learn from the child's expectations of what learning is like. The key to this rests in the notion of project learning.

Project Learning

Much of the work of the primary school is now conducted by means of discovery learning and organised projects. A project takes a theme and allows the child to explore the theme from as many angles as possible. Slowly the classroom is taken over by the theme as the children's work develops and as the teacher displays and structures what the children have produced. The children work together towards a final end product, a display or open day which can be shared with other classes, parents and friends.

In order to make an explicit link between the project work of the primary school and the Eucharist, Paul Jenkins and I devised the illustrated Communion books for seven to eleven year olds, *The Lord is Here*[1] and *At the Lord's Table*.[2] In these books the whole text of the Communion service is spread over thirty-one double pages. Each page presents only one basic idea, and each idea is associated with a picture. For example, the Nicene creed has three basic ideas, belief in God the Father, belief in God the Son, and belief in God the Holy Spirit. The creed, therefore, occupies three pages and is associated with three illustrations.

It is the illustrations which form the link between the Communion service and the project work of the primary school. *His Spirit is with us* now suggests ways in which each of these thirty-one pictures becomes the basis for a project. Each project concentrates upon the practical things which the child can make or do. In this way the child's understanding can be built up about each of the components of the Communion service in turn.

A good example of a project which is often covered at some stage during the primary school is a project on 'My Neighbourhood'. Children of different ages and different abilities are all in their own way able to contribute to a study of their own neighbourhood and of the people who live and work there. A study of this nature is able to utilise all the different aspects of the primary school curriculum from drama to mathematics. The project on the local neighbourhood finds a natural place in the Communion service at the section of the prayer for the church and the world where in the Rite A order we pray for our families, friends and neighbours. The illustration in the children's Communion book draws attention to some of those familiar people. Thus, a project on 'My Neighbourhood' becomes part of a programme of Christian nurture when the whole project is related to a specific part of the Eucharist, and the celebration of the Eucharist becomes the culmination of the programme of work. The church building itself becomes the place in which the project is displayed, and the intention of the Eucharist becomes the offering of this project to God. The sacrament is where the secular and the sacred meet.

By way of a further example, I return to the third section of the creed where we state our belief in God the Holy Spirit. The illustration in the children's Communion book shows a group of children flying kites on a windy day.

---

[1] For use with Series 3 Communion Service. 1981 edition revised for use with Rite A Holy Communion.
[2] For use with An Australian Prayer Book, Second Order for the Holy Communion.

The link is the obvious one that in the language of the bible, both Hebrew and Greek, the same word stands for wind and for Spirit. Thus the wind has become one of the primary Christian images for God the Holy Spirit.

In the project associated with this part of the service, we have explored the many facets of the wind. We have made kites and visited the park to fly them. We have made windmills and taken a trip to see one. We have blown up balloons and had a party with them. We have pretended that we were out on the mountain struggling against the gale, or on some tropical island basking in the warm breeze. We danced the dance of leaves caught up in the wind. We have written stories and poems about the wind and painted pictures. By doing these things we have learnt about the mysterious movement of the Holy Spirit. And along the way we have encountered extracts from scripture, as well as modern and traditional hymns about God the Holy Spirit.

Finally, we have taken the results of our project to church on Sunday. A hot air balloon hung from the pulpit. Flags waved from the rood screen. Kites fluttered from the rafters. A windmill stood on the font. Balloons were suspended above the pews and let down at the end of the service. Our drawings, poems and stories were mounted – and the photographs of our visit to the park and the windmill were displayed. Our dance and drama about the wind were presented before the whole worshipping community as that community came together to celebrate its faith in the Christ of the Eucharist.

The children enjoyed their project on the Spirit. Their families and friends enjoyed seeing their work contribute to the celebration of the Eucharist. Most of all, each time the third section of the creed is recited, the illustration of flying kites will remind them of the mysterious wind-like quality of God the Holy Spirit.

His Spirit is with us

His Spirit is with us suggests separate projects for all thirty-one sections of the Communion service. In this way, it is possible over a period of time to develop the child's understanding of the Communion service, and liking for the worship of the church. The barrier between the religious and the secular is dissolved, and the child feels at home in church.

The opening Greeting of the Communion service 'The Lord be with you' is accompanied by a picture of two children. The picture introduces a project on 'Getting to know you'. The Collect for Purity is illustrated by the picture of baptism and is supported by a project on water. The 'Lord have mercy' shows the prodigal son's return being welcomed by his father and prepares for the theme of 'the royal welcome'. The happy mood of the 'Glory be' is portrayed by children playing instruments and the project 'Making Music'. The Collect provides an opportunity to study the clergyman, and the lessons from scripture introduce the bible through a theme based on books, libraries and newsprint.

The first part of the Creed carries the illustration of a flame. The project examines the theme of signs to discover how God makes himself known in terms of images like father and the flame of the burning bush. The second part of the Creed shows the cross and leads on to a project on the life of Jesus. The third part of the Creed, concerning God the Holy Spirit, offers the theme of wind.

The Prayer for the Church and the World has six sections. The invitation examines the notion of prayer as communication between friends and shows children at play. The other five sections look at the countries of the world (the peoples and their flags), the church (the ministers and the laity), the local community (the postman, milkman, lollipop person), the sick (a nurse and an ambulance driver), and the departed. This final section of the prayer has chosen the illustration of candles and the theme of 'Light and Life' as a way of exploring the idea of the communion of saints.

The Confession introduces the theme of barrier builders and the Absolution the theme of the mender. The Prayer of Humble Access explores birthday parties. The Peace is introduced by a project on hands and the Offertory is related to a project on shopping.

The Prayer of Thanksgiving is divided into five sections. The five associated projects are to do with bird watching, journey into space, the wedding reception, bread and wine and carnival time. The Lord's Prayer is related to a project on picnics and the Fraction introduces the theme of sharing.

The administration of Communion provides an opportunity to base a project on journeys and pilgrimages. The Prayer of Thanks after communion is explored through a project on dancing. The Blessing is illustrated by the rainbow as a symbol of God's goodwill and involves a project on the biblical imagery of the Noah story. Finally, the Dismissal leads to a project on Christian involvement in the world.

How to use the projects

His Spirit is with us has thirty-one chapters to parallel the thirty-one illustrations in the children's Communion books. Each chapter contains two parts. The first part of each chapter, called Background Material, informs the teacher about the theological background to the part of the Communion service under consideration. This material is not, generally speaking, intended for direct use with the children. The principle behind this part of each chapter is that the meaningful and relevant presentation of the Eucharist among children is enhanced by the teachers' own theological insight. In this part, the text of the Communion service is reviewed and the relevance of the pictures from *The Lord is Here* is discussed. Then a few comments, together with extracts from biblical commentaries and other books, are presented to help to illuminate the ideas and concepts involved in the text of the service and the children's project work. Each section of Background Material leads to a collect and three scripture readings which can be used at the celebration of the Eucharist for which the project work prepares.

The second part of each chapter, called Teaching material, provides some very practical suggestions for teaching the theme to the children. Ideas are presented for the kind of work children can contribute towards a final display – things they can make and do. Suggestions are made for written work, both of a factual and creative nature. Ideas are presented on the way in which the children's finished work can be organised and displayed at the Eucharist. Activities are suggested in the form of relevant games, drama, outings and visits.

The Teaching Units are full enough to enable the person who is not a professional teacher to make a good job of the project theme. On the other hand, they are not intended to be a substitute for creative originality. The units will serve their purpose if they suggest one or two lines which the teacher then pursues in his or her own way. Each chapter contains enough suggestions to keep a school well occupied for a whole term. Others may prefer to take just one aspect of a chapter as material for a single lesson. Each chapter is completely self-contained – and the chapters can be used in any order.

Church and School

The thirty-one projects are intended for two different kinds of environment. First, the nurturing of the young into the worship of the church is, I believe, an appropriate activity for church aided primary schools. The projects demonstrate the way in which the whole curriculum of the church aided primary school can at the same time be part of a programme of Christian nurture. The material can be used in a number of ways in a church school. For example, a chapter can be adopted by a single class and the whole project contained within the classroom. The project can be concluded with a celebration of the Eucharist in the classroom itself. On the other hand, the whole school can decide how to divide a chapter among a number of classes. In its own way each class can contribute towards organising the final display in the local church. The Eucharist in church can provide the climax to the project. In church the project can be shared with the whole people of God in the parish.

Second, where church aided schools are not available to offer this kind of teaching, I envisage the development of 'children's workshops' – small groups meeting in parents' homes, the vestry, the school or the church itself, for an hour or so during the week, at weekends, or during school holidays. At these workshops specific projects from the Eucharist can be worked out in very practical ways. A number of small groups can meet throughout the week at different times and in different places, as proves most convenient to the children and the organisers. The groups are given a unity by working on a common theme. Several groups can work for several weeks on one project, and afterwards the project can be summed up at a Sunday celebration of the Eucharist. For example, on the first Sunday in the month the work produced by the children's workshops can be brought to church to become the framework from which the parish Eucharist develops. This is the celebration of the Eucharist for which the children have prepared. In fact, it is from the children's work that the adults also learn.

Postscript

The aim of this programme of Christian nurture is to introduce children into the worship of the church and to break down the barriers that stand between the church and the child. It is a programme which offers a vision of the church's future and a commitment to the child. The next step is simply to choose a chapter – any chapter between 1 and 31 – and to put the vision to the test.

1. GREETING

Getting to know you

The Preparation

The Lord be with you.
And also with you.

☐ TEXT

The phrase 'The Lord be with you' is an ancient form of greeting. At the opening of the service this Greeting has three functions:

1 The greeting declares the service started. In effect it says that the service begins when the people of Christ greet each other and acknowledge that the Lord is with them.

2 The greeting sets up the relationship between the president and the people. The president takes the initiative in greeting the people. By accepting and responding to this initiative the people acknowledge his authority to preside at the celebration.

3 By making the response together the people acknowledge from the start that they are stepping forward into the Eucharist as a body rather than as each person alone.

☐ PICTURE

The picture of two children, a boy and a girl, not only serves to illustrate the greeting as the opening part of the service – it is also the opening picture of the child's book. The picture focuses attention on each child himself or herself as one of the special individuals who come together to be the people of Christ who celebrate the Eucharist. The intention is that the child using the book should identify with one of the figures. From the outset we want the child to say 'this book is about me', and more especially 'this service is for me'.

☐ COMMENT

Joseph Gelineau comments on the function of the salutation as establishing a relationship between the president and people, J. D. Crichton speaks about the importance of human relationships in liturgy, and Michel Quoist's prayer demonstrates the Christian's concern for his neighbour and brother. The Old Testament reading shows the scriptural origin of the salutation 'The Lord be with you'. In the New Testament reading Paul greets the church in Corinth. In the Gospel reading Jesus walks with two disciples and they recognise their Lord's presence with them in the breaking of the bread.

Joseph Gelineau, *The Liturgy Today and Tomorrow*, (Darton, Longman and Todd 1978, pp. 78–9):

When the president says: 'The Lord be with you' and we reply 'And with your spirit', we can of course reflect on the deep meaning of these words. But the act of speaking remains valid even if we don't: it introduces the assembly's celebration by establishing a relationship between the president and the people.

J. D. Crichton, 'The Church and the Worshipping Community', in Cheslyn Jones, *The Study of Liturgy*, (SPCK 1978, p. 19):

In the liturgy there is a vertical movement, the outgoing of man to God. But there is also a horizontal movement. Liturgy is celebrated *with* others and the relationships between the members of the worshipping community are of the highest importance . . . The sociologists tell us that in true community there must be a face to face relationship, and for the Christian this means that the members of the community are *persons* bound together by faith and love. In principle they are already related to one another. In the worshipping community this relationship is deepened and enhanced.

Michel Quoist, *Prayers of Life*, (Gill 1963, p. 17) provides a meditation on the theme of 'My Friend':

I shook hands with my friend, Lord,
And suddenly when I saw his sad and anxious face, I feared that you were
    not in his heart.
I am troubled as I am before a closed tabernacle when there is no light to
    show that you are there.
If you were not there, Lord, my friend and I would be separated.
For his hand in mine would be only flesh in flesh.
I want your life for him as well as for me.
For it is only in you that he can be my brother.

Read 1 Corinthians 1:1–10 (St Paul greets the church in Corinth)
John Ruef, *Paul's First Letter to Corinth*, (Penguin 1971, pp. 1–4):

Paul follows the conventions of letter writing of his own day by beginning
with his own name and status and then the title of those addressed. He
expands the greeting form in order to make clear the relation which he has
to those addressed . . . Paul proceeds with the thanksgiving. This was
usual in the Hellenistic world in a formal letter between those sharing the
same religious background . . . In all his letters Paul follows the same
general formula: he (1) gives thanks, (2) always (3) to God (4) on behalf of
the Christians to whom he writes (5) because of things God has done for
them, which he proceeds to enumerate.

C. K. Barrett, *The First Epistle to the Corinthians*, (A & C Black 1971,
pp.34–5) examines in greater depth the meaning of Paul's greeting:

A non-Christian Greek would send his correspondent greeting; a Jew
would wish him peace. Paul prays for his readers grace and peace, and sees
both as coming from God our Father and the Lord Jesus Christ
. . . When one Christian wishes grace and peace to another he prays that
he may apprehend more fully the grace of God in which he already stands,
and the peace he already enjoys.

Read Luke 24:13–35 (The Lord's presence is recognised in the breaking of
the bread)
George Caird, *Saint Luke*, (Penguin 1963, pp. 257–9):

From the experience of this couple (on the road to Emmaus) we can learn
much about the resurrection appearances of Jesus. As they walked along
the road, Jesus suddenly appeared at their side, and they assumed that he
was a fellow traveller who had overtaken them; but later when he disappeared just as suddenly from the supper table, they realised the truth, that
he was no longer subject to limitations of time and place . . . The disciples
recognised Jesus by the way in which he broke the bread. Luke and his
friends would no doubt find in the solemn scene at the supper table an
anticipation of their own eucharistic observances.

☐ **WORSHIP**

Heavenly Father,
you know each one of us by name:
you love each one of us.
Help us to recognise your presence with us,
and to grow closer to each other
as we come to your holy table together;
through Jesus Christ our Lord.   Amen.

First reading: Ruth 2:1–12
Second reading: 1 Corinthians 1:1–5
Gospel reading: Luke 24:13–35

Teaching material

■ **CONTEXT OF UNIT 1**

The Greeting brings together a number of individuals and catches them up
in the beginning of the liturgy. For this experience to be real for the child,
three things are necessary:
1 The child needs to feel comfortable and at home in the liturgy.
2 The child needs to feel able 'to be himself' and to know that his individuality is valued by the worshipping community.
3 The child needs to know that he is among friends. Basically he needs to
   know the other children and adults who are present.

■ **OBJECTIVES**

1 To enable the child to explore himself and to realise something of his
   uniqueness.
2 To enable the child to tell the community about himself.
3 To enable the child to get to know the other children of his group. (The
   wider objective of getting to know the adults in the local church is
   reserved for Section 11.)
4 To encourage the child to think about different forms of greetings.

■ **DISPLAY WORK**

a Group work Here the unit of study is the whole class. The aim is to
display information about the whole class. The method is to develop a series
of wall charts – HERE WE ARE charts. In this way both the individual child
and the visitor can see the characteristics of the whole class at a single glance.

1 The children make pictures of themselves and the pictures are organised on a wall chart. There are a number of attractive ways to organise these pictures:

  a) Just faces are drawn. The wall chart is intended to provide a sense of unity and to show that all these faces belong together ('HERE WE ARE TOGETHER').

  b) The wall chart is a large house or bus – with a window for each member of the class. The pictures are placed in the window spaces and named.

  c) The wall chart is a tree – with an apple for each member of the class. The children's pictures are placed on the apples.

  d) The wall chart is a ship. Each child draws himself as a sailor with his name on the hat band. The ship can be named after the school/church.

  e) Complete self portraits are drawn. The wall chart is intended to provide a context and to show what the children do in common. The context could be a large outline of the church, the school or the Sunday school building ('HERE WE ARE GOING TO CHURCH').

2 The children report how they are like each other and how they differ from each other. Similarities and differences can be organised around a number of key variables, for example: a) age, b) height, c) colour of eyes, d) length of span, e) street or village where they live, f) number of brothers and sisters, g) weight.

  The collecting of this kind of information has a number of educational consequences. It enables the child to see himself in relationship to the other class members. It encourages the child to take an interest in the other children of the group. In order for the child to find out about a number of the variables it is necessary for him to gain the help of other members of his group (e.g. in discovering the colour of his eyes, in measuring his height etc.).

The information can be displayed in the form of wall chart histograms. For example each child may be given a square of coloured paper and asked to write his name and his height on it. The teacher prepares the histogram and the children stick their paper in the appropriate place.

3 Encourage the children to talk about the different ways people greet each other, e.g. the wave through the window, the handshake, the kiss. Examine the different forms of verbal greeting. Look at the customs and language of different countries. Discuss the way people greet each other on the telephone or in letters. Finally produce a large mural of the children greeting each other, e.g. by using words written in balloons emerging from the children's mouths.

b Individual work Here the unit of study is the individual child. Each child is encouraged to produce a book about himself – a 'HERE I AM' book. The child's motivation for producing the book is the idea that the book is to be displayed in church as the child's way of saying 'Here I am: get to know me!' A good form for such a book is the zig-zag book so that the pages can be unfolded and displayed at a glance. Each page is for a different piece of information. Class discussion can list carefully the headings for each page, e.g. a picture of me, a description of me, my height, age, etc., a picture of my house, a description of my house etc.

For display purposes the zig-zag books can be mounted under each other to allow for cross reference to be made.

■ WRITING

1 The children can be asked to write a letter, say to the Vicar, telling him all about their group – and about the work which they have done in order to understand the Greeting.

2 Read and write about the two disciples on the road to Emmaus.

■ ACTIVITIES

1 Games provide another way of exploring individual differences. Histograms can be developed on the basis of
 a) how far we can jump
 b) how long we can stand on one leg
 c) how many eggs we can carry in an egg and spoon race.

2 A variant of pass-the-parcel can be used as an opportunity to get the children talking about themselves. Forfeits can be simple things like
 a) what is my favourite colour

b) what do I want to be when I grow up
c) recite my favourite poem.

3 A number of country dances require the child to change partners frequently. This provides a good way of letting children mix with each other and get to know each other.

4 Older children may care to present a 'This is Your Life' programme.

5 Older children may like to act out the situation of strangers meeting and trying to get to know each other – say in a doctor's waiting room.

6 Individual voice differences can be discovered by tape recording the children talking to each other. Play back the recording and ask 'Guess who is speaking'.

7 Let the children interview each other, using a list of questions, like 'what is your favourite sport?' 'what food do you like best?'

8 A dance-drama can be devised to symbolise the individuality and isolation of each child being brought together through the Eucharist. Begin by asking the children to space themselves out around the edge of the room or corners of the church. Each performs his or her own isolated dance movement. They move towards one part of the room (the centre or the communion table) and begin to co-ordinate their movements. At some stage in the dance the salutation 'The Lord be with you' and the reply 'And also with you' can be used to express the change of mood. Appropriate music for the drama would begin discordantly, each line of music following its own pattern or rhythm without regard to the other lines, and gradually the music resolves itself into harmony.

■ **DISPLAY HEADINGS**

The wall charts and the zig-zag books are good for displaying both in school and in church. Useful headings are
  1 Getting to know *You*
  2 Here we are together, etc.
  3 The Lord be with You: And also with You
  4 Greetings
  5 Class four comes to church

A short explanation might run like this, 'Our Communion Service begins with the greeting "The Lord be with You" – and it means with each one of us. So here we are to introduce ourselves'.

The Lord is Here or *At the Lord's Table* open at pages 2–3 can be displayed also.

2. COLLECT FOR PURITY

Ways with water

> Almighty God,
> to whom all hearts are open,
> all desires known,
> and from whom no secrets are hidden:
> cleanse the thoughts of our hearts
> by the inspiration of your Holy Spirit,
> that we may perfectly love you,
> and worthily magnify your holy name;
> through Christ our Lord.
> Amen.
>
> 4

Background material

☐ **TEXT**

The Collect for Purity emphasises at the beginning of the service that we are not worthy to approach God in the Eucharist unless he takes the initiative to prepare us for meeting himself. In this Collect we acknowledge four things:

1 We cannot conceal ourselves from God.
2 As we stand, we are not worthy of God.
3 Only God can make us fit for himself by filling us with his Holy Spirit.
4 By the inspiration of the Holy Spirit we can approach God in worship – to magnify his holy name.

☐ **PICTURE**

The picture of people watching a baptism suggests three themes on the idea of man's need for preparation before he can come before God in worship:

1 Water as the Christian symbol for cleansing and preparation.

2 Baptism as the sacrament of the restoration of man's relationship with God.

3 Baptism does not take place in secret. The people watch it take place. Baptism, like the Collect for Purity, is an open acknowledgement of man's recognition of his state before God.

☐ **COMMENT**

Two ideas in the Collect for Purity need some comment, the use of the word 'inspiration' and the notion of God's omniscience raised by the phrase 'from whom no secrets are hidden'. The Old Testament reading, which illustrates the cleansing and healing function of water, has been associated with baptism from the early days of the Christian church. The New Testament reading shows Philip bringing a new member into the church through baptism. In the Gospel reading John the Baptist baptises Jesus and points to the baptism with which Jesus will baptise.

Inspiration This word comes from a root meaning 'to breathe into'. This is an attractive idea when we remember that in the languages of the bible the same word is used to stand for our three English words 'Spirit', 'wind' and 'breath'. We are asking God to cleanse the thoughts of our hearts by breathing into us his Holy Spirit.

From whom no secrets are hidden This phrase raises the question of God's omniscience. 'Omniscience' means knowledge of everything, all knowing.
  D. Shaw, *Who is God?* (SCM 1968, p. 113):

> The divine knowledge is not that of the detached outside observer. It is rather 'inside' knowledge, of one who knows the situation from the inside and whose motive is love. This rules out the possibility that the divine knowledge is in any way comparable to that of a 'Big Brother', spying on everything that goes on in order to pounce on any irregularity and put a decisive stop to any dangerous or unwelcome development. It is rather the knowledge of love, the untyrannical knowledge of complete sensitivity to everything that is.

Read 2 Kings 5:1–19 (The cleansing of Naaman)

  The early Church Fathers very soon saw a prefiguring of the Christian rite of baptism in certain passages of the Old Testament. This passage from 2 Kings was regularly interpreted as referring to baptism. For example Ambrose, *On the Sacraments*, wrote:

> The prophet said, 'Go to Jordan, dip and thou shalt be healed'. He began to reflect and say 'Is that all? . . . as if there were not better rivers in my own

native land' . . . Then he went to Jordan, dipped, and arose whole. What, then, does it mean? . . . It is not all water that heals, but that water heals which has the grace of Christ (translation by Thompson and Srawley, SPCK 1919, p. 81).

Read Acts 8:26–40 (Philip baptises the eunuch)

The interesting issue about this passage concerns verse 37 – the verse relegated to a footnote in modern translations like the New English Bible and the Jerusalem Bible. The verse is a question and answer confession of faith before baptism is permitted. Since this verse is not in all the ancient manuscripts of the book of Acts, scholars like James Dunn, *Unity and Diversity in the New Testament*, (SCM 1977, p. 55) argue that 'Acts 8:37 has to be recognised as a baptismal formula of a later generation' inserted into the text of Acts by the scribes who copied out the early manuscripts. This insertion shows how the church's later baptismal practice of demanding a confession of faith before the administration of baptism became read back into the New Testament itself.

Read Mark 1:1–13 (Jesus is baptised by John the Baptist)

In the New Testament and in the Christian church water is a powerful symbol associated with the beginning of the Christian life in baptism. Thomas Fawcett, *Hebrew Myth and Christian Gospel*, (SCM 1973, p. 123):

> The use of water as a cleansing agent in a physical sense led naturally into its use as a sacramental symbol. As the body needed to be washed clean of accumulated filth, so also did the soul. That this was the primary meaning of John's baptism Mark has no doubt.

Similarly Oscar Cullmann, *Baptism in the New Testament*, (SCM 1950, p. 11): 'Just as ordinary water takes away the physical uncleanness of the body, so the water of baptism will take away sins.' But Cullmann is careful to note that the idea of washing away sin is only a small part of the Christian idea of baptism. The sacrament of baptism means rebirth or incorporation into the body of Christ.

☐ **WORSHIP**

Almighty God,
you sent your servant John
  to cleanse your people with the water of baptism
  and to prepare them for the coming of your Son.
Send now your Holy Spirit upon us
  to cleanse the thoughts of our hearts
  and to prepare us for his coming in the eucharist,
Who is alive and reigns

with you and the Holy Spirit,
one God, now and for ever.   Amen.

First reading: 2 Kings 5:1–14
Second reading: Acts 8:35–39
Gospel reading: Mark 1:1–13

Teaching material

■ CONTEXT OF UNIT 2

The Collect for Purity invites us to become aware that we need God to prepare us before we can approach his holy table and offer him true worship. A powerful symbol for this preparation is the sign of water and the sacrament of baptism. Water cleanses – and more than that, water gives life. For the child to experience the significance of the Collect for Purity two things are necessary:

1 The child needs to know something about the everyday functions of water as a lifegiving force and as a cleansing agent, since it is on the basis of analogy with these everyday functions that the religious understanding is developed.

2 The child needs to be aware of the specific Christian understanding of baptism.

■ OBJECTIVES

1 To enable the child to understand the importance of water in everyday life and the many ways in which we are dependent on water.

2 To introduce the child to the rite of Baptism.

It is best to start from what the child already knows about water, and then gradually to draw out the parallels with baptism.

■ DISPLAY WORK

a **Water** Begin by letting the children talk about the uses of water. Help them to experience and to understand the many important functions fulfilled by water.

1 Water is necessary to support life. Observe the importance of water for a cut flower. Place two flowers in identical containers: fill one container with water and leave the other empty.

2 Water is necessary to give growth. Observe the importance of water for the

growth of plants. Place beans on two sheets of blotting paper: keep one moist and the other dry.

3 Water is used for drinking. Produce a collage of different drinks – using advertising materials etc.

4 Water is an important part of food stuffs. Observe the moisture in fruit and vegetables. Observe dehydrated food stuffs and the process of reconstitution. Produce a collection of packets of dehydrated foods and pictures of fruits etc.

5 Water is necessary for washing. Collect pictures concerned with washing, i.e., baths, showers, sinks, washing machines, car washes, etc.

6 Study rainfall, streams, rivers, wells, etc.

7 Study how people used to obtain their water. Make a large model of a well.

8 Study how fish live in water and how different animals drink and store water (e.g. elephants, giraffes and camels).

9 Study the way in which a town's water supply works – the water tower, the purifying system, the pipes running under the street. Study the way in which the water supply works in the school or in a house, running from the tank in the roof.

10 Study the power of water. Make a water wheel from a circle of stout card. Fold the edges to produce a flange. Use a pencil as a spindle and operate the wheel by placing it under gently running water. This could form part of a larger model.

11 Study the other uses of water – steam drives a toy engine or a railway engine; ice keeps food fresh; hot water works central heating and hot water bottles; jets of water put out fires; water is used to cool the car engine, etc.

b Baptism Let the children talk about the baptisms which they have attended. In particular let them discuss i) who is there, ii) what happens, iii) why it happens.

Four creative activities can help to develop the child's understanding of these issues and also be useful for display purposes.

1 The production of a model font.
   a) If clay is available this is a good medium for individual children to work on.
   b) Papier mâché on a cardboard base can be used by a group of children to produce a life sized font.

2 The production of a collage of a baptism scene – depicting vicar, font, child, parents, godparents, countless onlookers, etc. Set alongside this another collage of baptism by total immersion as in the time of Jesus.

3 A number of churches present the godparents with a lighted candle in a special cardboard holder. Ask the children to design and make such a candle holder.

4 Show the children the kind of cards which are used to record the time, date and place of baptism. Ask them to design a baptism card, and to record the details of their own baptism.

■ **ACTIVITIES**

a Water

1 Attempt to visit the local water works – and do a project on the visit.

2 Study how water is used for recreation. Visit the local swimming pool, the local river, centres where there are small boats, etc.

3 Encourage the children to produce a short play about what happened the day that 'the men dug up the road and the water was turned off' – let them

explore how much we depend upon our regular supply of water.

4 The theme could provide an opportunity for doing some real washing – or even cleaning the vicar's car.

b Baptism

1 Visit the church, look at the font, attend a baptism service.

2 Act out a baptism service, using a doll, with children taking the part of the priest, the parents, the godparents, friends, etc.

3 Interview people from different Christian churches and discover how the practice of baptism differs – especially try to discover something about the Baptist church.

■ WRITING

1 Ask the children to write about some aspect of their project on water and baptism – for example their visit to the local waterworks, or their presence at a baptism service.

2 Imaginative writing can be stimulated by a title like 'Searching for water on a desert island': the children can be asked to imagine that they are stranded on a desert island without supplies of water – they need to search quickly. This project allows room for the drawing of maps, etc.

3 Read and write about Jesus' baptism.

4 Look up the promises made during the baptism service and write about them.

■ DISPLAY HEADINGS

Useful headings for displaying with the work produced in the course of this unit are
1 'Cleanse the thoughts of our hearts'
2 Water cleanses
3 Water revives
4 Water gives growth
5 The font contains the water for baptism
6 Class 4 goes to a baptism service

A short explanation might run like this: 'The Collect for Purity reminds us that we need God to prepare and cleanse us before we come to meet him in the Holy Communion'.

The Lord is Here or *At the Lord's Table* open at pages 4–5 can be displayed also.

3. KYRIE ELEISON

The royal welcome

Lord, have mercy.
Lord, have mercy.

Lord, have mercy.
Lord, have mercy.

Christ, have mercy.
Christ, have mercy.

Background material

☐ TEXT

The Kyrie is a brief prayer for divine mercy. It has been used in Christian worship from the fourth century onwards. Now the Kyrie is placed in the Communion service before the Gloria. In some churches during the penitential seasons of Advent and Lent the Kyrie is used on its own instead of the Gloria. Although originally, as used in the Eastern church, the Kyrie does not appear to have been specifically penitential, its penitential use is now well established by tradition. The penitential use of the Kyrie indicates two things:

1 Man's awareness of his need for God's mercy.
2 Man's confidence that God is a God of mercy.

☐ PICTURE

The picture illustrates the two central aspects of the Kyrie Eleison:

31

1 Man's need for God's mercy.
2 God's ready welcome for those who come seeking his mercy. The imagery of this picture is based on the parable of the prodigal son. It is the son who comes, head bowed. It is the father who welcomes with outstretched hands.

☐ **COMMENT**

Kyrie Eleison is simply the Greek version of the short prayer 'Lord have mercy.' In the Shorter Oxford English Dictionary 'mercy' is defined as 'forbearance and compassion shown by one person to another who is in his power and who has no claim to receive kindness'. The Old Testament reading is described by W. O. E. Oesterley as the most heart-searching of all the penitential psalms. This is followed in the New Testament reading by the author of the Epistle to the Hebrews giving his grounds for confidence in God's mercy and acceptance. Two alternative Gospel readings are given, one illustrating man's penitential approach to God and the other illustrating God's forgiveness and welcome.

Read Psalm 51 (A psalm of penitence)
W. O. E. Oesterley, *The Psalms*, (SPCK 1939, pp. 270–1) writes that this is

the most heart-searching of all the penitential psalms . . . For the realisation of the sense of sin, set forth with unflinching candour, it has no equal in the Psalter . . . In outward form the psalm is beautifully and skilfully constructed, and reveals most exquisitely the emotions which succeed one another in the penitent's heart: first, the cry to God for mercy; then, confession of sin, uttered in deep contrition; this is followed by prayer for forgiveness, and the resolution to amendment of life; and finally, in certainty that God in his love answers prayer, thanksgiving and praise.

Read Hebrews 4:14–16 (the compassionate high priest)
Hugh Montefiore, *The Epistle to the Hebrews* (A & C Black 1964, pp. 91–2):

Jesus is not said to sympathise with these weaknesses in the sense that contemplation of them arouses in him feelings of pity and compassion. He sympathises because he has, through common experience, a real kinship with those who suffer. His temptations had not been confined to certain compartments of his life (e.g. to those particular temptations which are specially mentioned in the gospels), but they covered the whole range of human experience . . . Precisely because Christians have a compassionate high priest, they have grounds for confident assurance that the barriers between God and man have been removed.

Read Luke 18:9–14 (Man's approach before God)
William Barclay, *Gospel of Luke* (St Andrew Press 1953, p. 234):

True prayer comes from setting our lives beside the life of God. No doubt all that the Pharisee said was true. He did fast; he did meticulously give tithes; he was not as other men are; still less was he like that tax-collector. But the question is not, 'Am I as good as my fellow men?' The question is, 'Am I as good as God?' . . . It all depends what we compare ourselves with. And when we set our lives beside the wonder of the life of Jesus, and beside the holiness of God, then all that is left to say is, 'God be merciful to me – the sinner'.

Read Luke 15:11–32 (the Prodigal Son)
Eta Linneman, *Parables of Jesus*, (SPCK 1966, p. 76):

For a man to come to recognise his sins and repent under the pressure of self-incurred misery is not unusual, and is credible in its effect. What the parable next narrates, however, is far from commonplace. Even if he is in a great hurry for an aged oriental it is beneath his dignity to run. When the father falls about his son's neck, he is stopping him from going down before him on his knees to him and humbling himself . . . The kiss on the cheek is for an equal. When the father embraces and kisses his returning son, he has shown him without a word that 'you are to be my son, in spite of all that has happened' . . . His confession of guilt is answered by abundant mercy.

Part of the son's experience is that he must approach a father who is both welcoming and overshadowing. The Christian knows that he can approach the loving father and yet rightfully never presumes to come except in penitence. This is in fact the essence of the 'Religious Experience' described by Rudolph Otto in *The Idea of the Holy* (OUP 1923). Otto writes of the two poles of man's religious experience. The divine is seen at the same time as both *tremendum* (that from which man wishes to escape because it is so much greater than he is and therefore induces fear) and *fascinans* (that towards which man is irresistibly drawn).

] **WORSHIP**

Lord God,
you are our powerful King,
and we are your people.
You are our loving Father,
and we are your children.
Be gentle with us, and make us confident to come to you boldly.
We make our prayer in Jesus' name.   Amen.

First reading: Psalm 51:1–17
Second reading: Hebrews 4:14–16
Gospel reading: Luke 15:11–32 or Luke 18:9–14

Teaching material

■ **CONTEXT OF UNIT 3**

The Kyrie reminds us of the Christian's position before God. At one and the same time God invites us to come to himself and yet we remain aware of our unworthiness to come to him. For this experience to be real to the child two things are necessary:

1 The child needs to be aware of the awesome majesty of God. God is the great ruler whom we approach with fear.

2 The child needs to be aware of the kind and welcoming nature of God. God is the loving father who welcomes us home when we come to him. In the New Testament these two aspects of the Christian's position before God are expressed by two kinds of parable – those presenting God as a king, and those presenting God as a loving father.

■ **OBJECTIVES**

1 To enable the child to experience what it means to respond to God as king.

2 To enable the child to experience what it means to respond to God as loving father.

The issues of penitence and confession are explored in Unit 16.

■ **DISPLAY WORK**

a God the King Let the children talk about their knowledge of kings and queens. Two sorts of information will emerge: a mixture of history, legend and fairy tale, and current information about our royal family, probably derived from television and newspapers. In leading this discussion good use can be made of press cuttings and children's story books. Let the children give attention to the outward signs of kingship – the crown, the royal robes, the throne, the palace. All these emphasise that the king/queen is someone who is set apart and is different. Let the child also examine the way in which royalty has been treated with a mixture of fear and respect throughout history.

The following projects can help to develop the child's understanding of God as King.

1 The production of puppets of kings and queens. Puppet heads can be made by covering balloons with papier mâché. The balloon can be withdrawn

when the paper is hardened. Noses can be made from egg boxes. The heads are transformed into kings and queens by making cardboard crowns and splendid robes. The finished puppets can either be displayed on stands or used by the children as hand puppets.

2 The production of a mural showing a large palace in the background and royal figures in the foreground. The royal robes, crowns, etc. can be the basis for a rich collage using all kinds of material remnants. The mural could take the form of a royal procession with the crowds standing back and cheering.

3 Produce a scrapbook of press cuttings and magazine articles about the British royal family.

4 Look at a specific period in history and organise a project on the royal household of that time.

5 Look at pictures of the crown jewels and make model or life-size jewels, crowns, etc., in whatever materials are available to the children.

6 Look up some of the bible references to God as King and produce a collage of texts, stories and pictures.

b God the Loving Father The following projects can help to develop the child's understanding of God as Loving Father.

1 Let the children talk about their experiences of adults who love them and welcome them even when they are naughty. Ask them to write about this experience or to produce a story illustrated by a cartoon sequence of pictures.

2 Make a class study of the parable of the Prodigal Son (perhaps in association with the drama suggested in the next section). Produce a sequence of murals telling the story and leading to the climax of the welcome the son receives on his return home.

ACTIVITIES

a God the King Drama helps the child to know what it feels like to be in the presence of royalty. It is possible to enact a state occasion which includes a royal procession. Some of the children can dress up as royalty: others can be part of the crowd watching on. The child's whole understanding of himself can be changed by using a simple curtain as a robe or a cardboard circle as a crown. In this way they can explore the difference between the royalty and the common folk – how both feel and how they react to each other. Part of the procession can be accompanied by the music of a royal march.

b God as Loving Father Again the parable of the prodigal son provides a good basis for dramatic activity. A number of small scenes can be devised and the feelings of the characters in each scene explored, the son leaving home, the son taking his possessions to a new land, the good life of the new land, the feeding of pigs, the return home, the father's welcome and the brother's rejection. Give particular attention to the gestures which the father makes in welcoming the prodigal home – for example the open arms and the warm embrace and kiss.

■ WRITING

1 A well known nursery rhyme speaks of a cat who went to London to see the queen. Ask the children to pretend to be that cat and to write their experiences of their visit to see the queen.

2 Write the story of the Prodigal Son as it is seen by one of the main characters – the father, the older brother, the person who offers the Prodigal Son a job, the people who work on the father's farm, the Prodigal Son himself, etc.

■ DISPLAY HEADINGS

The organisation of the display of this project needs to bring together the two themes of God the King and God the loving Father. Display the work created in the course of this unit with such headings as:

1 In some places the bible speaks about God as the great king. We look up to God like we look up to a king or queen – and sometimes we are overwhelmed by him.

2 The bible also speaks about God as the loving father. God welcomes us like a loving father – even when we have been naughty.

A short explanation might run 'When we say the Kyrie Eleison we have mixed feelings – we feel that God ought to be severe with us like a cross king, and yet we know that he welcomes us back like a loving father.'

The Lord is Here or *At the Lord's Table* open at pages 6–7 can be displayed also.

4. GLORIA

Making music

Glory to God in the highest,
and peace to his people on earth.

Lord God, heavenly King,
almighty God and Father,
we worship you, we give you thanks,
we praise you for your glory.

Lord Jesus Christ,
    only Son of the Father,
Lord God, Lamb of God,
you take away the sin of the world:
have mercy on us;
you are seated at the right hand
    of the Father:
receive our prayer.

For you alone are the Holy One,
you alone are the Lord,
you alone are the Most High,
Jesus Christ,
with the Holy Spirit,
in the glory of God the Father.
Amen.

9

Background material

TEXT

The Gloria is one of the earliest Christian hymns outside the bible. It consists of three main sections:

1 The key note of the first section is praise. The opening sentence of this hymn of the church echoes the angelic salutation of Luke 2:14. The next sentence piles up shouts of praise.

2 The second section strikes the note of penitence. It is the Christian's response to the greatness of God underlined in the first section.

3 The third section returns to shouts of praise.

At this early stage in the service the Gloria prepares us for the fact that the word 'eucharist' itself means 'to give thanks'. As a great shout of thanks and praise, the Gloria sets the mood for what is to follow.

☐ **PICTURE**

The picture suggests the theme of celebration. Such celebration is to do with music, movement and happiness. The children are playing all sorts of musical instruments, drum, cymbal, trumpet, recorder, guitar – and they are obviously enjoying it. Whether said or sung, the Gloria of the church shares in this rhythm of music and movement.

☐ **COMMENT**

Gloria in Excelsis is simply the Latin version of the opening words of this hymn, 'Glory in the highest'. In the Shorter Oxford English Dictionary 'Glory' is defined as 'praise, honour, and thanksgiving offered in adoration'. The Old Testament reading is a call for everything that has breath to praise the Lord and to make music to his name. Similarly, the New Testament reading is an invitation to sing and make music in your hearts to the Lord. The Gospel reading culminates in the angelic hymn from which the first lines of the Gloria are derived.

Read Psalm 150

Artur Weiser, *The Psalms*, (SCM 1962, p. 841):

> The keynote of all the last hymns of the Psalter has been that of praise, and at the very end the great Hallelujah (= praise the Lord), now swells the final chord. The last psalm is simply and solely a call to sing the praise of God, in which all the voices on earth and in heaven unite to the accompaniment of the triumphant strains of the entire orchestra of the Temple-music . . . in a tremendous symphonic hymn of praise . . . In praising God the meaning of the world is fulfilled. To praise the abundance of his power is the purpose which links together the most diverse voices in heaven and on earth in a tremendous symphonic hymn of praise.

Read Ephesians 5:18–20 (Sing and make music in your hearts to God)

Making reference to this passage, Robin Leaver, 'Music in Church Today', in *Anglican Worship Today*, (Collins 1980, p. 50) writes

> The music of worship, truly understood, is always God-centred and God-directed. But this vertical dimension explodes horizontally to draw all the worshippers together. The music of worship is not merely notes and sounds. It is essentially an expression of the heart and mind as, filled with the Spirit, the people of God address one another in psalms and hymns and spiritual songs, singing and making melody to the Lord with all their hearts (Ephesians 5:19). Such music is an expression of our faith in God in Christ.

Read Luke 2:8–14 (The angels greet the birth of Christ)

George Caird, *Saint Luke*, (Penguin 1963, pp. 61–2):

According to the book of Job (38:7), when God laid the cornerstone of the earth, 'The morning stars sang together, And all the sons of God shouted for joy'. So now the same chorus gathers to celebrate the new creation, in which God's full glory will be displayed by the accomplishment of his eternal purpose, and man's true peace realised by the establishment of God's kingdom. The promise of peace or welfare is to men with whom God is pleased – a phrase which remains obscure until it is caught up by the words which Jesus hears at his baptism (Thou art my beloved son; with thee I am well pleased – 3:22).

There is a problem in the Greek text of Luke's Gospel at this point. The translation which the Authorised Version of the Bible offers, 'Peace, good-will towards men' is the reading of the majority of the Greek manuscripts. However the really important manuscripts support the alternative reading 'on whom his favour rests'. This alternative reading is adopted by the New English Bible.

The angelic hymn given in Luke's Gospel has become the springboard for a number of Christian hymns and prayers. For example, Bishop Thomas Ken (1637–1711) composed the following prayer based on this theme:

Glory be to God in the highest, and on earth peace, goodwill towards men; for unto us is born this day a Saviour who is Christ the Lord. We praise thee, we bless thee, we glorify thee, we give thanks to thee, for this greatest of thy mercies, O Lord God, heavenly King, God the Father Almighty. Amen.

WORSHIP

Dear Lord God,
You gave us an ear for music,
   a heart for song,
   and limbs for movement.
Help us to praise you
   with tambourines and dancing,
   with recorders and singing,
   with the clash of cymbals and the fanfare of trumpets.
We make our prayer in the name of Jesus Christ,
   who lives and reigns in harmony
   with you and the Holy Spirit,
   now and for ever. Amen.

First reading: Psalm 150
Second reading: Ephesians 5:18–20
Gospel reading: Luke 2:8–14

■ **Teaching material**

■ **CONTEXT OF UNIT 4**

The Gloria is a great hymn or shout of praise. It is the Christian's response of joy in the presence of God. One of the main ways in which this experience of joy can be expressed is through worship and liturgy. For this expression to be real, the child needs to be allowed to respond to worship and to contribute to worship in ways which are natural and enjoyable to himself. A natural way to give expression to joy and praise in the presence of God is through the making of music, song and dance. In this way the child can really enjoy praising God.

■ **OBJECTIVES**

1 To enable the child to see the relationship between music and praise.
2 To enable the child to experience the joy of praising God – and to express this joy through the making of music.

■ **DISPLAY WORK**

Three projects can help to develop the child's understanding of the joy of music in worship.

a Produce a mural about music and musicians
1 Talk about the different kinds of instruments the child knows and make a complete list of them. Look at the musical instruments in the school. Ask children who can play these instruments to demonstrate their sounds. Look at pictures of different instruments. Listen to different musical sounds on record. Look at choirs and orchestras where lots of people sing or play together.

2 Encourage the children to talk about the pop groups they see on television – the sounds produced and the instruments used. Enable them to see that all music can be used to praise God.

As a consequence of this discussion a large mural can be produced showing classical musicians and pop groups – and all sorts of musical instruments, etc.

b Make musical instruments
By way of example, the following kinds of instruments can be made:

1 Instruments which you bang with hand or stick
  a) Different sounds can be made by banging different kinds of 'drums' – from empty tins to empty boxes. Both tins and boxes can be decorated

with paper collage – using coloured magazines.

b) Beer bottle tops can be nailed loosely onto the sides of a broom handle. When the handle is banged gently on the floor or hit with a stick a tinkling sound is made.

c) Different lengths of wood or metal can be suspended from a string line. The different lengths produce different sounds when hit.

2 Instruments which you shake or rattle

Different kinds of containers can be filled with different kinds of objects to produce different sounds. Useful containers are yogurt pots, tins, boxes, plastic squash bottles. The containers can be decorated. Pebbles, sand, dried peas, cotton wool balls can be used inside. Two peas in a pot make quite a different sound from twenty peas in the same pot. An interesting shape is produced when two yogurt pots are glued mouth to mouth.

3 Instruments which you pluck
   a) Rubber bands improvise as strings for instruments. Empty tissue handkerchief boxes provide a ready-made sound chest. The bands need to be raised either end of the box on pencils or something similar. The sound is changed by adjusting the length and tightness of the rubber bands.
   b) A large string instrument can be made from a tea chest and broom handle.

4 Instruments which you bang together
Useful things to bang together to make interesting sounds are coconuts, metal rods and wooden sticks.

5 Instruments which you rub together
A nice rasping sound is produced by rubbing together two blocks of wood covered by sandpaper.

6 Instruments which you blow
   a) The paper-covered comb is an old favourite in this category.
   b) Blow into the top of a bottle.
   c) Bamboo pipes.

c Make a model organ
After taking the children to see the church organ (or, possibly, the organs in several churches) and after they have listened to its sound, invite them to make a model of an organ case, using cardboard tubes for pipes, etc.

■ **ACTIVITIES**

The following two activities will help the child to experience the place of music in praise and worship.

1 The children can use in the context of worship the instruments which they have made. For example, where it is usual to sing the Gloria at the church's eucharist, the children can learn how to use these instruments to accompany the Gloria at a special celebration of the eucharist.

2 The children can be given the chance to know better the instrument usually used in church worship – the Organ. A useful method is this. Familiarise the children with the richness of the organ's sound by using a record in the classroom. At this stage the emphasis is on the sound not the church connection. J. S. Bach's 'D Minor Toccata' is an excellent starting point. Encourage the children really to learn this piece of organ music. Talk about the shapes and colours which the music suggests. Allow them to paint their feelings in response to this music. Allow them to explore in dance movement the different moods of the Toccata – its climaxes and its dying away moments. Develop this exploration into some form of pattern of

movement which is known and accepted by the children and into which they naturally lapse when they hear the music. Then take them along to the church and arrange for the D Minor Toccata to be played there and for the playing to take them by surprise. In this way they will discover that their joy of movement, colour and music can be transferred directly to the building in which the church worships. Try to use this dance movement at the parish Eucharist one Sunday.

WRITING

1 Ask the children to draw all the musical instruments they know, and to write something about them.

2 Ask the children to write about the visit to see the church organ and their experience of the D Minor Toccata.

3 Ask the children to write about their favourite pop group.

4 Research the life of a famous musician, perhaps a church musician like J. S. Bach, or Cliff Richard.

5 Write a poem based on Psalm 150.

DISPLAY HEADINGS

Useful headings for displaying with the work produced in the course of this unit are
1 Class 4 makes music
2 Making music
3 Praise the Lord with the sound of music
4 Praise the Lord with pop music
5 Praise the Lord with classical music

A short explanation of the unit might run like this 'The Gloria is a great Christian hymn of praise. Music helps us to express the joy and happiness in our praise.'

The Lord is Here or *At the Lord's Table* open at pages 8–9 can be displayed also.

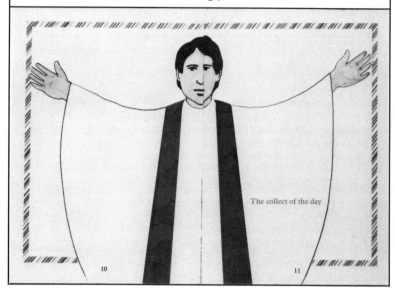

The collect of the day

10   11

Background material

☐ **TEXT**

The prayer book has appointed special Collects for 1) every Sunday of the church's year, 2) festivals and holy days like Christmas and All Saints day, 3) lesser festivals and holy days like the festivals of a bishop or harvest festival, and 4) various occasions like days of prayer for the unity of the church or civic occasions. The Liturgical Commission, *The Alternative Service Book 1980* (CIO 1980, p. 69) writes 'The principle upon which the Collects have been provided is that the "Theme" which has emerged from the controlling lesson has in turn controlled the content of the Collect.'

☐ **PICTURE**

The Collect is the first point in the service when the president asserts his position as the one who acts on behalf of the worshipping community. The picture focuses attention on the priest himself. At this point in the service the priest is offering a prayer on behalf of the people. Soon he will perform his two unique functions of pronouncing the absolution (section 17) and presiding at the Prayer of Thanksgiving (sections 21 onwards).

☐ COMMENT

This section looks first at the traditional construction of the Collect, then it turns attention to the significance of the words President and Priest. Finally, comment is made on two New Testament passages which have been quoted as providing biblical authority for the Church's pattern of ministry. One of these passages is suggested as the New Testament reading at the Eucharist. Both the Old Testament reading and the Gospel reading are passages appointed by the *Alternative Service Book* for the Ordination of Priests.

Collect

A Collect is a short prayer of a formal construction. Often a Collect is composed of three parts. This structure can be conveniently illustrated by reference back to the Collect for Purity discussed in Service Section 2

1 Part one is an invocation, usually including reference to some divine attribute or act as a ground for prayer (Almighty God . . . no secrets are hidden).
2 Part two is the prayer proper, a short, simple and definite petition, usually including a statement of consequence (Cleanse . . . your holy name).
3 Part three is a pleading of Christ's name or an ascription of glory to God (Through Jesus Christ our Lord).

President

This is the term used by Rite A to describe the minister who presides over the whole service. *The Alternative Service Book 1980* (p. 115):

> The president (who, in accordance with the provisions of Canon B12 'Of the ministry of the Holy Communion', must have been episcopally ordained priest) presides over the whole service. He says the opening Greeting, the Collect, the Absolution, the Peace, and the Blessing; he himself must take the bread and the cup before replacing them on the holy table, say the Eucharistic Prayer, break the consecrated bread, and receive the sacrament on every occasion. The remaining parts of the service he may delegate to others. When necessity dictates, a deacon or lay person may preside over the Ministry of the Word.

Priest

The ministry of the Christian church has evolved over a period of nearly two thousand years. A lot of different factors have determined the shape of this evolution. In the Anglican Church the priest is one who is episcopally ordained and who is seen to stand in the succession of the apostles. His ordination gives him authority to do certain things that laymen are not authorised to do, i.e. celebrate communion and pronounce absolution. Traditionally he is also expected to exercise two other functions, namely pastoral care and teaching or preaching. These two other functions he is able to share with lay members of the Christian community.

Alec Graham, in G. R. Dunstan, *The Sacred Ministry*, (SPCK 1970, pp. 50–53) sees three contemporary functions for the Christian priest:

1 *to display* or represent the Christian's response to Christ
2 *to enable* the church to be itself
3 *to involve* the church in what he is and does.

Graham argues that ordination means that

certain Christians publicly, unambiguously, with particular solemnity, at a mature age, renew that total dedication to their master which, no doubt, they made some years earlier and which should characterise the life of every Christian: as they reaffirm their discipleship in this public and solemn manner, they accept further particular responsibilities. These responsibilities are pastoral, prophetic and priestly.

While this ministry belongs to the whole church, the ordained minister is specially 'commissioned to make explicit this threefold responsibility'.

Read Acts 6:1–6 (the appointment of the seven)
Read 1 Timothy 3:1–13 (instructing the leaders of an early Christian community)

These two passages have been quoted as giving New Testament authority to the church's pattern of ministry. It needs to be stressed that in the New Testament the words bishop, elder and deacon are not used with that kind of precision. Regarding the passage from Timothy, C. K. Barrett, *The Pastoral Epistles*, (OUP 1963, p. 31) writes: 'It is important to note the names which are given to these ministers, though the terminology is too fluid to allow firm historical conclusions.' Regarding the passage from Acts, Austin Farrer in K. E. Kirk, *The Apostolic Ministry*, (Hodder 1946, p. 138) writes 'The supposition that the seven are regarded by Luke as deacons is a very old error'.

In his review of the New Testament foundations for priesthood and for the church's ministry, Hans Küng, *Why Priests?*, (Collins 1972, p. 36) writes

The New Testament recognises various types of organisation and administration of the community; they cannot be reduced to one another even though they have fused in the course of time. Hence, the New Testament does not allow us to 'canonise' any one form of community constitution . . . This gives it the freedom to get in step with the times . . . It is not just a question of searching the New Testament for isolated models which we then try to imitate: instead the New Testament offers determinative elements which have to be maintained and confirmed in quite different circumstances if we are to claim the title of Christian.

⊐ **WORSHIP**

Almighty God,
you call priests to serve your church in many ways;
   specially to preside at the Eucharist,
   and to pronounce the forgiveness of sins.
Strengthen those whom you have called
that they may faithfully serve you,
   to the glory of your name
   and to the benefit of your church.
We make our prayer in the name of Jesus Christ,
   our great high priest.   Amen.

First reading: Malachi 2:5–7
Second reading: 1 Timothy 3:8–13
Gospel reading: John 20:19–23

Teaching material

◼ **CONTEXT OF UNIT 5**

The Collect is the first point in the service where the president exercises his function of acting on behalf of the worshipping community. The Collect therefore focuses attention on the person of the priest and his special role in the Christian community. For the child to appreciate the nature of priesthood two things are necessary:

1 The child needs to understand that the priest is an ordinary man. He is not especially good, especially clever, or superhuman in any way. He has an ordinary job to do. Some aspects of the priest's job are purely administrative: running the church can be like running any other business, and places a number of pressures on the priest, especially when he lacks the secretarial and financial support necessary to do the job well. Like anyone else, the priest can become tired, rushed and cross. This understanding is important if the child is to formulate reasonable expectations of the clergy.

2 The child needs to understand that the priest is in some ways different from other people:

  a His ordination gives him a special job to do. He presides at the Eucharist. He pronounces the Absolution. He enables the Christian community to be the Christian community before God.

  b His training gives him special skills and a specialist knowledge in such areas as scripture, church history and especially regarding the claims God makes on his people.

  c His own prayer life should help him to set an example in the way of spiritual awareness.

d He should have expertise in helping and counselling people.

e In particular when he is presiding at the Eucharist, the individual priest is pointing beyond the limitations of his own personality to the universal priesthood in which he shares. The use of robes and vestments help to symbolise this aspect of priesthood. Thus the child needs to understand the significance of the vestments and the way in which they help to point our attention beyond the priest to Christ himself.

■ OBJECTIVES

1 To enable the child to explore the priest's daily pattern of life.

2 To enable the child to see the way in which the priest is set apart by the church to act in a special way and on behalf of the whole worshipping community.

3 To enable the child to appreciate the significance of the robes which the priest wears when he celebrates the eucharist.

■ DISPLAY WORK

Three different projects can help the child to explore the nature of priesthood. The first is concerned with the priest's daily life. The second is concerned with the special role he has in liturgy and the vestments he uses at the eucharist. The third is concerned with the clergy through the ages.

a This is your priest's life

Let the children begin by talking about the priests they know. Let them speculate about what the priest does – how he was trained and why he became a priest. Then begin to make a list of the things he is likely to do in a day:

answer the phone; answer the door to visitors; write letters/references; fill in forms; visit hospitals, schools, factories; organise Sunday's worship; say the daily offices and spend time in prayer; attend to building problems at church; go shopping; prepare couples for marriage; visit family about baptism; deal with staffing shortage for sunday school; cope with problem that the organist has mumps; some one comes for advice.

All of these things (and many more) can now be organised into a form of board game (Priest's Progress). The children can design and make the board game for themselves and then play the game with dice.

b The vestments

The vestments of the Eucharist symbolise the objective side of the priest's role. Vested he represents the Christ before the altar. It is important for the child to recognise this formal aspect of the priest's appearance. Encourage the children to talk about the priest's vestments – the cassock, the alb, the stole, the chasuble. These vestments come in different colours for different seasons:

> white for Easter and Christmas; red for Whitsun and martyrs; purple for Lent and Advent; green for the rest of the year.

Show the church's vestments to the children and give them the chance to study them. Two creative activities can help them to become familiar with the vestments:

1 On a large sheet of paper draw round a child and then draw in the outline of the vestments – including a simple pattern on the chasuble. A good way of colouring the picture outline is by sticking balls of coloured tissue paper onto the paper background. Different groups of children can produce vestments in the four liturgical colours.

2 A real set of vestments can be made for the local priest to use at a special celebration of the eucharist. A number of different needlework skills can be employed in producing the basic shape of the vestments and then in decorating them.

c The clergy through the ages

Try to discover the names of the clergy who served your local church since it was built or, if your own church is very recent, base the project on an older church not too far away. Try to discover pictures or photographs of some of the former clergy. See if there are memorials inside the church or gravestones outside commemorating former incumbents. It is possible to make rubbings of these memorials. Talk about the life of clergy in earlier times. If local information is lacking, look at the lives of one or two well-known priests.

■ ACTIVITIES

1 The well-known television programme 'This is Your Life' can form the basis for drama. Encourage the children to explore the life story of a priest. They can assume the role of his parents, his school friends, his college friends, his wife, his children, his parishioners. They can pose questions like 'What do you think of him becoming a priest?' 'Was he different from you when he was at school?' 'What is it like having a priest for a father?' They can speculate about his day off – his hobbies – his sport etc.

2 Arrange for the children to meet some clergy from different denominations and from different parishes. They can be encouraged to think of questions to ask them – about their job and about their understanding of themselves. 'Why are you a priest?' 'When did you first want to be a priest?' 'How were you trained as a priest?' Since all clergy are not equally good at handling children's questions, it is wise to prepare the ground for this exercise carefully.

3 Devise and then record an interview with the local parish priest or, possibly, the Diocesan Director of Education.

4 Visit other churches and museums to look at different vestments.

5 See if it is possible to visit a church or cathedral which has a brass figure of a priest and arrange to let the children make a brass rubbing of it.

■ **WRITING**

1 Ask the children to pretend that they are priests and ask them to write about 'A day in my life as priest'.

2 Write letters which you think your parish priest is likely to receive or to write to other people.

■ **DISPLAY HEADINGS**

Useful headings for displaying with the work produced in this unit are
   1 Here is a stole
   2 Class 4 made this chasuble
   3 The vestments are a symbol of the priest's special job
   4 Meeting the priest
   5 A day in the life of the priest
   6 The Priest's Progress: a board game

A short explanation might run like this: 'When the priest says the Collect, he is praying on behalf of the whole congregation. The Collect makes us think of the priest's special function in the church.'

The Lord is Here or *At the Lord's Table* open at pages 10–11 can be displayed also.

6. MINISTRY OF THE WORD

Hear all about it

The Ministry of the Word

Old Testament Reading

This is the word of the Lord.
Thanks be to God.

New Testament Reading (Epistle)

This is the word of the Lord.
Thanks be to God.

The Gospel

Glory to Christ our Saviour.

This is the Gospel of Christ.
Praise to Christ our Lord.

The Sermon

12

Background material

☐ **TEXT**

At the heart of the ministry of the word is the reading of passages from scripture. The Book of Common Prayer established the pattern of two readings, the Epistle and the Gospel. The lectionary in *The Alternative Service Book 1980* has restored the pattern of three lessons, including a reading from the Old Testament as well as the Epistle and Gospel. As in the early church, the sermon immediately follows after the Gospel as a climax of the declaration and application of the word of the Lord.

The responses after the readings 'This is the Word of the Lord' and 'This is the Gospel of Christ' are in the present tense to indicate that God speaks today through the reading of the Word.

☐ **PICTURE**

The picture portrays a group of children enjoying the library corner in school. On this occasion they are not reading for themselves: the teacher is reading to them. The aim of the picture is to draw attention to the bible as itself a complete library of books – books which, either read silently or proclaimed aloud, are to be enjoyed alongside other books.

☐ **COMMENT**

In this section the Liturgical Commission's Commentary explains the principles on which the Alternative Service Book's Lectionary was constructed. Then a short comment is made on the content of the bible, and four different authors, Maurice Wiles, Christopher Evans, Joseph Gelineau and Trevor Lloyd, give different perspectives on the use of the bible by the church and in worship today. The Old Testament reading shows Ezra the priest proclaiming the Law and the people's response. The New Testament reading illustrates the respect shown to scripture by the writer of the Second Letter to Timothy. The Gospel reading shows Jesus' use of scripture in the synagogue at Nazareth.

The Lectionary (ASB 1980)
The Liturgical Commission's Commentary on *ASB 1980* (CIO 1980, p. 29):

the purpose of a biennial scheme for the readings at Holy Communion is to achieve a fuller presentation of scripture . . . On the nine Sundays before Christmas, the Old Testament reading is marked by an asterisk. This indicates that it is the 'controlling' reading, and that the others have been chosen to support it. During this season, in preparation for Christmas, they trace the story of Creation, the Fall, and the saving purposes of God revealed in the Old Testament to lead up to the celebration of the Incarnation and as it were to set the scene for the whole recital of Our Lord's ministry as it unfolds during the year. From Christmas to Easter the gospel is the controlling reading and sets out the life and ministry of the Incarnate Lord in more or less chronological order. From Easter to Pentecost the gospel still controls, presenting the Resurrection appearances in one year and in the other the concept of eternal life in the 'I am' passages from St John's gospel. From Pentecost the New Testament reading is the controlling reading . . . The concern is with the life and mission of the people of God, who live between Pentecost and Parousia and are on pilgrimage to the ends of the earth and to the end of time. Accordingly the appropriate theme for the last Sunday after Pentecost is 'Citizens of Heaven'. No matter how many Sundays after Pentecost there may be in the year, this Sunday always brings the series to a close.

The bible and worship
The word 'bible' is derived from the Greek work *biblia* meaning books. The

books of the bible are divided into two sections, the Old Testament and the New Testament. The books of the Old Testament date from before the birth of Jesus. These books are held in common by the Christian Church and the Jewish Synagogue. The books of the New Testament are the early writings of the Christian Church. They comprise the four Gospels of Matthew, Mark, Luke and John, Luke's second book, the Acts of the Apostles, a set of Epistles written by people like Paul, and Revelation of John. The word Gospel translates the Greek word *euaggelion* which means good news. The word Epistle is derived from the Greek word *epistole* which means simply letter.

Maurice Wiles in M. Hooker and C. Hickling, *What about the New Testament?*, (SCM 1975, p. 155):

> In the course of Christian history the distinctive character of 'holy scripture' has often been asserted in ways which were epistemologically absurd and religiously disastrous. Its composition has been ascribed to forms of dictation which left human writers no more than an instrument in the hand of the divine author but ensured the inerrancy of the resultant text. Then, in obedience to its commands, witches have been burnt to the glory of God or else a divine authority claimed for all one's own immediate concerns by the Midas touch of allegorical interpretation.

Christopher Evans, *Is 'Holy Scripture' Christian?*, (SCM 1971, pp. 22–3) argues that in order to assess the authority of the bible in the church we ought to start from the question:

> How did the New Testament come to be regarded as holy scripture? Anyone who has studied what is called the history of the Canon, which is the history of the process by which the New Testament writings came to have the status of holy scripture, knows how difficult it is to answer. The difficulties arise chiefly from the paucity of evidence in the vital period concerned, the first half of the second century AD, and from the often indirect character of such evidence as there is.

Joseph Gelineau, *The Liturgy Today and Tomorrow*, (Darton, Longman and Todd 1978, p. 75–6):

> The Bible is a word from elsewhere, another time and another place. It comes to us in the form of scripture written in other languages, languages of the past. It cannot be re-written even though it must always be freshly interpreted. In order to pass it on, it must be translated. And translated in a way which preserves the spirit of its own, other, language . . . We should therefore translate the Bible in a way that can be understood by us today, into our common speech and ways of thinking. But our translation should not obliterate the text's socio-historical context because this is ancient, oriental and agrarian.

Trevor Lloyd 'Worship and the Bible', in *Anglican Worship Today*, (Collins 1980, pp. 14–18) writes that the bible is

> not just a beautiful ceremonial volume carried in on a velvet cushion, but the vehicle which prompts and assists our response to God himself in Christian worship. Consider four areas of stimulation to worship: response to revelation, response to life, response to example, and response to precept.

> 1 *Response to revelation*. Christian worship is determined by the worshippers appreciation of the worth of God. How does the Christian know how much God is worth? Simply because God has revealed himself – in nature, in history, in our experience, in his Word. As important and essential as those other areas of revelation are, it is God's Word which actually gives articulate meaning and context to them.

> 2 *Response to life*. We see God taking ordinary things and consecrating them, taking them over, investing them with a real meaning beyond what is obviously apparent . . . It is the principle of the Incarnation, of God penetrating our ordinary life in order to open the gates of heaven to us.

> 3 *Response to example*. Because of the way that God uses his revelation of himself in words and actions, and his invasion of the whole of ordinary life, to stimulate us to worship him, it is ridiculous to expect him to give us a detailed set of instructions about how to do it . . . The Bible gives examples to stimulate our own response to God rather than to be slavishly re-enacted.

> 4 *Response to precept*. The church today does not only follow biblical examples and fill its worship with biblical quotations. It also obeys some of the precepts, rules, commands, suggestions laid down in the Bible.

☐ **WORSHIP**

Blessed Lord,
You have given the bible to your church,
 and for the benefit of your people.
Help us to hear your word,
 and to learn from it,
That we may come to know you more clearly,
 to love you more deeply,
 and to serve you more fully.
We make our prayer in the name of Jesus Christ,
 who is your Living Word.   Amen.

First reading: Nehemiah 8:1–8
Second reading: 2 Timothy 3:10–17
Gospel reading: Luke 4:14–21

Teaching material

■ CONTEXT OF UNIT 6

The Ministry of the Word points to two important aspects of the Christian's way of life. First, the Christian is committed to serious study about his faith in order to learn more about God's purposes for his people. Second, the Christian gives a special place to the holy bible both in his study and in his worship. For these two aspects of the Christian faith to become important to the child, two things are necessary

1 the child needs to discover that learning about the Christian faith can be interesting and worthwhile.

2 the child needs to become aware of the nature and importance of the bible in the life of the church.

■ OBJECTIVES

1 To enable the child to become familiar with the bible as a library or collection of books. A library contains all sorts of different books – history, poetry, stories and so on. These books are written for many different purposes and need to be read in many different ways.

2 To enable the child to appreciate that the bible contains old books. They are not written like books today. The people who wrote the books of the bible thought differently from us. They wrote in Hebrew and Greek. We have their books in many different translations.

3 To enable the child to understand how the books of the bible became written. They were written by many different people. Many of the stories were passed on by word of mouth for many years before they were written down. Other parts of the bible, like Paul's letters, were written specifically to certain people whom the writer knew well, as we write to our friends.

4 To enable the child to understand how the bible is used and treasured today within the Christian community. At the Eucharist an extract is read from the three different parts (Old Testament, Epistle and Gospel). The bible is used by preachers as the basis for proclaiming God's message to his people.

■ DISPLAY WORK

Begin by talking about the school library – and the public library. If possible, let the children look round a library and make a note of all the different kinds of books. Note how they are organised on the shelf – by subjects, size or reading difficulty. Then look at the books which make up the bible. Note the difference between the Old Testament and the New Testament. Explore the different lengths, styles and contents of the books of the bible. There are a number of creative activities which will enable the children to develop the idea of the bible as a library.

1 **Make a Bible Library** Each book of the Bible can be represented as a different volume. Empty cardboard packets can be covered with different sorts of 'binding' and the names of the books of the Bible inscribed on the spines. Different colour bindings can be used to distinguish the Old Testament books from the books of the New Testament, or to distinguish the different kind of books in each testament. Different size packets can be used for different lengths of books. When made, the books can be manipulated into different groupings, i.e. the order they appear in the New English Bible, the order they appear in the Jerusalem Bible, the categories of writing etc.

2 **Bible Game – 'Roll a Book'** It is important to understand that the books of the bible were written in different times and for different purposes. A simple approach is to concentrate on the main categories of literature in the bible and to establish which books belong to each category. Show the children how to fold a piece of card so as to produce an eight sided tube. The tube can be given body by inserting something like an empty washing up liquid container. A category of Bible book can be written on each of the eight sides. On another tube the names of eight books of the Bible can be written – for example

Tube One	*Tube Two*
New Testament	Acts of the Apostles
Old Testament	Amos
Stories of the old days	Genesis
God's work in history	Samuel
Prophecy	Jeremiah
Poetry	Psalms
Letter	Romans
Gospel	Mark

The game is played by two people. Each takes it in turn to roll his tube first. When tube one comes to rest, the word at the top becomes the key word. If the second tube comes to rest with a matching key word the second player receives a point – unless he fails to recognise that the words match. A number of different forms can be made of Tube Two.

3 **Old forms of writing** The books of the bible are old. Talk about the ways in which these books used to be written. If possible look at Hebrew, Greek and Latin Bibles – scrolls and illuminated manuscripts.

a Encourage the children to imitate the early forms of writing – perhaps a copy of a Greek or Hebrew character or a few Latin words.

b Some children will enjoy making illuminated script. They can begin by writing their name or the name of a book of the bible. Some may care to take this work further.

c Scrolls can be made from cardboard tubes. The handles can be nicely decorated. Some children may care to experiment with writing a scroll for themselves – either using the scroll for creative writing or for copying a passage from scripture.

4 The class newspaper The Bible contains a lot of material of many different kinds, rather like a newspaper. Encourage the class to produce its own newspaper of Biblical material – 'Good News According to Class 4'. The children can write about and illustrate their favourite bible story in a way suitable for news print. There is plenty of room for enjoyment and initiative to produce cartoons, advertisements, headlines etc. *The stars* can foretell the coming of the wise men. Hosea can run a *problem column*. Joseph *the weatherman* can prophesy seven years of drought. The *travel correspondent* can describe the Exodus. The *Government news agency* can describe the empty tomb on Easter Sunday. The Psalms can provide a *literary/poetry* page. The official steward can advertise wine for wedding feasts, etc.

5 Build a pulpit and lectern In church the bible is given a particular importance by virtue of its special place on the lectern. Similarly, the preacher is given importance by the pulpit. Encourage the children to appreciate this importance by making and decorating their own pulpit and lectern. An interesting lectern can be made on the basis of a bird table with a slightly sloping top. The front view of the table can be decorated with the traditional lectern shape of an eagle cut out of cardboard (the eagle symbolises the carrying of the gospel). Tracery can be painted onto it. Many pulpits are decorated with a 'Pulpit-fall' – a piece of rich cloth extending from the book rest a little way down the front. Such a pulpit-fall can be made in a number of ways, possibly in patchwork or in weaving.

■ **ACTIVITIES**

1 Arrange a competition to use the 'Roll a Book' game.

2 Use the lectern and pulpit described in the previous section to practise reading the scriptures aloud. Record the children's voices.

3 Visit some neighbouring churches and chapels to discover the different styles of pulpits and lecterns generally in use. Note the translation of the bible used in these different places.

4 Visit museums or libraries to look at ancient manuscripts.

5 Show a film or slides on the history of the bible.

6 The bible contains the account of God's people. All sorts of people worked to make this account and to write it down. The accounts differ greatly in terms of accuracy, interest, etc. Encourage the children to appreciate the

problems involved in writing such an account by asking them to write an up-to-date account of what has happened in their own church in recent years. Ask them to talk about the history, development, and practice of their own church with a number of different people, and then to write that account in a class book. Gradually a picture will emerge, but it will be a picture with problems, ambiguities and contradictions – in fact, something rather similar to the four gospel accounts of the times of Jesus. A good name for the class project could be 'Today's Bible: God's People at St Mary's'.

■ WRITING

1 Read and write about Jesus' visit to the synagogue in Nazareth (Luke 4:14–21).

2 Ask the children to write the 'life story' of one of the books of the bible – to relate the history of that book as it has been handed from person to person and translated into different languages, and to tell how it is used today.

■ DISPLAY HEADINGS

Useful headings for displaying with the work produced in this unit are
  1 The bible is a whole library of books
  2 The Old Testament was first written in Hebrew
  3 The New Testament was first written in Greek
  4 The bible used to be written on scrolls
  5 The monks made copies of the bible by hand, and they took great care to make their bibles very beautiful

A short explanation might run like this, 'The Ministry of the Word reminds us of the very important place which the Bible has in the Church.'

The Lord is Here or *At the Lord's Table* open at pages 12–13 can be displayed also.

7. CREED : GOD

Follow the signs

We believe in one God,
the Father, the almighty,
maker of heaven and earth,
of all that is,
seen and unseen.

Background material

☐ **TEXT**

The creeds are concise, formal and authorised statements of the important doctrines of the Christian faith. Originally they had two functions:

1 a formula to be accepted by candidates for Christian baptism.

2 a standard to distinguish between orthodoxy and heresy.

The Creed has been used in some eucharistic rites since the late fifth century. The Creed used here is known as the Nicene Creed. The name derives from the fact that this Creed has been erroneously attributed to the Council of Nicaea (AD 325). Its precise origin is somewhat later.

The first section of the Creed confesses faith in God the Father.

☐ **PICTURE**

The representation of God in pictorial form gives rise to many problems. The illustrated communion book has deliberately rejected two possibilities,

1 the representation of God in the form of a man. While it is helpful to think of God in human terms, it is not helpful to encourage children to be satisfied with this model of understanding.

2 the representation of God in highly stylised ideograms, e.g. the triangle symbolising The Trinity or the circle symbolising his Eternity.

The pictorial option taken is that of the flame. The flame is God's mode of self revelation to Moses in Exodus 3:2. It also suggests a number of the divine attributes, e.g. light, power, movement, transformation. The flame is one of a number of signs or symbols by which we can give expression to an understanding of God.

□ **COMMENT**

The word Creed comes from the Latin *Credo* meaning I believe. In this section comment is made on the two problematic concepts employed in the first part of the Creed, Almighty and Maker. Then Thomas Fawcett discusses the way in which symbols are used to talk about God. The Old Testament reading illustrates how fire is used as one specific symbol to talk about God. Both the New Testament reading and the Gospel reading illustrate the Christian experience of God as Father, and Joachim Jeremias comments on the uniqueness of this experience.

Almighty John Burnaby, *Belief of Christendom*, (SPCK 1959, p. 27) explains that neither the Greek word *pantocrator* nor the Latin word *omnipotens* 'convey the strict notion of "omnipotence" . . . viz power to do anything. They are adjectives of "glorification", which . . . express little more than the contrast between human weakness and divine strength.'

Maker Wolfhart Pannenberg, *The Apostles Creed*, (SCM 1972, p. 36):

All experience of redemption and liberation, however intense, remains ultimately without guarantee if in these experiences we have not to do with the creator of the world.

Commenting on the biblical tradition of creation from Genesis 1:1–2:4, Alan Richardson, *Genesis 1–11*, (SCM 1953, pp. 41–2) writes:

Creation in the biblical sense is *creatio ex nihilo* – out of nothing. It is utterly beyond the power of man to perform; it is essentially miraculous, and can be accomplished only by the living God . . . The Hebrew mind did not arrive at the idea of creation by way of philosophical speculation . . . The Lord who had been encountered in history was revealed to Israel as the almighty ruler of the destinies of nations; and it was inevitable that the prophets should conclude that the world of nature – the theatre and stage of history – was also his handiwork and empire.

Thomas Fawcett, *The Symbolic Language of Religion*, (SCM 1970, pp. 34–36) argues that symbols work deep down psychologically. They lead to what he calls 'emotionally experienced meaning', and they demand a response from us. He continues:

> When God is characterised as a father, the symbol calls upon men to play the part of sons. If the symbol of the husband is attributed to God, it implies the correlative that there is a wife, an image which Israel developed at some depth and which helped to shape the concept of religious chastity and loyalty. The shepherd symbol directed the Hebrew mind towards the need for a sense of trusting dependence on the part of man when confronted by God. The kingship symbol inculcated loyalty, respect and obedience. A symbol is never neutral, but always calls upon man to play his part in the dialogue between God and man which it opens up. In this lies the power of symbols to direct the life of men, to determine their moral behaviour and bring out their spiritual potentialities.

Read Exodus 3:1–6 (Moses and the Burning Bush)
Wheeler Robinson, *Religious Ideas of the Old Testament*, (Duckworth 1913, p. 105):

> Yahweh is also manifested by the phenomenon of fire in general, as by the stove vomiting smoke and flame that passed between the pieces of Abram's sacrifice, the burning bush seen by Moses, the pillar of cloud-shrouded fire that led the Israelites, the cloud that filled the temple.

Read Romans 8:14–17 and Luke 11:1–13 (the Christian addresses God as Abba, Father)
Joachim Jeremias, *The Prayers of Jesus*, (SCM 1967, pp. 57–63):

> Whereas there is not a single instance of God being addressed as Abba in the literature of Jewish prayer, Jesus always addressed him in this way . . . To address a father as *Abba* is a mark of the everyday language of the family . . . To the Jewish mind it would have been disrespectful and therefore inconceivable to address God with this familiar word. For Jesus to venture to take this step was something new and unheard of. He spoke to God like a child to his father, simply, inwardly, confidently. Jesus' use of *Abba* in addressing God reveals the heart of his relationship with God . . . The giving of the Lord's Prayer to the disciples authorised them to say 'Abba', just as Jesus did. In this way Jesus gave them a share in his relationship with God.

☐ **WORSHIP**

Dear Lord God,
you are a mighty rock,
   protect us.
You are a shepherd,
   care for us.
You are a vinedresser,
   shape us.
You are a king,
   rule over us.
You are a father,
   love us.
You are a still small voice,
   speak to us.
We make our prayer
   in the name of Jesus Christ our Lord.   Amen.

First reading: Exodus 3:1–6
Second reading: Romans 8:14–17
Gospel reading: Luke 11:1–13

Teaching material

■ **CONTEXT OF UNIT 7**

The Creed speaks about God in terms of certain well known images, Father, Creator, the Almighty. The associated picture speaks about God in terms of an equally well known but different type of image, namely the fire. The problem with images is that they easily become mistaken for the reality to which they point: and this is particularly the case among children. The danger is that when we begin by saying that God is *like* a father, we conclude by being content with the idea that God is an old man in the sky.

There are a number of different images which tell us something about God. Our knowledge of God develops by our willingness to see what each image has to say, by treasuring what it says, and then by passing onto the next image. No image is sufficient in itself. The purpose of this unit is to enable the child to explore some of the images used to speak about God – and to help him to understand that these images are not the final truth of the matter but only means to an end – they are signs and symbols which point beyond themselves. We begin by enabling the child to explore the idea of signs and symbols as they apply to everyday life before proceeding to examine their use in talk about God.

OBJECTIVES

1 To enable the child to explore the concept of signs and symbols. Signs and symbols play a very important part in everyday life. The child needs to begin by understanding how everyday signs and symbols function.

2 To enable the child to explore the images used to speak of God. It is necessary for him to come to see how these images function as signs and symbols which are not ends in themselves but rather point beyond themselves.

3 In particular attention is given to eight images which are used to speak of God – Father, King, Creator, shepherd, vinedresser, rock, fire, small voice. It is important for the child to experience some of the meaning of these key Christian images.

4 To enable the child to appreciate both the fun and the difficulty involved in talking about God. It is important to strike the balance between
   a) the child thinking that he knows all there is to know about God – and later rejecting it.
   b) the child thinking it is too difficult for him to bother with.

DISPLAY WORK

It is useful for the teacher to begin this unit by listening to the children's own ideas and without offering much by way of initial stimulation. Begin by asking the children to tell you about God – to talk about God, to write about God, to draw God. Accept the children's own ideas and use these as a starting point. The first key lies in recognising which of the ideas are really important to the child, and in respecting these ideas. The aim of the unit is not to undermine the child's own belief structure, but to offer him ways of developing a more adult perspective when he needs to do so.

The display work is divided into two sections – a section dealing with the signs and symbols encountered in everyday life and a section dealing with the images we use to speak about God.

a Signs and Symbols

There are a number of different kinds of signs and symbols which the child meets in his everyday life.

1 *Traffic signs.* Encourage the children to remember and describe as many traffic signs as they can. Look at the highway code. Explore what the signs mean and how we have to respond to them. Then road signs can be painted and drawn. More interestingly road signs can be made – perhaps even as life size models. For example, orange beacons can be made by using cardboard tubes as the poles (carpet stores have this kind of tube) and an orange balloon as a globe. The zebra crossing can be made by painting black stripes onto a large roll of white paper. Simpler signs can be made from cardboard.

2 *Trade marks.* There are a number of well known trade marks associated

with brand name food stuffs, certain supermarkets, and trades (like the barber's pole and pawnbroker's three balls). When the child sees these signs he is immediately aware of the meaning to which they point. A scrap book can be made to illustrate these signs.

3 *Other signs*. There are a number of other signs which may be of particular interest to different groups of children, for example,

   a petrol signs
   b coats of arms (the local county, the cricket club, local families)
   c badges and scarves (football teams, the school)
   d car signs (the rolls royce radiator grille)
   e pub signs (the King's Head etc.)
   f the international picture signs (public lavatories etc.)

b Images for God

The bible speaks about God in terms of two different kinds of images

   a images based upon analogy from human relationships, for example, father, shepherd, king.

   b images based upon analogy from natural phenomena, for example, fire, thunder.

Ask the children to examine the following images and to explore what they say about God

1 *Father*. In Luke 15:11–32 God is likened to the father who welcomes back the Prodigal son. This theme is explored fully in Teaching Unit 3.

2 *King*. In Matthew 18:23–27 God is likened to the King who commands respect and who forgives. This theme also is explored fully in Teaching Unit 3.

3 *Creator*. In Genesis 1–2 God is likened to a craftsman who creates things, and who on the seventh day rests from his labour, pleased with all that he has made. Let the child talk about things which he has made and of which he is particularly proud. Explore the way in which he takes special care of the things which he has made. Look at craftsmen and their fine work; see how the craftsman becomes attached to his work and takes particular care of it. In such a way does God care for the world which he made. Illustrate the theme by asking the children to write about something they have made and of which they are proud, and by collecting pictures of craftsmen.

Be prepared for the puzzle that when we make something we merely transform existing material: God makes the material in the first place. Apart from God there is no material at all. He brings *all* into existence.

4 *Shepherd*. In Psalm 23 God is likened to a shepherd who cares for his people and looks after them like a shepherd looks after his sheep. (See also, John 10:1–18 and Luke 15:3–7.) This image is based on the Palestinian model of sheep farming which is somewhat different from the way in which

shepherds work in this country. The basic idea, however, is still useful. Let the children talk and write about the work of a shepherd – the sheep wandering off, the difficulty of rounding them up, etc. Wordsworth's poem 'Michael' gives an idea of their work as it was in Grasmere around the year 1800. A large collage or model can be made of sheep, the shepherd etc., perhaps using scraps of real wool.

5 *Vinedresser*. In Isaiah 27:2–6 God is likened to a vinedresser who plants, prunes and cares for his vines. Let the children talk about their own experience of gardening, and explore the skill and care of a good gardener.

6 *Rock*. Psalm 18:2, 31 speaks of God as a rock and as a fortress. The image implies strength and dependability. God is strong and can be relied upon. Collect pictures of strong rocks and fortresses. Build a cardboard castle on a 'rock' of papier mâché covered wire netting.

7 *Fire*. Exodus 3:1–6 speaks of God appearing to Moses in the burning bush. Encourage the children to talk about the qualities of fire and to explore the Moses story. The story is an image to present an aspect of God's self revelation. Give particular attention to Moses' feelings when he met with God.

8 *Small voice*. In 1 Kings 19:11–13 God appears to Elijah as a small voice. Explore with the children the idea of meeting with God in quiet and stillness. This story also helps to illustrate the transitory nature of the images we use to express our experience of God. Fire, wind, earthquake are all good images in themselves, but for Elijah on this occasion they did not work – their place needed to be taken by something else, and something which Elijah may well have found surprising.

ACTIVITIES

a Signs and Symbols

1 Take the children for a walk or outing in order to spot as many signs as possible – road signs, shop signs, etc.

2 When a number of road signs have been made they can be arranged in appropriate places
   a inside the church – the zebra crossing at the chancel step, water splash at the font, a speed limit on the organ, etc.
   b outside to provide a cycle track etc.

3 Highway code snap. A set of playing cards can be made showing
   a pictures of traffic signs
   b the meaning of these signs. Play as for snap.

b Images for God
(Activities related to the images of King and Father are explored in Unit 3.)

C

1 *Creator* a) encourage the children to make something really well – something which each one of them really wants to make and in which he will take a pride.

b) arrange a 'hobbies' exhibition of all the things which the children have made, collected, etc.

2 *Shepherd* If it is possible to visit a sheep rearing area arrange to do so. Quite often it is possible to collect little pieces of wool from the hedges and fences. Use this to make a collage about the visit.

3 *Vinedresser* Let the children plant a small garden and then observe the care and effort which is needed to cultivate it properly.

4 *Rock* Arrange to visit an old castle built on a strong mound.

5 *Fire* Let the children act out the story of Moses and the burning bush – giving attention particularly to Moses' feelings when he meets with God.

6 *Small Voice* Use appropriate music and poems about quietness and stillness to create an atmosphere of stillness and peace. Then encourage the children to create their own music, poetry and dance to illuminate this image of God.

WRITING

1 Ask the children to think of new images which they could use to talk about God. Draw upon their experience of everyday life in the same way as the ancient Hebrew people did when they spoke in terms of shepherds, vine-dressers, etc.

2 Creative writing can be stimulated by such techniques as
  a) a title like 'The day I made something very well'.
  b) ask the children to pretend to be sheep and to describe their shepherd.
  c) ask the children to imagine that their lives depend upon a strong fortress built upon a rock.

DISPLAY HEADINGS

Useful headings for displaying with the work produced in the course of this unit are
  1 signs are there to tell us things
  2 road signs help us to understand our journey
  3 some road signs tell us about the law
  4 some road signs tell us about the hazards of the road
  5 we use signs and images to talk about God
  6 God is like a father who loves us
  7 God is like a shepherd who leads us
  8 God made himself known to Moses like a burning flame
  9 I believe in one God, the Father, the Almighty . . .

A short explanation might run like this: 'The Creed sums up what we believe about God the Father'.

The Lord is Here or *At the Lord's Table* open at pages 14–15 can be displayed also.

8. CREED : JESUS

Meeting Jesus of Nazareth

We believe in one Lord, Jesus Christ,
the only Son of God,
eternally begotten of the Father,
God from God, Light from Light,
true God from true God,
begotten, not made,
of one Being with the Father.
Through him all things were made.

For us men and for our salvation
he came down from heaven;
by the power of the Holy Spirit
he became incarnate of the Virgin Mary,
    and was made man.
For our sake he was crucified
    under Pontius Pilate;
he suffered death and was buried.

On the third day he rose again
in accordance with the Scriptures;
he ascended into heaven
and is seated at the right hand
    of the Father.
He will come again in glory
to judge the living and the dead,
and his kingdom will have no end.

17

Background material

☐ **TEXT**

The section of the Nicene creed about the second person of the Trinity is the longest and fullest part of the Creed. This is because much of this section was drawn up specifically to combat the heresy of Arius: and this heresy was about the person of Christ. First, the Creed defines at some length the relationship between the Father and the Son. Then it states the church's faith in

1 the Incarnation
2 the Crucifixion and death
3 the Resurrection
4 the Ascension
5 the second coming and judgement.

PICTURE

The picture focuses attention on the cross as the symbol of faith in Jesus, and as the primary symbol of Christianity itself.

COMMENT

In this section comment is made on thirteen key words or concepts which appear in the second part of the Creed. Then six New Testament references are noted to help locate these concepts within a biblical context. The Old Testament reading is a well known passage which has been interpreted by the church as pointing forward to the Christ. The New Testament reading relates the Ascension, and the Gospel reading relates the discovery of the empty tomb.

We believe John Burnaby, *The Belief of Christendom*, (SPCK 1959, p. 60):

> The Jesus of whom we speak is a certain Nazarene who was called the Christ and on that account was put to death under Pontius Pilate. That there was such a person is not a matter of belief but of historical knowledge, whereas the creed as a whole is concerned not with what we may reasonably claim to know but with what we believe.

Lord The word can simply mean master, but it can also mean much more than this. Wolfhart Pannenberg, *The Apostle's Creed*, (SCM 1972, p. 69):

> The word Lord, *Kurios*, is used in the Greek translation of the Old Testament as a paraphrase for the Old Testament name for God, Yahweh, which the devout Jew avoided pronouncing. Jesus may perhaps have been called 'The Lord' before Easter, in the more commonplace sense of a polite form of address. Later this custom merged, at least, with the weightier meaning of the word 'Lord', as a paraphrase for the name of God.

Jesus is the Greek form of the Hebrew word Joshua meaning 'God is salvation'. John Fenton, *Saint Matthew*, (Penguin 1963, p. 43) writes 'As Matthew points out the name is applicable to Jesus who will save *his people*, Israel, *from their* sins.' (Mt 1:21)

Christ is the Greek translation of the Hebrew 'Messiah' meaning 'Anointed One'. Burnaby, *The Belief of Christendom*, p. 65, writes, 'The ceremony of anointing was the setting apart and empowering of a chosen individual for a sacred office, especially the office of priest or king.'

Son of God By the time this creed was written the term had come to stress the divinity of Christ. Earlier on when St Mark used the term it meant something quite different. Christopher Evans, *The Beginning of the Gospel*, (SPCK 1968, p. 72) writes that it is a Semitic idiom

> according to which 'son of' means not 'belonging to', nor even primarily 'the physical offspring of', but the special object of a father's regard, who owes his father obedience and is to reproduce his character. In the Old Testament Israel, as a people which had been redeemed by God and which knows his will through the Law, is called the Son of God.

Eternally begotten   The juxtaposition of these two ideas intentionally presents a paradox intended to safeguard two truths, 1) that the relationship between the first and the second person of the Trinity is precisely that of Father and Son, and 2) that the Son exists, and has always existed, eternally with the Father.

God from God ... were made   The second person of the Trinity is in no sense inferior to the first. The theological importance of these statements is that they stress that the Christ who saves us is none other than God himself. On this issue John Burnaby, *The Belief of Christendom*, p. 76, writes,

> To acknowledge with the Creed that our Lord is of one substance with the Father, is to acknowledge that what God gave in the giving of his Son was *himself* – and that nothing less than God's giving of himself could bring into this world of change, sin, and death the power of his own endless life.

For our salvation   The work of Christ, that is the salvation of mankind, is the central tenet of faith around which the creed's statements of belief in the second person of the Trinity are constructed.

Incarnate of the Virgin Mary   The idea of the virgin birth may be understood to refer to something historical; or it may be a way of expressing a theological truth. Raymond Brown, *The Virginal Conception and Bodily Resurrection of Jesus*, (Chapman 1973, p. 28):

> Matthew and Luke are interested in virginal conception as a sign of divine choice and grace, and as the idiom of a Christological insight that Jesus was God's Son or the Davidic Messiah from birth, etc. – in other words, they are interested in it as a phenomenon with theological import.

Pontius Pilate   was Procurator of Judaea from AD26 to AD36 when he was recalled because of his cruelty.

Resurrection   Norman Perrin, *The Resurrection Narratives*, (SCM 1977, p. 5):

> We live and move and have our being in a world in which Jesus has risen

from the dead. A quality of life is possible for us in that world which would not be possible for us without the faith we celebrate each Easter morning. 'Jesus is Risen!' we cry, and we share his victory over the last enemy, death.

Ascension The story of the Ascension provides the link between Luke's two books, Luke's Gospel and the Acts of the Apostles.

He will come again Mathias Rissi, *The Future of the World*, (SCM 1972, p. 18):

> The future of the church and the world is Jesus Christ. His appearance is certain and will be seen by all. That is the testimony of the entire New Testament . . . no one knows when the hour will come, not even the church. He will come like a thief. The parousia is thus still one of God's secrets, the unveiling of which he has reserved to himself. Not only the date, but the entire event is shrouded in mystery.

Some New Testament references
1 Luke 1:26–35 Birth of Jesus
2 Mark 15:1–end Death of Jesus
3 Luke 24:1–11 Resurrection of Jesus
4 Acts of Apostles 1:6–11 Ascension of Jesus
5 1 Thessalonians 4:13–18 Second coming of Jesus
6 John 1:1–14 Significance of Jesus

WORSHIP

Almighty Father,
you made the shepherds glad at the news of your Son's birth;
you made the disciples glad at the sight of their risen Lord.
Give us that same knowledge of his presence with us,
that we may live the new life in him.
He lives and reigns with you and the Holy Spirit, now and always.   Amen.

First reading: Isaiah 9:6–7
Second reading: Acts 1:6–11
Gospel reading: Luke 24:1–11

Teaching material

■ **CONTEXT OF UNIT 8**

The church's belief in Jesus is built up in two parts. First, it is committed to faith in a person who lived at a specific time and place in history. Second, it is committed to the belief that this person was none other than God incarnate and that he is worthy of our worship and praise. For the church's faith in Jesus to be meaningful to the child two things are necessary. First, he needs to be able to understand Jesus as a real person in time and place – who lived a real life in every respect. Without this emphasis Jesus becomes an insubstantial and mythical figure. Second, he needs to be able to direct his praise and intercession to Jesus. Without this emphasis Jesus becomes a mere figure from the past.

Since the whole emphasis of the Eucharist is on Jesus as the focus of worship, the particular emphasis of this teaching unit is on Jesus in time and history. The presence of Christ in the Eucharist is dealt with in a later unit.

■ **OBJECTIVES**

1 To enable the child to become familiar with the place and conditions in which Jesus lived.

2 To enable the child to know some of the traditions associated with Jesus.

3 To enable the child to become especially familiar with one Gospel account of the life and significance of Jesus.

■ **DISPLAY WORK**

The display work is divided into two sections. The first deals with the Palestine in which Jesus lived and the second deals with the life and significance of Jesus himself.

a The Palestine of Jesus

Begin by talking about where Jesus lived. Look at a map and look at pictures and film strips of Palestine as it is today and as it was at the time of Jesus. Talk about how Palestine is different from this country and how things were different two thousand years ago.

1 Draw up a long list of all the things we have which Jesus did not have in first century Palestine. Draw or cut out pictures to illustrate this list – like cars and taps and supermarkets. A large display can be arranged.

2 Older children will enjoy studying a map of Palestine and drawing it – giving place names, etc. An ambitious group could make a three dimensional map of papier mâché on a board base.

3 Organise pictures of Palestine and the Palestinian way of life, today and two thousand years ago.

4 Create a model of a Palestinian village – say Nazareth. Include
   a houses with a flat roof and outside steps.
   b the carpenter's shop with a bench, tools, and his finished work of chairs, tables, door, cartwheels, farm implements, etc.
   c the market place with corn, olive oil, sheep, goats, bales of wool, fancy goods, spices.
   d the well – with women carrying water in pitchers.
   e the synagogue.
   f small figures – clothes pegs or pipe cleaners dressed in Palestinian clothes – storytellers, traders, shepherds, farmers, wine makers, wedding guests, the robbed and wounded traveller.
   g outside the village there could be vines, corn and sheep, etc.

b The Life and Significance of Jesus

Begin by talking about the things Jesus did and said – and the main events of his life.

1 See how Jesus has been portrayed during the past two thousand years in writing and art. Look at different pictures etc. Christmas cards provide one source of representation, and some of these reproduce 'old masters'. Encourage the children to produce their own art work based on this experience.

2 The three synoptic gospels, Matthew, Mark and Luke, are all closely related. Mark was used as a primary source by the other two. Encourage the children to write out a few passages (which are held by all three gospels) side by side and see how they differ, for example.
   a) the account of John the Baptist in Matthew 3:1–6, Mark 1:2–6 and Luke 3:3–7. Luke omits the description of John's manner of dress and extends the quotation from Isaiah about the voice crying in the wilderness.
   b) the account of the arrest in Matthew 26:47–56, Mark 14:45–51 and Luke 22:47–53. Neither Matthew nor Luke include the account of the young man who fled naked. Matthew adds some teaching about those who live by the sword. Luke identifies the precise ear which was cut off, and gives an account of its healing!

3 Encourage the children to study one Gospel and to see how the events of that Gospel follow on in sequence. St Luke is the best Gospel for this purpose. Create either a large frieze or a work book of St Luke's Gospel. Encourage different children to write about and to illustrate different sections of the gospel and then recreate the whole gospel from their work. A useful structure and sequence of headings is:

1:26,46	The angel announces the birth of Jesus and Mary sings the Magnificat
2:4	Joseph and Mary go to Bethlehem
2:15	The shepherds go to see the baby Jesus
2:22	Jesus is presented in the temple and the old man Simeon greets him
2:42	Jesus visits the temple at the age of 12 years
3:21	Jesus is baptised by John the Baptist
4:1	Jesus is tempted in the wilderness
4:16	Jesus preaches in the synagogue at Nazareth
4:35	Jesus heals a man in the synagogue
5:1	Jesus calls Peter, James and John to be his disciples
5:13	Jesus heals a leper
5:24	Jesus heals a paralytic
5:27	Jesus calls Levi to be a disciple
6:1	Jesus walks through the corn field
6:6	Jesus heals a man with a withered arm
6:12	Jesus calls twelve men to be his disciples
6:20	Jesus teaches the crowds in the plain
7:1	Jesus heals the centurion's son
7:11	Jesus restores the widow's son to life
8:22	Jesus stills the storm
8:26	Jesus heals the mad man
9:16	Jesus feeds the five thousand
9:29	Jesus is transfigured
11:1	Jesus teaches his disciples to pray
18:15	Jesus blesses the children
18:35	Jesus heals the blind man
19:1	Zacchaeus climbs the tree to see Jesus
19:35	Jesus rides into Jerusalem on a colt
19:45	Jesus clears the temple
20:19,27	The Pharisees and Sadducees ask Jesus trick questions
22:19	Jesus celebrates the Last Supper with his disciples
22:45	Jesus goes to the mount of Olives and prays, but his disciples fall asleep
22:54	Jesus is arrested
22:61	Peter denies Jesus and the cock crows
22:63	Jesus is mocked
23:1	Jesus is brought before Pilate
23:8	Jesus is brought before Herod
23:21	The people shout for Jesus to be crucified
23:33	Jesus is crucified between two thieves
23:53	Jesus is placed in the tomb
24:1	They come to the tomb and find it empty
24:13	Jesus meets the two disciples on the road to Emmaus

24:30   Jesus is recognised when he breaks the bread
24:50   Jesus blesses his disciples and departs from them
24:52   Jesus' disciples praise God and are very happy.

If it is impracticable to cover the whole Gospel, select a few sections. Look at a healing story, the calling of a disciple, a parable, the birth story, the baptism, the trial, the resurrection. These episodes then can be arranged as a display.

ACTIVITIES

1 Arrange for the children to see some illustrations of Jesus – stained glass windows in nearby churches, or paintings in local museums or art galleries.

2 The gospel narratives provide a lot of opportunity for drama and dressing up, e.g.:
   a enact the calling of the disciples (Mark 1:16–20, Mark 2:13–17)
   b experience being the leper who was healed by Jesus (Mark 1:40–45)
   c experience being Zacchaeus trying to see Jesus in the crowd (Luke 19:1–10)
   d enact the trial scene (Mark 14:53–72)
   e enact the parable of the sower (Mark 4:1–20). Let the children be the corn withered by the sun, the birds of the air which eat the seed, etc.

WRITING

1 Creative writing can be stimulated by a beginning like 'My name is Peter/Mary Magdalene and I was a close friend of Jesus . . .'

2 Ask the children to write about life in Palestine.

DISPLAY HEADINGS

Useful headings for displaying with the work produced in the course of this unit are
   1 We believe in one Lord Jesus Christ
   2 Jesus lived in Palestine nearly two thousand years ago
   3 Jesus is our Lord
   4 The Gospels tell us what Jesus did and how the early Christians believed in him
   5 Class 4 has interpreted the life of Jesus

A short explanation might run like this: 'The creed sums up what we believe about Jesus'.

The Lord is Here or *At the Lord's Table* open at pages 16–17 can be displayed.

9. CREED : HOLY SPIRIT

A windy day

We believe in the Holy Spirit,
the Lord, the giver of life,
who proceeds from the Father
    and the Son.
With the Father and the Son he is
    worshipped and glorified.
He has spoken through the Prophets.

We believe in one holy catholic
    and apostolic Church.
We acknowledge one baptism
    for the forgiveness of sins.
We look for the resurrection of the dead,
and the life of the world to come.
Amen.

Background material

☐ **TEXT**

This section of the Creed concerns belief in the Holy Spirit. The Church's teaching about the Holy Spirit was the last stage of the trinitarian doctrine to be worked out in detail. Therefore, this section of the Creed is not written as fully as the previous section on the second person of the Trinity.

Closely associated with the section on the Holy Spirit are three other tenets of faith, concerning
1 The holy catholic and apostolic church.
2 One baptism for the forgiveness of sins.
3 The resurrection of the dead and the life of the world to come.

☐ **PICTURE**

The intention of the picture is to illustrate the relationship between the Holy Spirit and wind

1 Both are represented by the same word in Hebrew *(ruach)* and in Greek *(pneuma)*.
2 Both are invisible, but readily seen in their effect.
3 Both are free to act as they will in a way which can be unpredictable.
4 The picture reflects the happiness of life in the Holy Spirit, and on a breezy day.

☐ **COMMENT**

In this section comment is made on three phrases from the third part of the Creed. Then Wheeler Robinson comments on the appropriateness of the image of the wind to speak about God the Holy Spirit. The Old Testament reading illustrates the life giving force of the Holy Spirit. The New Testament reading and the Gospel reading both focus on Jesus' promise and gift of the Holy Spirit to his disciples.

Proceeds from the Father and the Son   The argument is that the Holy Spirit is not created, but *proceeds* from both the Father and the Son. John Burnaby, *The Belief of Christendom*, (SPCK 1959, p. 135):

> What 'proceeds' from God belongs to his divine being, whereas all created things are called into being by his command; and their being cannot have the eternity which is his.

Is worshipped and glorified   The point which the Creed wants to make is that the Holy Spirit is God in the same sense that the Son is God and the Father is God. Thus the Holy Spirit is said to be worshipped and glorified with the Father and the Son.

We believe in one holy catholic and apostolic Church   'Catholic' means world wide. 'Apostolic' means founded on the apostles. Through these words the Creed stresses the continuity of the church both in space and time, linking together people who live in different places and in different ages.

Holy Spirit   can be seen as a way of talking about the immanence or presence of God in the world. Both in the Old and New Testaments the wind is an image used of the Spirit. Wheeler Robinson, *The Christian Experience of the Holy Spirit*, (Fontana 1962, pp. 14–15):

> The primitive and fundamental idea of 'spirit' in the Old Testament is that of active power or energy, power superhuman, mysterious, elusive, of which the *ruach* or wind of the desert was not so much the symbol as the most familiar example. When we read books of travel in Arabia, such as Doughty's *Arabia Deserta* or Lawrence's *Revolt in the Desert*, we are often made to feel the overwhelming power of the wind across the desert, scorching heat by day and piercing cold by night. This elemental force,

incalculable and irresistible and invisible, was surely akin to that which could shape a man's behaviour as strangely as the desert sand was shaped before the blast.

Read Acts 2:1–13 (The day of Pentecost)

To understand this episode it must be remembered that Acts is written by the same writer as Luke's Gospel. James Dunn, *Baptism in the Holy Spirit*, (SCM 1970, pp. 44–6):

> For Luke Pentecost is the climax of all that has gone before. From the start of the ministry of Jesus we are pointed forward, not to the death of Jesus, but beyond that to the baptism which he will give (Luke 3:15–17) . . . It was only at Pentecost by the gift of the Spirit that the benefits and blessings won by Jesus in his death, resurrection and ascension were applied to the disciples . . . Pentecost is a new beginning – the inauguration of the new age, the age of the Spirit – that which has not been before. Luke makes this clear in several ways . . . Clearest of all, it was only at Pentecost that the Joel prophecy was fulfilled. In the old two-age view of Jewish eschatology the gift of the Spirit was *the* decisive differentia which marked off the old dispensation from the new. The 'last days' did not begin for the disciples till Pentecost. Only then did they enter into the distinctively Christian dispensation and into the distinctively Christian experience of the Spirit.

Read John 14:15–18 (The Promise of the Paraclete)

The translators of the New Testament have had problems with the Greek word 'Paracletos'. The New English Bible settles for the translation 'Advocate' – in a legal sense one who pleads your case in court. Sanders and Mastin, *St John's Gospel*, (A & C Black 1968, pp. 326–7) write that the root of the word 'means literally "call to one's side" . . . the word conveys the general sense of one who supports another by his presence and his words'. They suggest that 'champion' makes a good translation.

☐ **WORSHIP**

Almighty God,
you sent your Holy Spirit to the disciples
on the day of Pentecost
like the wind from heaven
to enable them to preach the gospel.
Fill us with the same Spirit,
and enable us to share in their work;
to your honour and glory.
We make our prayer through Jesus Christ our Lord.   Amen.

First reading: Ezekiel 37:1–10
Second reading: Acts 2:1–13
Gospel reading: John 14:15–18

Teaching material

CONTEXT OF UNIT 9

The key image used to speak about God the Holy Spirit is the wind. The image of the wind and the reality of God the Holy Spirit are so closely associated that in both Hebrew and Greek the same word is used for 'wind' and for 'Spirit'. In order for the child to comprehend what the church means when she speaks of God the Holy Spirit it is first necessary for him to experience and to grasp the nature of the wind. The wind is full of mystery. It is difficult to explain where it comes from or where it goes to. It is difficult to explain what it is. We know that the wind is there and yet we cannot see it. We can experience only its effects. And it is so with God the Holy Spirit. We cannot see him. We cannot predict his activity and yet we can experience his effect on us.

OBJECTIVES

1 To enable the child to experience and to think about the mystery of the wind.

2 To enable the child to study the effect of the wind on simple things like kites and windmills.

3 To enable the child to see the connection between the image of the wind and the reality of God the Holy Spirit.

DISPLAY WORK

There are a number of things which the child can make and through which he is able to learn about the activity of the wind.

1 Paper darts and aeroplanes can be made in a number of different ways from folding paper. Most children already know their own ways of making these things. Allow them to compare their different methods and different models, and to experiment with their flight patterns. The models can also be coloured.

2 Balsa wood gliders can be made in a number of different ways. Some children may want to produce quite sophisticated models.

3 Ordinary balloons can be blown up and decorated with such slogans as

'God is Spirit', 'Happy Whitsun'. Use them to decorate the church or school.

4 Model hot-air balloons can be made by covering ordinary balloons with papier mâché. Margarine tubs can be used to represent the basket. The completed hot-air balloon can then be coloured and suspended for display.

5 There are a number of ways of making kites from balsa wood and paper. The kites can be painted and the string can be decorated with coloured tissue paper bows.

6 Model windmills can be made from large wooden boxes or cornflake boxes. Sails can be made from a sheet of cardboard from which a + shape can be cut. In order for the windmill to work the sails need to have flanged edges for the wind to push against.

7 Small sailing boats which really float can be made simply from a piece of shaped wood. A sail can be made from card.

8 Large sailing boats not intended to float can be made by a group of children working together from cardboard packing cases. At the simplest level two boxes can be fixed together to form an oblong hull. A pointed bow and a rounded stern produces a familiar boat shape. A broom handle or piece of dowelling can make a mast. Sails and rigging can be produced from card, paper, material, string, etc.

■ ACTIVITIES

The purpose of these activities is to enable the child to experience the many aspects of the mysterious nature of the wind.

1 Allow the child to use and to enjoy all the wind toys produced in the creative section of this unit.

2 Candles are a real fascination for the child. Under careful supervision allow the child to experiment with the effect of draught and wind on a candle flame.

3 Talk about the noise of the wind and try to manufacture that noise. Tape record it.

4 Talk about the feeling of being out on a windy day. While the tape recorded wind is being played back allow the children to enact their experience of a windy day. Then encourage them to be trees beaten by the wind, leaves blown by the wind, windmills turned by the wind, kites taken up by the wind, gliders supported by the wind, washing blown about by the wind on the clothes line, a candle being extinguished by the wind, etc. Find appropriate music for each of these different experiences.

5 Visit a windmill, or a place where sailing boats can be seen.

WRITING

1 Ask the children to imagine that they are washing on a washing line, and to write their experience. It is a windy day. They are blown away . . .

2 Ask the children to read about the coming of the Holy Spirit at Pentecost in Acts 2:1–21, and then to write and draw about the account given in the Acts of the Apostles.

DISPLAY HEADINGS

Useful headings for displaying with the work produced in the course of this unit are
    1 In Hebrew *ruach* means both *Spirit* and *Wind*
    2 In Greek *pneuma* means both *Spirit* and *Wind*
    3 The Holy Spirit came to the disciples like a rushing wind
    4 You cannot see the wind but you can feel its effects
    5 Our windmill speaks to us of the Holy Spirit

A short explanation might run like this – 'We have to speak about God in a kind of picture language. The picture which tells us most about God the Holy Spirit is the picture of the wind.'

The Lord is Here or *At the Lord's Table* open at pages 18–19 can be displayed also.

10. INVITATION TO PRAYER

Between friends

The Intercession

Let us pray for the Church
and for the world,
and let us thank God for his goodness.

Almighty God, our heavenly Father,
you promised through your Son Jesus Christ
to hear us when we pray in faith.

Background material

☐ **TEXT**

This section is the invitation for the people to join with the president in prayer for the church and the world. This prayer is interpreted by the rubric to include the giving of thanks as well as intercession.

☐ **PICTURE**

The picture stresses that prayer (intercession and thanksgiving) is not an isolated activity: prayer is not something which we do apart from the other things of life. In his prayer the priest at the centre of the picture is catching up all the other activities which are going on around him. He is telling God about them because he knows that God is interested in all that is going on. There is a two-way interaction between prayer and the kind of activities portrayed in the picture

1 Prayer feeds on all that we do in life. For example, when we make a model or enjoy a game we want to tell God about it.

2 We deliberately do things in order to prepare for prayer. For example, we go out to visit friends who are sick before praying for them at the Eucharist.

COMMENT

This section is concerned specifically with two aspects of prayer, namely intercession and thanksgiving. Intercessory prayer presents certain theological and philosophical problems. These problems are discussed by Alan Richardson and John Drury. Then Michel Quoist complements the picture by reminding us that in prayer we need to listen to God as well as to speak to him. The Old Testament reading is an example of answered prayer. The New Testament reading and the Gospel reading are both exhortations to pray.

Alan Richardson, *A Dictionary of Christian Theology*, (SCM 1969, pp. 262–3):

> The NT requires and indeed assumes that Christians will pray without ceasing. It also teaches that prayer should be made 'in the name of Jesus' . . . Christian prayer thus contains only those petitions which can be genuinely offered in the name (character, spirit) of Christ . . . This rules out all selfish requests and every suggestion that prayer is a kind of magic by which God's attention can be caught or his will influenced . . . It is often objected that, if God is a loving Father who knows that his children have need of all sorts of things, there is no purpose in intercessory prayer. Yet Jesus himself says 'Ask . . . knock . . . seek' (Mt 7:7f), shortly after saying 'Your heavenly Father knows that you need all these things' (Mt 6:32). This implies that intercession is not begging for necessities which might otherwise be withheld; in fact we are not to worry about our own food and clothing. Our prayer should be concerned with God's kingdom of righteousness . . . A father expects his children to be concerned, as he is, for other members of his family in distress . . . If our communion with God is even a faltering reflection of Jesus' own intimate sonship, we shall not be able to prevent ourselves from bringing to our heavenly father all the concerns which press upon us . . . But can we expect God to interfere with the laws of nature for our or others' benefit when we pray to him (e.g.) for rain in time of drought? Much depends upon the way in which this question is formulated . . . We must first clarify our conception of the God to whom we pray. Christian prayer is possible only if we believe in the God whom Jesus called Father . . . If our belief in God is the child-like (not childish) trust in one to whom we can always turn quite spontaneously, there is nothing that can be asked 'in the name of Jesus' about which we cannot pray to God. But will our prayers be answered? Yes, though not necessarily in the way we would have chosen: there is much to

be learned from the so-called unanswered prayers of Jesus . . . Of course, we still pray for deliverance from danger or for rain: the child cries to his father for help, even though he knows that his father is doing the best that can be done in the situation.

John Drury, *Angels and Dirt*, (Darton, Longman and Todd 1972, pp. 67–8) examines the question 'is praying to someone an attempt to change his mind and does it work?' He writes

genuine asking observes and respects the other's freedom of decision and keeps its distance. It is a discourse between two centres of freedom . . . When someone prays he expresses himself and his needs in a free and uninhibited way. The only restraint he acknowledges is that his prayers should allow an equally free and uninhibited answer. He seeks to move the other. He asks God to see and to act, but he leaves to him just how he should see and just how he should act. There is no grovelling. Like the early Christians he makes his plea standing upright on his feet. In this sense he is strong and active. But he does not attempt to control the answer, which rests with God. In this sense he is helpless.

Michel Quoist, *Prayers of Life*, (Gill and Macmillan 1963, p. v) stresses that before being written his prayers

were both lived and prayed. They stem from the lives of committed Christians offered to God day by day. We record these experiences to help others to bring to God every aspect of their lives and to transfigure their lives through prayer . . . They are meditations on life, and should help Christians to discover the riches of a contact with God arising from the daily events of their existence . . . God is always the initiator in his dialogue with man . . . The Christian must listen to him actually speaking in his life and in the world. God addresses us through every event, even the most insignificant.

☐ **WORSHIP**

Almighty God,
your Son Jesus Christ taught us to talk with you like a father.
Listen to us as we relate to you the things that are important to us.
Help us also to listen to you and to appreciate the things that are important to you;
so that we may learn to pray the prayers you desire from us.
Through the same Jesus Christ our Lord.   Amen.

First reading: 2 Kings 4:31–37
Second reading: 1 Timothy 2:1–4
Gospel reading: Matthew 7:7–11

Teaching material

CONTEXT OF UNIT 10

The Invitation to Prayer reminds us that God is concerned with all that takes place in our lives and that he wishes us to share our lives with him. He wants us to talk with him about all that makes us happy or sad. He wants us to share our fears, sorrows, frustrations and joys. God also wishes us to share in his concern for his world. For these experiences to be real to the child four things are necessary:

1 The child needs to understand God as a friend who is concerned with and interested in all that he does.

2 The child needs to become aware of the many ways in which the ordinary things of his everyday life can be and should be shared with God in prayer.

3 The child needs to understand the concerns for which God wishes him to pray.

4 The child needs to see God as the source of all that is good and to give thanks to him.

OBJECTIVES

1 To enable the child to understand the concept of prayer as communication between friends.

2 To enable the child to appreciate that everything he does – all his activities, all his joys, sorrows, fears, etc., are important to God.

3 To enable the child to become more aware of the people, the situations and the issues regarding which God wishes him to pray.

4 To enable the child to experience the feeling of giving thanks to God for all his good gifts.

DISPLAY WORK

a Prayer as communication

1 Encourage the child to establish a form of news book called 'My Prayer Book', and to record in that book the things which are important to him. Nothing is too mundane for God's attention: he is even interested in what we have for dinner. This is all part of saying, 'God, this is what is happening in my little world.'

2 Encourage the children to explore different modes of communication and to produce a display of some of them, like the television, radio, film projector, telephone, newspaper, books, letters, people talking – also television aerial, telephone wires, post box, etc.

3 'Televisions' can be made from cardboard boxes: 'films' can be drawn on rolls of paper and wound inside the television on wooden dowelling.

4 Post boxes can be made from cardboard and painted red. The children can be encouraged to communicate with each other by 'post'.

b Everything in life can become part of prayer
1 Begin by talking about all the things the class enjoys doing. Make a list of these things. Ask the children to illustrate some of them, and to think of ways of presenting them to God as prayer. For example, the illustrations can then be taken into church and displayed as part of our prayers.

2 Produce posters of some of the children's favourite activities. These too can be displayed in church as part of our prayer, as part of our way of telling God about ourselves. For example
    a some children might like to make a mural of a football match. Each child could draw one player: these can be cut out and arranged against an appropriate background.
    b perhaps there is a special place in the neighbourhood which the children enjoy – a park, a place by a river, an adventure playground. Encourage the children to talk about it and then to produce a poster or a model describing it.

3 Arrange for something special to happen – a day's trip to a place of special interest for example. Encourage the children to base a project on that visit – making models, writing about and illustrating the things of interest. All this can be done as part of offering ourselves and our whole environment to God in prayer.

c Spotting God's goodness

An emphasis in the invitation to the prayer for the church and the world is on God's goodness. Ask the children to think of ways in which God's goodness is seen. Produce a large collage with the heading 'We thank God for his goodness' and incorporate in this pictures of the things for which the children wish to thank God, for example, their homes, their parents, their toys, their food, their friends, etc.

d Our responsibility to pray

The prayer for the church and the world emphasises that there are certain areas regarding which God wishes us especially to pray. Ask the children to look through the whole of this prayer and make a list of the areas regarding which we ought to pray, e.g. for the sick. Discuss the various sections of the prayer and develop the children's understanding of them. Encourage them to think of particular people, places and situations regarding which they could/should pray. Ask them to copy out the prayer and to write in their own special prayers of thanksgiving and petition.

Begin a 'prayer board' – a notice board divided into the five sections of this prayer i.e.

1 the church
2 the world
3 the local community
4 the sick
5 the Saints and the departed

Encourage the children to write short prayers to be pinned onto the board in the appropriate place. Help them to become aware of the issues and people around them for which they should pray.

WRITING

1 The children can be asked to think of their school friends who have moved away to live in a different place. They are to write to them explaining what they have done in the course of this teaching unit.

2 Read and write about Elijah's prayer in 2 Kings 4:31–37.

ACTIVITIES

1 In small groups the children tell each other about what they have been

doing the previous evening. First, simply let them enjoy the experience of communicating with each other. The next stage is to let the children record their accounts for a specific audience – for example a child who has been away from school through sickness, or an elderly housebound member of the church congregation, etc. Careful editing could introduce singing or recorder playing onto this tape.

2 Let the children experience the fun of conversation over a toy telephone. For example, telephones can be made from two cocoa tins. A hole is punched in the bottom of each tin and string is knotted through the hole. When the string is pulled tight the tins act as a form of telephone. Telephone conversations of this nature can be used to stimulate a number of role–play situations.

3 Help the children to experience the importance of speech in communication. Set up games in which the children have to communicate without speech, for example one group acts out an idea and another group has to guess what it is. All kinds of themes can be acted out; an easy one is based on the miming of different occupations.

4 Help the children to experience the joy of listening to other people talking about themselves. For example, enable the children to talk with some elderly people about what things were like when they were young, etc.

5 Let the children experiment in communicating with each other by means of such devices as morse code, semaphore, the deaf and dumb alphabet.

■ **DISPLAY HEADINGS**

Useful headings for displaying with the work produced in the course of this unit are
1 Prayer is conversation with God
2 We like to tell God about the things which are important to us
3 We like playing football – so we tell God about it
4 God likes us to pray about the things which are very important to him
5 We pray for our friends by name
6 We thank God for his goodness

A short explanation might run like this: 'The Prayer for the Church and for the World reminds us that God wants us to talk with him about everything that is important to us and at the same time to share in his concerns for his people.'

The Lord is Here or *At the Lord's Table* open at pages 20–21 can be displayed also.

11. PRAYER FOR THE CHURCH

Meeting the church

Strengthen our bishop and all your Church
in the service of Christ;
that those who confess your name
may be united in your truth,
live together in your love,
and reveal your glory in the world.

Lord, in your mercy
hear our prayer.

Background material

❑ TEXT

This section is part of the prayer of the people of God for the Church and for the World. The purpose of this section is to bring before God our intercessions and thanksgivings for the whole Christian church. We pray for all the people who are the church of God, bishops, priests, deacons, and laity. We pray for the church of God

throughout the world
in our own country
in our own diocese
in our own rural deanery
in our own parish

❑ PICTURE

The church is first and foremost the people of God. The picture portrays the people of God assembled around the bishop.

The people are neither sitting in church nor at prayer. It is the pilgrim church on the move in the world.

☐ **COMMENT**

In this section comment is made on the church and the church's ministry. The Old Testament reading shows Israel as the assembled people of God. The New Testament reading illustrates Paul's care for the churches. The Gospel reading is Matthew's account of Jesus founding his church on Peter the Rock.

The church

In the New Testament the word church translates the Greek *ecclesia* which always means an assembly of people and cannot mean a building, i.e. 'the people of God called together to be about God's business', or more simply 'God's People'. A number of images are used to express this fact. In the NT the church is described as the 'New Israel', 'Body of Christ', the 'Fellowship of the Holy Spirit'. In the Christian creeds it is described as 'one, holy, catholic and apostolic'. There is always a tension between what the church is called to be and what it actually is here and now. John Macquarrie, *Principles of Christian Theology*, (SCM 1966, p. 372):

> As an actual historical association, the Church exhibits 'more or less' the unity, holiness, catholicity and apostolicity which will fully belong to it only when it gives itself up in order to become the Kingdom of God.

A similar point is made by Stanislaus Lyonnet in *Rethinking the Church*, (Gill and Macmillan 1970, p. 18):

> One of the main difficulties encountered when speaking of the Church stems from the fact that, although a reality of the supernatural order, realities of the natural order must be used to express it and these are always inadequate for the purpose.

When praying for the church throughout the world, it is necessary to remember that the world wide church of Christ involves not only many different races and languages, but also many different denominations and sects. The World Council of Churches provides some link amid the diversity.

The Church's Ministry

The Church of England follows the ancient pattern of the threefold form of the sacred ministry, involving bishops, priests and deacons. Generally a clergyman begins his ministerial work as a deacon for one year before being ordained priest. As a deacon he cannot celebrate the eucharist, pronounce the absolution or give the blessing. These three acts are the privilege of the priest. The priest cannot administer the sacraments of confirmation and ordination. The administration of these sacraments is the privilege of the bishop. The bishop as head of a diocese may be assisted by suffragan bishops. Dioceses are organised into provinces: provinces are presided over by archbishops. The Church of England also recognises the lay ministry in the form of readers. Readers are laymen trained and licensed to conduct services and to preach. Some dioceses also recognise lay elders who are licensed to conduct worship, but not to preach. Neither readers nor elders can celebrate the eucharist.

Read 2 Kings 23:21–23 (The People of God assemble for the Passover)
Victor de Waal, *What is the Church?*, (SCM 1969, p. 55):

> The church is called *ecclesia*, which simply means the 'assembly' . . . Already in the Old Testament the 'assembly', meeting together in one place, is thought of as fundamental to Israel, as is witnessed by the desire to gather together all adult Jews in Jerusalem for the great festivals, a principle extended and necessarily mitigated by regarding the synagogue as a reflection of the Temple . . . Thus while the Hebrew word *qahal*, variously translated *ecclesia*, assembly, or church, came in fact to designate the people only theoretically assembled, in God's sight as it were, the basic idea of actual meeting was never totally abandoned. And it is this aspect that takes on new life and meaning in the church, to which, as to the idealized Israel of old, God has promised his presence and guidance night and day. It was for this reason, as Dom Gregory Dix pointed out so forcefully, that the early Christians, even in virtual certainty of arrest, clung to the eucharistic *assembly* (not just to communion, which they often in any case had privately at home from the reserved sacrament) as to a life-line, for without it they did not constitute the church of Jesus Christ.

Read Matthew 16:17–19 (Jesus and the Church)
This is one of the two occasions when the word church occurs on Jesus' lips in the Gospels themselves – the other is Matthew 18:17. There remains a lot of debate in New Testament scholarship as to whether these texts are authentic. Newton Flew, *Jesus and his Church*, (Epworth 1939, p. 97):

> But if the promise to Peter be regarded as authentic, it cannot be separated from the promise to the larger company of disciples, nor can the promise be regarded as unconditional. There is no contradiction between the 'thou' of 16:19 and the 'ye' of 18:18. The community which is built on Peter has his privileges and his duties, and both the privileges and the duties are determined by the mission of Peter and his fellow apostles, which is the age-long mission of the Church of God, to carry the divine revelation to mankind.

☐ **WORSHIP**

Almighty and everlasting God,
you call men and women, boys and girls, of all races
    into membership of your church.
Hear the prayer which we make for all your people;
that they may all serve you faithfully
in their calling and ministry
to the glory of your holy name;
Through our Lord and Saviour Jesus Christ.   Amen.

First reading: 2 Kings 23:21–23
Second reading: 1 Thessalonians 1:1–5
Gospel reading: Matthew 16:13–19

Teaching material

■ **CONTEXT OF UNIT 11**

The first section of the Prayer focuses on the church. In order to give meaning to this section of the prayer the child needs to have some understanding of four areas:

1 The child needs to know something about the specific church with which his own worship is associated.
2 The child needs to know something about the different denominations which go to make up the whole church of Christ.
3 The child needs to know something about the structure of the ministry and the organisation of the Anglican Church.
4 The child needs to be aware of the world-wide context of the church of Christ.

■ **OBJECTIVES**

1 To enable the child to explore his local church in the two senses of the building and the people.
2 To enable the child to see the work of the church in its world wide context.
3 To enable the child to appreciate the historical perspective of the church as an institution which goes back a long way in time.
4 To enable the child to see how the different denominations all contribute to the church of Christ.
5 To enable the child to understand the function of the bishops.
6 To enable the child to understand the meaning of such terms of church organisation as 'deanery' and 'diocese'.
7 To help the child to pray for the church.

▌DISPLAY WORK

1 Begin by talking about the people who go to the local church. Build up a list of these people – the vicar, curate, readers, organist, choir, church wardens, PCC members, treasurer, sidesmen, bellringers, verger, sacristan, servers, cleaners, flower arrangers, the congregation, the different organisations and committees like the Mothers' Union, Sunday School, etc. Talk about their different jobs: invite some of them to talk with the children about what they do. Two activities can help the children to get to know these people:

a) produce a mural of 'The people at our church' and include some writing about their various jobs.

b) ask the children each to make a book called 'The people at our church'. They can write and draw something about one person on each page and then try to get that person's signature.

2 Encourage the children to get to know an old church very well – preferably the church with which they are associated if it is an old church. Talk about the people who used to worship there and who built it.

a Allow the children to make rubbings of the different surfaces inside and outside the church. The rubbings can be mounted for display. Give particular attention to the memorial stones, etc. noting their dates.

b If there are a number of tomb stones or memorials, the children can be set a competition to find out information in response to questions like, 'When did Thomas Smith die?' or 'How many people named Brown are buried in the churchyard?'

c If the church has a list of previous incumbents ask the children to copy out this list and to compare the dates with pictures in their history reference books. They may care to use these pictures as the basis for an illustrated history of their church linked around the names of the past incumbents.

d It might be possible to see some of the old church registers: find out how far these books go back in time.

e Let the children make a plan of the church and draw on the plan all the important features like the font, pulpit, altar, pews, etc.

f Let the children make a large model of their church.

3 Talk about the different denominations – the Church of England, the Roman Catholic church, the Methodist church, the United Reformed church, the Baptist church, the Salvation Army, etc. Try to arrange for the children to visit some of these different buildings. Draw attention to the features which really characterise the denominations, e.g., the font in the Baptist church, the central pulpit in the non-conformist church, the altar and reserved sacrament in the Catholic church, the musical instruments in the Salvation Army citadel. Ask the children to write about their visits. Some may like to make models of the different buildings and others may care to draw their impressions of them.

4 Talk about the ways in which the children can recognise the bishop, and then talk about the work he does. There are three activities by which the children can learn more about the bishop:

    a mitres can be made from cardboard sheets painted or covered in cloth, and the pastoral staff can be made from a walking cane covered in silver paper.

    b some children might like to make a bishop's cope from patchwork.

    c a life size figure can be drawn and coloured in as a collage.

5 Help the children to understand how their own church and parish fits into the wider structure of a deanery, an archdeaconry and a diocese. Older children may care to produce a map of the area – showing the parishes of their own deanery. The names of the churches, the clergy and the church-wardens etc. can be readily found in the diocesan handbooks. Try to find photographs/pictures of the local churches, clergy and the diocesan bishop. These can be stuck onto the map.

6 Talk about the work of the church in other countries. Make use of the children's materials produced by the missionary societies etc. and construct a project around this material. Find out if there is someone locally who would be able to talk to the children about their own work in the church overseas.

■ ACTIVITIES

1 Take the children on a special visit to a church: prepare for the visit with work sheets etc.

2 Arrange for the children to be able to talk with some of the people who go to the church and have a special job to do there.

3 Take the children to visit the churches and chapels of different denominations. Let them talk with the ministers or someone in authority.

4 Visit a local cathedral and see where the bishop has his 'chair' or throne. (The word 'cathedral' comes from the Latin word *cathedra* meaning a chair. The cathedral is the building built around the bishop's chair!)

5 Making use of the mitres and the pastoral staff the children can act out some of the functions of the bishop – like confirmation. A whole class dressed as bishops can attend a special eucharist and pretend that they are representing the whole world-wide church of Christ – they can be dressed as representing different nationalities.

■ WRITING

Ask the children to write a guide book to their own church – a guide book which deals with

a the building
b the people who meet there
c the worship and other activities

DISPLAY HEADINGS

Useful headings for displaying with the work produced in the course of this unit are

1 The word 'Church' means the people of God
2 Our old church buildings remind us of the people who worshipped God a long time ago
3 These people make up part of the church at St Mary's
4 We pray for the Church of Christ throughout the world
5 We pray for our bishop, William
6 We pray for all the different denominations

A short explanation might run like this: 'When we pray for the Church of Christ we think of millions of Christian people throughout the world.'

The Lord is Here or *At the Lord's Table* open at pages 22–3 can be displayed also.

12. PRAYER FOR THE WORLD

Around the world

Bless and guide Elizabeth our Queen;
give wisdom to all in authority;
and direct this and every nation
in the ways of justice and of peace;
that men may honour one another,
and seek the common good.

Lord, in your mercy

hear our prayer.

25

Background material

☐ **TEXT**

This section is part of the prayer of the people of God for the Church and for the World. The purpose of this section is to bring before God our intercessions and thanksgivings for his world.

We pray for our own nation, and all the nations of the world; we pray for the Queen and for all those in authority. We pray especially for causes of national or international concern. We pray that men will

1 care for justice
2 work for peace
3 honour one another
4 seek the common good.

☐ **PICTURE**

The picture makes use of the imagery of national flags to represent the diversity and identity of the many peoples of the world. These people are different in their outward appearance but alike in their importance to God.

COMMENT

In this section comment is made on the Christian understanding of the world and on prayer for the world. The Old Testament reading traces the divisions in the world to man's exaltation of himself as over against God. The New Testament reading shows God's reversal of these divisions on the day of Pentecost, and the Gospel reading looks forward to the establishment of unity among mankind through Jesus.

The Christian understanding of the world The word 'world' can be used both to mean the created universe in which we live and the peoples who inhabit it. The Christian believes that

1 the world was created by God and therefore ultimately belongs to God
2 God loves and cares for the world
3 the world rejected God
4 the purpose of Christ is to bring the world back into right relationship with God
5 everything that happens in the world is of importance to God
6 God wishes his people to share his concern for the world and to work with him in the job of reconciliation

Prayer for the World On the subject of praying for the world Sister Edna Mary, *This World and Prayer*, (SPCK 1965, p. 27) writes:

The task of the Christian is to be deeply involved in the world, but to see that involvement always in the light of his relationship with God. There can never be two parts of his life, labelled respectively 'God' and 'the World' – for he ought never to be able to see the one apart from the other. St Gregory the Great is reported to have said, 'As often as I go to God I am sent to men; as often as I go to men I am sent back to God'; but the unity is closer even than this swing of the pendulum. There must be the constant recognition of God as one has dealings with other people, the constant bringing with one of other people in every approach to God.

Read Genesis 11:1–9 (The Tower of Babel); Acts 2:1–13 (The Day of Pentecost)

Alan Richardson, *Genesis 1–11*, (SCM 1953, pp. 125–6) writes that one of the great biblical themes is given expression in the parable of the Tower of Babel. This theme

is that of the unity of mankind shattered by reason of man's sin. The Bible tells the story of God's plan to recreate the lost unity of the human family.

D

In Genesis we read of all mankind as originally one family, the sons of Noah, and of the differentiation of mankind into all the many races and kindreds of the earth. The parable of the Tower of Babel emphasizes that it is man's exaltation of himself as over against God which is the prime cause of divisions and rivalries, of which the different languages are symbolic. Men cannot speak to one another in a common tongue because they have no common interest or mutual regard. God seeks to recreate mankind into one great family, the Universal Church, united in one covenant of love in the blood of Jesus Christ, and speaking one common language of the Holy Spirit of God. The story of Pentecost with its miraculous reversal of the Babel confusion of languages, is itself a parable of the power of the divine love to bind together 'men from every nation under heaven' in the New Covenant of grace (Acts 2:5–11); the story of the Gift of Tongues at Pentecost is nothing other than the Babel story in reverse. When men in their pride boast of their own achievements, there results nothing but division, confusion and incomprehensibility; but when the wonderful works of God are proclaimed, then every man may hear the apostolic Gospel in his own tongue.

Read John 10:7–16 (One flock, one shepherd)

William Barclay, *The Gospel of John Volume 2*, (St Andrew Press 1955, p. 75):

The only possible unity for men is in their common sonship with God. In the world there is the division between nation and nation; in the nation there is the division between class and class. There can never be one nation; and there can never be one class. The only thing which can cross the barriers and wipe out the distinctions is the Gospel of Jesus Christ telling men of the universal fatherhood of God.

☐ **WORSHIP**

Dear Lord God,
you created the world, and intended mankind to live in peace and unity.
Forgive the divisions we have made in your world.
Help us to share your concern for healing those divisions;
that we may work with you to recreate peace and unity.
We make our prayer through Jesus Christ,
   who is alive and reigns with you and the Holy Spirit,
   now and for ever.   Amen.

First reading: Genesis 11:1–9
Second reading: Acts 2:1–13
Gospel reading: John 10:7–16

Teaching material

CONTEXT OF UNIT 12

The prayer for the world reminds us of God's concern for the whole world and his desire that we should share his concern. For this concern to be real to the child three things are necessary:

1 The child needs to be aware of the size and diversity of the world – and the smallness of his own community in relationship to the whole globe.
2 The child needs to be aware of the differences between peoples of different races and to be able to respect them all as equals.
3 The child needs to be aware of our responsibility for the less well developed parts of the world.

OBJECTIVES

1 To enable the child to know a little more about the world and the people who live in it.
2 To teach the child to respect peoples of other races and cultures.
3 To direct particular concern towards the underdeveloped parts of the world.
4 To help the child to pray for the world.

DISPLAY WORK

Begin by letting the children talk about the world and the things they already know about it.

1 Make a list of some of the continents, countries, races of people, languages, mountains, rivers, lakes, etc. Look at a globe and find these locations on it. Often children are fascinated by learning names and by knowing facts like the longest river and the tallest mountain.

2 Encourage the older children to draw maps of parts of the world and to write in the place names etc.

3 A good way to learn about the world is through studying the food we eat. Make a list of our foods and the places from which they come. A collage can be produced of food wrappings arranged according to countries.

4 Examine a few foods in detail and learn about the life styles of the people who produce them, for example: the wheat growing countries; the cocoa/ chocolate producing areas; the tea growing countries; the rice growing areas.

5 Flags are a very important symbol of nationalities. Encourage the children to study the different flags of the world and to make as many large flags as

possible. Some can be painted on paper. Some can be made by patchwork on cloth. Some designs can be produced by weaving or tapestry.

6 Many children like collecting stamps. Arrange a display of the stamps of the world and try to say something about the countries from which they come.

7 It is important for the child to realise that not everyone in the world is well off. Arrange for material to be available from organisations like Christian Aid and Oxfam. Produce a display of world poverty and famine.

8 Draw up a list of the foods eaten in different parts of the world. Illustrate these by encouraging the children to set up a table with different places for different countries. Instead of real food life size models can be made from dough or clay and then painted. Give the contrast between a meal of many courses and the simple bowl of rice.

9 Collect newspapers and books in different languages and make a display of them.

10 Collect pictures of different places in the world and of different races of people. These can be stuck onto large wall maps of the world. Travel brochures are a good source of such pictures.

11 Many children are fascinated by national dress. Some collect dolls dressed in national costume. Arrange a display of national dress. One way of achieving this is to make life size drawings. Draw round a child and colour in the costume.

12 Give particular attention to television news items about world affairs. Follow up television news items by cutting out extracts from the daily newspapers. Encourage the children to talk about world situations and to bring these situations before God in their prayers.

13 In this prayer we pray for our Queen and country. Create a display which includes:

photographs of the Queen and royal family (including the royal dogs); photographs of the prime minister and some other MPs; the royal palaces; the Houses of Parliament; a large map of this country.

■ **ACTIVITIES**

1 Make use of films and film strips about the way of life in different parts of the world.

2 Listen to music which comes from different parts of the world and try different forms of national dances.

3 Learn to sing different National Anthems.

4 Listen to tapes/records of people speaking different languages.

5 Arrange for people who have lived or worked abroad to talk to the children about the country they know well. Invite them to bring photographs and to give attention especially to the foreign customs, festivals, meals, etc.

6 Some children may like to make national costumes and to wear them in pageant. They could 'dress up' for a special eucharist based on the theme of this unit, and also bring in the flags which they have made.

7 Encourage a number of friends, staff or parents to talk about their holidays in foreign places.

8 Arrange a visit from a representative of Christian Aid or Oxfam.

9 Encourage the children to take an active involvement in world development. Seek guidance from Christian Aid or Oxfam as to ways in which the children could raise a specific sum of money for one of these charities.

WRITING

1 Creative writing can be stimulated by a theme like 'My journey round the world by balloon . . .'

2 Read and write about the Tower of Babel.

DISPLAY HEADINGS

Useful headings for displaying the work produced in the course of this unit are
   1 We pray for the world.
   2 We pray for Queen Elizabeth.
   3 We pray for the people in Japan, etc.
   4 We pray for the work of Oxfam.

A short explanation might run like this: 'In our prayers we are reminded of God's care for his world. We too need to share in his care for the world.'

The Lord is Here or *At the Lord's Table* open at pages 24–5 can be displayed also.

13. PRAYER FOR OUR NEIGHBOURHOOD

Meet the neighbours

Give grace to us, our families and friends,
and to all our neighbours;
that we may serve Christ in one another,
and love as he loves us.

Lord, in your mercy

hear our prayer.

Background material

☐ **TEXT**

This section is part of the prayer of the people of God for the Church and for the World. The purpose of this section is to bring before God our intercessions and thanksgivings for our immediate environment. We pray for

    our family
    our friends
    our neighbours
    our local community.

Prayer for our community can be seen as an opportunity to bring all aspects of local life before God, for example

    different churches and their congregations
    different roads and their occupants
    different places of work and their workers
    different schools and their pupils and staff
    different organisations and their members
    those who serve the community in different ways.

PICTURE

The picture focuses attention upon some of the many people who go to make up the local community. Our prayer is for our immediate circle of family and friends, but it is also for all those with whom we come into contact. It is prayer of this nature which translates an impersonal community into a personal community – it sees the milkman as a person, not as a service industry.

COMMENT

In this section Roger Bush brings his own city before God in prayer and Michel Quoist meditates on the meaning of love for others. The Old Testament reading contains the command to love your neighbour like yourself, and in the Gospel reading Jesus develops this command through the parable of the Good Samaritan. In the New Testament reading Paul makes intercessions and thanksgiving for the church in Rome.

Roger Bush, *Prayers for Pagans*, (Hodder 1968, section 20) composes a prayer over his own city:

This is my city, Lord.
I've flown over it,
Driven round it,
Walked through it,
And I love it.
Its concrete chasms, its quiet parks.
Golden beaches and shabby streets.
Its massive buildings and its tiny homes.
Its suburbs, rich and poor.
But most of all, Lord, its people.
The bustling throngs on their way to work,
The peak hour driver, and the kids at school.
The casual shoppers, the tired mums.
The rich, the poor, the young, the old.
Take out the people and the city's dead.
Faces under bright lights,
Tired old men sleeping in the park.
My city, Lord, your city,
Remember, Lord, there was one city over which
you stood and wept,
Do you weep over this city?
With its hunger, its greed, its cruelty.
Its foolishness and heartbreak.
Lord, I believe you do.
For sometimes I too lay awake at night,
And listen to the agony of God,
Your people's cry.   Amen.

Michel Quoist, *Prayers of Life*, (Gill 1963, p. 79) meditates on the theme of love:

There are two loves only, Lord,
Love of myself and love of you and of others,
And each time that I love myself, it's a little less love for you and for others.
It's a draining away of love,
It's a loss of love,
For love is made to leave self and fly towards others.
Love of self is a stolen love.
It was needed for others, they need it to live, to thrive, and I have diverted it.
So the love of self creates human suffering,
So the love of men for themselves creates human misery,
All the miseries of men,
All the sufferings of men.

Read Romans 1:8–12 (Paul's prayer for the church in Rome)
William Barclay, *The Letter to the Romans*, (St Andrew Press 1955, pp. 6–7):

Although Paul did not know the people at Rome personally he nevertheless constantly prayed to God for them. It is ever a Christian privilege and duty to bear our loved ones and our fellow-Christians to the throne of Grace.

Read Luke 10:25–37 (The Good Samaritan)
According to the Shorter Oxford English Dictionary, a neighbour is 'one who lives near or next to another; e.g. in an adjoining house, or in the same street or village'. Jesus offers a different kind of definition of neighbour by telling the parable of the Good Samaritan. According to Jesus' definition my neighbour is anyone who needs my care, my help and my prayers. Eta Linnemann, *Parables of Jesus*, (SPCK 1966, pp. 53–4):

It was, however, surprising and offensive for Jesus' hearers that it should be a Samaritan that was given the role of the merciful man. Between the Jews and this heretical mixed people there reigned implacable hatred. On the Jewish side it went so far that they cursed the Samaritans publicly in the synagogues . . . Why does Jesus mention a Samaritan here and not a Jewish layman – as his listeners were certainly expecting after a priest and a Levite? The only thing the Samaritan had in common with the Jews in the eyes of the listeners was that he too was human. If it is he who shows mercy, this mercy is something that man as such shows to man. Any possibility of ascribing it to a common nationality or religion is excluded.

WORSHIP

Heavenly Father,
you taught us through your Son
   to regard all people as our neighbours,
   and to love our neighbours as ourselves.
Help us to be alert to the needs of those around us:
and give us grace and strength to be of service to them;
through Jesus Christ our Lord.   Amen.

First reading: Leviticus 19:15–18
Second reading: Romans 1:8–12
Gospel reading: Luke 10:25–37

Teaching material

CONTEXT OF UNIT 13

This section of the prayer reminds us of our responsibility to pray for our own community, our families and our friends. For this kind of prayer to be real for the child three things are necessary:

1 The child needs to be aware of the importance of his own community to God.
2 The child needs to be alert to the many different people in his own community and to the jobs which they do. He needs to respect them and to realise their value before God.
3 The child needs to be conscious of the value and importance of his own family and friends – and desire to bring these people regularly before God in prayer.

OBJECTIVES

1 To enable the child to know about the place where he lives.
2 To encourage the child to recognise the way in which his own life is helped and enriched by others in his community.
3 To help the child to appreciate his parents, family and home and to learn to pray for them.
4 To encourage the child to think about his friends and to recognise his responsibility of praying for them.
5 To encourage the child to establish a pattern of prayer for his neighbourhood, family and friends.

■ **DISPLAY WORK**

a **The local community**

Begin by talking about the area in which the children live – get them to name the streets and places of interest and importance. Give particular attention to the people who live and work there. Many Local Authorities produce guides or handbooks which can be useful for this kind of information. A number of creative activities can further the child's understanding of his community. First, let the children concentrate on the place itself.

1 A map can be drawn showing the roads and places of interest.

2 Pictures can be drawn of some of the places of interest, the church, the school, the shops, etc.

3 Older children may like to make a model of part of the community. The model can include toy cars, trains, etc.

4 The children can be asked to think of all the information a newcomer to the community needs. Lists can be prepared of the shops, postboxes, public telephone boxes, bus routes, etc. Useful information can be recorded, e.g.
    a nearest chemist and opening times
    b doctors' surgery hours
    c shop hours
    d when the local garages are open
    e times of the church services
    f when groups like the guides, brownies, towns women's guild meet
    g when the library is open

Second, let the children concentrate on the people in the local community. Talk about the different people who work in the community and in neighbouring communities and on whom we depend:

1 Make a list of those who are employed in the community in one way or another, for example, the baker, barber, butcher, chemist, crossing patrol person, dentist, district nurse, doctor, dustman, fireman, grocer, milkman, paper boy, policeman, postman, roadsweeper, school caretaker, shop assistant, teacher, vicar, etc.

2 Make a list of those who do voluntary work in the community, for example, the brownie/cub leaders, meals on wheels, Oxfam shop, school managers, WRVS, etc.

3 Life size models can be drawn of these people, giving attention to their special uniform or characteristics.

4 The children can make some of the things which characterise these people, e.g.
    the policeman's/fireman's helmet from papier mâché

the crossing patrol sign from cardboard and card tubing
the postman's bundle of letters
the milkman's milk bottles
the fruiterer's stand

5 Encourage the children to prepare a book of the people who work in their local community – either each child can compile his own book, giving a page to each key person, or the whole class can produce a large folder, each child working on part of it.

6 The children can prepare a large map of their walk to school. The map can begin by showing their own house and end by showing the school. En route they can illustrate the places of interest which they pass and the people whom they meet – 'the milkman delivers milk along Borchester Way' – 'Gran waves to me as I pass her house', etc.

b Home, family and friends
The exploration of home and family can be a delicate issue. The teacher's discretion must decide both whether it is appropriate to tackle this area with any given group of children, and also the degree of sensitivity with which the area should be covered. The aim of studying it is to help the child to understand that his home and family are important to God.

1 Here the emphasis is on each child's home and immediate family in relationship to the whole local community. Produce a large diagram or map of the catchment area from which the children come. Ask each child to draw a picture of his or her own family and to name each person in the picture: arrange these pictures on the map.

2 Here the emphasis is on the child's extended family. Talk about the concept of family trees. Encourage the children to draw their own family trees and to illustrate and write about them.

3 Here the emphasis is on the child's friends, and the intention is to encourage the children to remember their friends in their prayers. Two activities can help the children to think about their friends.
  a encourage the children to talk about the games they enjoy with their friends: a class book can be produced on 'The Things We Do Together'.
  b invite each child to make a list of all the groups of children with whom she or he interacts:
    1 their immediate brothers/sisters
    2 their cousins and extended family groups
    3 the children in the immediate neighbourhood of their homes
    4 the class at school
    5 the children at Sunday school
    6 the brownies/cubs/guides/scouts etc.
    7 the under ten football team.

Each of these groups can be illustrated on a circular sheet of paper. Each child can draw his/her own picture on a similar sheet of paper. The illustrations of the groups can then be arranged around the illustrations of the individual child. The effect is that of the petals of a flower arranged around the centre – and the children can see very clearly the different groups with which they each interact.

◼ ACTIVITIES

1 Arrange a walk around the local neighbourhood and note all the things of interest. Give special attention to the shops, the places of work and the people we meet there.

2 The child's understanding of his area can be increased by a whole series of 'number games'. It is possible to count the number of people who pass by the school gate – the number of cars that stop at the traffic lights – the number of shops that have 'special offers' in their windows, etc. Distances can be measured between different places in the community.

3 Arrange visits to meet some of the people who work in the community. For example the police are often very willing to visit schools, and often the firemen are willing to allow schools to visit the fire station etc.

4 The children can make use of the things which they have produced to characterise the different jobs (like the policeman's helmet), and wear or carry them for a special Eucharist.

5 These different articles symbolising the different jobs which people have in the community can also encourage the children to engage in role play. Role play situations can be devised, like
  a visits to the local shops
  b the day the milk float broke down
  c the week the bakers were on strike
  d the work of the local policemen

6 Children are very familiar with the 'emergency services' of the fire brigade, police and ambulance service from their experience of television. Television programmes can provide a good basis for drama through which the importance of these services for the community can be explored.

■ WRITING

1 Ask the children to write a 'guide' to their local community.

2 Ask the children to choose one person in the community and to write a story, 'I am the headmistress', 'I am the dustman', etc.

3 The children's awareness of their dependence upon people in the community can be developed by writing on themes like, 'The day the milkmen were on strike'.

4 The children can write about 'A day with my friends'.

■ DISPLAY HEADINGS

Useful headings for displaying with the work produced in the course of this unit are
  1 We pray for Ambridge
  2 We pray for the people who help us
  3 We pray for our school
  4 We pray for the people who live in Borchester Road
  5 We pray for our friends
  6 We pray for our families

A short explanation might run like this: 'In the Prayers we pray for our families, our friends, for all the people whom we know, and for those whom we meet in our local community.'

The Lord is Here or *At the Lord's Table* open at pages 26–7 can be displayed also.

14. PRAYER FOR THE SUFFERING

Sick call

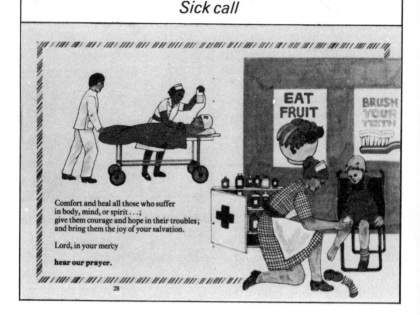

Comfort and heal all those who suffer
in body, mind, or spirit . . .;
give them courage and hope in their troubles;
and bring them the joy of your salvation.

Lord, in your mercy

hear our prayer.

28

Background material

□ **TEXT**

This section is part of the prayer of the people of God for the Church and for the World. The purpose of this section is to bring before God our concern for the health and healing of mankind. There are two ideas in this section

1 We pray for those who are physically sick, mentally disturbed, spiritually insecure, emotionally unhappy, materially poor.

We have the opportunity to mention individuals by name – or specific categories of people.

2 We give thanks for and pray for those concerned with the healing, health and welfare of mankind, for example doctors, nurses, hospital ancillaries, porters, technicians etc., psychiatrists and psychologists, counsellors, social workers, samaritans, marriage guidance counsellors, clergy.

□ **PICTURE**

The picture focuses attention upon those concerned with a ministry of healing. The emphasis is on the caring afforded by the medical profession as well as on the suffering of the sick. The international symbol of the Red Cross is given prominence in the picture.

COMMENT

In this section comment is made on the three problematic concepts of comfort, healing and salvation. Then Michel Quoist is prompted by a hospital visit to meditate on the problem of suffering, and Melvyn Thompson speaks from the perspective of a hospital chaplain about the need to have concern for the whole person and not just the sickness. In a reading from the Apocrypha the author of Ecclesiasticus traces the relationship between the healing profession and faith in God. The New Testament reading looks at the church's ministry of healing. In the Gospel reading Jesus brings sight to a man born blind.

Comfort and heal . . . salvation

In every day speech 'comfort' is now generally used to mean to make someone comfortable or to soothe or console someone who is in grief or trouble: originally the meaning is to strengthen, encourage, support and invigorate. The Christian does not see healing simply in terms of patching up or curing sickness. Healing has to do with the whole person and with the creation of 'wholeness' in relationship to God. In the New Testament there is a close relationship between the concepts of health and salvation. This relationship is seen very clearly by the way in which the same verb is used to mean both 'to save' and 'to heal'. In the Gospel miracles healing is used as a sign of God's salvation: it does not follow, however, that lack of healing is a sign of lack of salvation.

Michel Quoist, *Prayers of Life*, (Gill 1963, p. 65) provides a meditation on the theme of 'The Hospital', from which this is an extract.

Lord, suffering disturbs me, oppresses me.
I don't understand why you allow it.
   Why, Lord?
Why this innocent child who has been moaning for a week, horribly
   burned?
This woman with cancer who in one month seems ten years older?
Why this suffering in the world
   that shocks, isolates, revolts, shatters?
Why this hideous suffering that strikes blindly without seeming cause?
Why these people, Lord, and not others?
Why these, and not me?

Son, it is not I, your God, who has willed suffering, it is men.
They have brought it into the world in bringing sin.
Because sin is disorder, and disorder hurts.

But I came and took all your sufferings upon me, as I took all your sins,
I took them and suffered them before you.
I transformed them, I made of them a treasure.
They are still an evil, but an evil with a purpose,
For through your sufferings, I accomplish redemption.

Melvyn Thompson, *Cancer and the God of Love*, (SCM 1976, pp.79–81):

Theology claims to be dealing with suffering and what faith means within it – and it must therefore see the *whole* situation, and not just the part of it that relates to the medical condition. It is complex and contains both negative and positive sides. The sense of companionship for a person who is often lonely, the care and concern of the medical staff, receiving cards and flowers from neighbours and friends, and the general fact of being cared for – all these may become positive symbols of hope, and they are just as real a part of hospital experience as the disease . . . Our concern for the cure of disease is at all points secondary to our concern for the person who is sick; and if it is *not*, then we are not practising medicine, but only playing with medical possibilities.

Read James 5:13–16 (Anointing the sick with oil)
R. R. Williams, *The Letters of John and James*, (CUP 1965, pp. 138–9):

During the ministry of Jesus healings of all kinds are said to have taken place. His apostles were sent out with a commission to do the same kind of things. Miracles of healing are recorded in Acts. In James the 'miraculous' aspect is still there, but it is in process of being changed to a regular feature of the life of the church. The sick man is to send for the elders of the congregation. These elders will pray over him and anoint him with oil in the name of the Lord. The symbolic use of oil by the church has continued in varying forms to the present day. A growing number of clergy now make use of the laying-on of hands and anointing with oil as part of their ministry to the sick.

Read John 9:1–12 (The man born blind)
Sanders and Mastin, *The Gospel According to John*, (A & C Black 1968, pp. 237–8):

The question illustrates the common belief of the time that illness and other signals of misfortune were a punishment for sin . . . Jesus refuses to discuss the cause of the man's affliction; instead, he directs the disciples' attention to the opportunity which it affords of showing forth the works of God . . . Jesus proceeds to complete God's work of creation by giving sight to the blind man.

▌WORSHIP

Almighty and everlasting God,
your Son Jesus Christ healed the sick,
   and restored them to wholeness of life.
Look with compassion on those who suffer,
   and by your healing power
     bring them to wholeness of life
     and to the joy of your salvation;
through our Saviour Jesus Christ,
who is alive and reigns
   with you and the Holy Spirit,
     one God, now and for ever.   Amen.

First reading: Ecclesiasticus 38:1–14
Second reading: James 5:13–16
Gospel reading: John 9:1–12

Teaching material

▌CONTEXT OF UNIT 14

This section of the prayer reminds us of the Christian's responsibility both
to pray for those whose grasp on life is threatened in one way or another – by
sickness, unhappiness, poverty, etc., and also to pray for those who are
concerned with the healing and helping professions.

   For this kind of prayer to be real for the child four things are necessary:

1 The child needs to be able to feel empathy with those who suffer from
sickness, unhappiness, poverty, etc.
2 The child needs to understand that God also shares this empathy with
those who suffer. He needs to learn how this faith in God helps people to
make sense of their suffering.
3 The child needs to know about the caring professions, agencies and
institutions in his area. He needs to be aware of the way in which he can
aid their work and remember them in his prayers.
4 The child needs to become aware of the responsibility of the churches to
help those who are unable to help themselves.

OBJECTIVES

1 To enable the child to feel empathy for those who are in hospital; physically unwell; mentally unwell; unable to care for themselves; unhappy;
materially poor.
2 To enable the child to know about the caring agencies in his own area.

3 To encourage the children to do something practical to assist their local caring organisations.

4 To encourage the children to establish a pattern of prayer for the suffering and for those who care for them.

■ **DISPLAY WORK**

a Helplessness

Begin by encouraging the children to talk about the way in which they need others to care for them and to do the things they cannot do for themselves. Proceed to talk about the helplessness of a baby – list the things he cannot do for himself. Then consider the helplessness of old age. A mural can be produced on the theme 'Throughout life we need others to care for us and to help us'. On the one hand encourage the children to produce illustrations of the help needed by the very young child, the pushchair, the walking frame, the toys etc. On the other hand illustrate the elderly person's walking stick, hearing aid, etc. In the middle illustrate the help needed by the junior age child.

b Ill Health

1 Encourage the children to talk about their own experiences of ill health either concerning themselves or their near family. It is sometimes helpful for the children to listen to adults recount their own experience of ill health – but care needs to be taken to draw out the positive and creative side of this experience. Let the children write their experiences.

2 If the children know someone who is ill encourage them to make and to send 'Get Well Cards'.

3 The children's own sensitivity to others can be sharpened by people telling them about the way in which their specific disabilities handicap them. For example there might be someone in the community who is blind, deaf or lame and deals with that handicap creatively. They might be willing to talk with the children. Encourage the children to write or to draw about that experience.

c The Caring Agencies

1 Begin by talking about the caring professions which serve the local community:

doctors	district nurses	Red Cross
dentists	veterinary surgeons	St John's Ambulance
opticians	ambulance driver	teachers of the deaf
nurses	radiographer	school speech therapists
	school nurse	

Discover who these people are and the job they do. If possible invite some of them to talk with the children. Talk about the children's experience of these people. Three creative activities can help to stimulate the children's interest in these people:

a) Life size posters can be made showing the nurse in uniform, the doctor wearing his stethoscope etc.

b) A class book can be produced on each of these people.

c) It is easy to forget just how many different people are involved in maintaining the hospital health service. The children can be stimulated to produce a large pictorial diagram illustrating the relationship between all these people. The central illustration is a patient in bed and the rest of the hospital staff can be arranged at distances from the centre – i.e. the surgeon, radiographer, staff nurse, sister, doctor, porter, anaesthetist, cleaner, cook, ward clerk, student nurse, nursing ancillary, physiotherapist, ambulance driver, G.P., hospital administrator, pharmacist, etc.

2 Talk about the local places and buildings which are concerned with caring for the sick etc.:

hospitals	clinic
old people's homes	health centre
doctor's surgery	chemist's shop
dentist's surgery	chiropodist
	optician's shop

Discuss where these places are and what goes on there. If possible arrange visits to some of them and arrange for the children to be shown round. A class book can be produced describing these various places. Also models can be made of some aspects of these places, for example

a) a hospital ward showing the beds etc.

b) the chemist shop window showing the different coloured bottles etc.

c) the ambulance.

ACTIVITIES

1 Encourage the children to take an interest in the children's ward of their local hospital. Discover whether the hospital would welcome gifts of toys and books. Encourage the children to arrange a collection of some of their toys and, if the hospital is willing, arrange for the children to visit it and to present their gifts.

2 Encourage the children to arrange an 'entertainment' for a local old person's home or convalescence home. Apart from Christmas time these places are quite often ignored by the community. And frequently they appreciate children's music, song, dance, drama, etc. Some of the children's work can be displayed as well. Some hospitals like to decorate their entrance hall or waiting rooms with children's art work.

3 Encourage the children to take an active interest in a fund raising activity of their local hospital group. Some hospitals run fetes which would appreciate help. Some hospitals collect stamps, tinfoil or beer can rings in order to raise funds.

4 The children's awareness of specific handicaps can be sharpened by role play. Ask the children to imagine that they are blind, deaf, lame, etc. and to act out the consequences of that handicap and the way in which they could strive to overcome it.

5 The children's experience of television serials about hospitals etc. could provide the basis from which to develop some drama.

6 Encourage the children to keep a prayer board in church for the sick and for the caring professions and to keep this up to date.

■ **WRITING**

1 Encourage the children to write on the theme 'A day in the life of Doctor Smith' etc.

2 Read and write about the healing of the blind man in John 9:1–12.

■ **DISPLAY HEADINGS**

Useful headings for displaying with the work produced in this unit are
  1 God knows when we are helpless. He desires to help us
  2 Jesus knows what it is like to suffer. He cares about us
  3 We pray for the young and for the old
  4 We pray for those who are sick, especially
  5 We pray for those who are unhappy
  6 We pray for the doctors and nurses at St Mary's hospital
  7 We pray for the people who work in Boots the chemists

A short explanation might run like this: 'In our prayers we are reminded of God's care for the sick and the suffering. We need to share in his care.'

The Lord is Here or *At the Lord's Table* open at pages 28–9 can be displayed also.

15. PRAYER FOR THE DEPARTED

Light and life

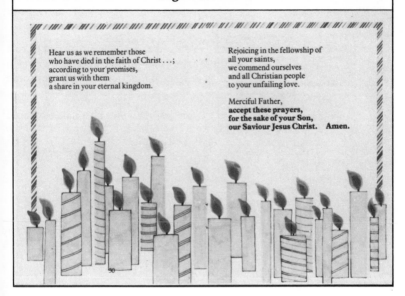

Hear us as we remember those
who have died in the faith of Christ . . . ;
according to your promises,
grant us with them
a share in your eternal kingdom.

Rejoicing in the fellowship of
all your saints,
we commend ourselves
and all Christian people
to your unfailing love.

Merciful Father,
**accept these prayers,
for the sake of your Son,
our Saviour Jesus Christ.   Amen.**

Background material

TEXT

This section is part of the prayer of the people of God for the Church and for the World. The purpose of this section is to bring before God our intercessions and thanksgivings for the whole of his creation, extending beyond ourselves in both time and space. There are three ideas in this section of the prayer

1 Commemoration of the departed – i.e. a bringing of the departed to mind before God: this may be interpreted to include prayer for the repose of the departed, including specific people mentioned by name.
2 Thanks for
   a) the lives and witness of the saints.
   b) the founders of our own community and church.
   c) those who have been important to ourselves and have now died.
   d) our sharing through the eucharist with the whole church of Christ, living and departed.
3 Commendation of the worshippers and all Christians to God.

☐ PICTURE

The picture deliberately moves away from the traditional imagery of angels and saints. Attention is focused upon the twin concepts of light and life: the picture emphasises that light and life in Christ persist in many shapes and forms. The poetry of the church has frequently used the imagery of light to speak of the departed; for example Isaac Watt's hymn, 'How bright those glorious spirits shine'.

☐ COMMENT

In this section F. L. Cross argues that the practice of praying for the dead is closely connected with the doctrine of purgatory, and then John Macquarrie comments on the doctrine of purgatory. Thirdly, A. M. Allchin looks at the practice of praying for the dead in the context of the concept of the communion of saints. In the New Testament reading the author of the Epistle to the Hebrews sets his readers in the context of the faithful witness of God's people in past ages. Both the Old Testament reading and the Gospel reading are suggested by the Alternative Service Book for the Feast of All Saints.

Oxford Dictionary of the Christian Church, ed. F. L. Cross, (OUP 1957, p. 378) writing on the subject of praying for the dead argues that

> The practice of offering prayers on behalf of the dead is closely connected with the doctrine of purgatory. The warrant for it is the belief that those in purgatory are still part of the Church and, as members of the Mystical Body of Christ who have not yet arrived at the beatific vision, can be helped by the intercessions of those still alive. Explicit scriptural justification for the practice has been found in 2 Macc. 12:40–6. There is ample evidence for its use in the inscription of the catacombs . . . and the early liturgies also commonly contain commemorations of the dead . . . At first the Protestant Reformers continued the traditional custom of praying for the dead. But before long they came to denounce it . . . Since the middle of the 19th century, however, the practice has been increasingly adopted in the C of E.

John Macquarrie, *Principles of Christian Theology* (SCM 1966, p. 328) writes on the subject of purgatory that

> If we think of heaven and hell as limits to be approached rather than final conditions in which to remain; if we refuse to draw any hard and fast line between the 'righteous' and the 'wicked'; if we reject the idea that God's reconciling work is restricted to the people living at this particular moment, and believe that his reconciliation can reach anywhere, so that it makes sense to pray for the departed; above all, if we entertain any universalist hopes of salvation for the whole of creation, then we are committed to the belief in an intermediate state, whether or not we call it 'purgatory' . . . The name 'purgatory' is, however, entirely appropriate,

for it points to the process by which we are fitted for that union with God which is our ultimate destiny. Heaven, purgatory, and hell are not sharply separated, but form a kind of continuum through which the soul may move, perhaps from the near-annihilation of sin to the closest union with God . . . The suffering envisaged in purgatory is not an external penalty that has to be paid, but is our suffering with Christ, our being crucified with him as we are conformed to him, the painful surrender of the ego-centred self that the God-centred self of love may take its place.

A. M. Allchin, *The World is a Wedding* (Darton, Longman and Todd 1978, pp. 68ff) writes regarding the communion of saints

At the heart of the Christian way there is a single life and a single death, which though it is situated in space and time, is, it is asserted, not limited by these things in the way in which our lives usually are. In a particular place and at a particular moment in history something new occurred, which had about it all the newness of the creation itself. The barriers of death were broken down, so that all times and all places, the ages which came before as well as the ages which follow after, are affected by this radically new and creative act. God is in man, and man is taken into God. The things of God become the things of man, and what is most distinctively divine becomes most distinctively human. Man at last realises in himself that for which he was made, that for which he has always longed. He becomes truly man in coming to share fully in the very life and nature of God. This is the faith which lies behind the words 'The Communion of Saints' . . . We pray for the departed because we love them in the love which comes from God, and believing them to be nearer God than we are, we are sure that they pray for us more strongly within that same love. In prayer, by God's gift, man rises up into the freedom of God and becomes a fellow worker with God. To ask the departed to pray for us, and ourselves to pray for them is a natural expression of a solidarity with them in the redemptive love of God in Christ. It is a gift of the Holy Spirit, an aspect of that communion in fellowship which he creates . . . But who are these Saints with whom we are said to be in communion, not, clearly, only those who are called 'Saints', who by one means or another had been publicly recognised and commemorated by the church as people who have reflected the character of God in some particularly shining way. Rather it must include all those who belong to God, to the God who is not a God of the dead but the living, all those who are in Christ, and are united with us in the power of the Holy Spirit.

Read Hebrews 11:1–12:2 (The Cloud of Witnesses)

To achieve its proper cumulative effect the whole of this passage needs to be studied. For a short reading at a service, good sense is conveyed by reading simply 11:13–16 and 12:1–2. About this passage, Hugh Montefiore, *The Epistle to the Hebrews*, (A & C Black 1964, p. 213) writes:

The present competitors are the last to take part in a kind of gigantic relay race. They are being watched by huge multitudes who have already handed on the baton of faith and who are waiting as invisible spectators to encourage those who run last. This great cloud of witnesses are not merely onlookers of the present contest, but they have given their own witness of faith by their own past lives, some even to the point of death.

☐ **WORSHIP**

Almighty God,
you have called out people to your service in every age,
    and you unite them in the fellowship of your Son.
Give us grace to follow in the footsteps of your saints,
    that we may share with them in your eternal kingdom.
Through Jesus Christ our Lord.   Amen.

First reading: 2 Esdras 2:42–48
Second reading: Hebrews 11:13–16 and 12:1–2
Gospel reading: Luke 6:20–23

Teaching material

■ **CONTEXT OF UNIT 15**

The prayer for the departed reminds us of the way in which the eucharist unites the whole church of God and brings together in Christ his followers once separated both in time and space. For this prayer to be real to the child four things are necessary:

1 The child needs to be aware of the wonder of life, and the natural cycle of birth, growth, death and rebirth.

2 The child needs to feel himself to be within the context of the whole church of Christ, living and departed – that is to see himself alongside the people who used to worship in his own church or community, and alongside the great saints of the past. He needs to know that the departed are alive in Christ.

3 The child needs to know something about the lives of the saints, the Church Fathers and the Church Leaders of the past.

4 The child needs to apprehend some of the images through which the Church expresses the continuity of life which it experiences in Christ. A central image is that of light.

■ **OBJECTIVES**

1 To enable the child to appreciate the wonder of life and to accept the

natural cycle of birth, development, death and rebirth as part of the God-given order of the world.

2 To enable the child to experience a sense of identity with past generations of Christian people and to be aware of their continued life in Christ.

3 To give the child access to information about the saints, church Fathers and church leaders of the past.

4 To enable the child to become familiar with the Christian symbol of light as a way of expressing our faith in the eternal life which is in Christ.

5 To help the child to appreciate the place of the departed and the saints in his pattern of prayer.

DISPLAY WORK

a The natural cycle of life, death and rebirth

Encourage the children to study the way in which new life springs out of death. Four creative activities help to develop this theme.

1 Study the life cycle of the butterfly: the butterfly lays an egg; from the egg comes the caterpillar; the caterpillar eats and grows; the caterpillar changes into a chrysalis; a skin covers the chrysalis; the butterfly takes shape inside the skin; the butterfly emerges.

The children can illustrate this life cycle in painting and by making large butterflies from tissue paper etc.

2 Study the life of the tortoise who hibernates during the winter and wakes up to a new life in spring. Ask the children to make model tortoises. Egg boxes provide an interesting texture for the shells. They can then write about the life of the tortoise and his experience of waking up into Spring.

3 Examine the way in which a flower produces seeds. The seeds are buried and 'die'. Then they give life to a new flower. Encourage the children to illustrate a description of this cycle.

4 Spring is the time for new life. Encourage the children to name all the things which burst into new life in Spring and to produce a large wall chart illustrating all these things – for example, flowers, trees, lambs, chicks, rabbits, etc.

b Identity with the past

Encourage the children to explore the history of their own community and to study the people who made that history.

1 Visit the local church:

    a see if there is a list of past incumbents/churchwardens etc. note their names and dates.

b examine the memorial tablets/brasses/monuments in the church: draw some of them and write down their inscriptions.

c inspect the tomb stones in the churchyard: note family names and make rubbings of some of them.

d ask to see the church registers of baptism/marriage/burial.

It is possible to reconstruct family histories from these documents.

2 Note the names of the local houses and streets. Try to discover the origin of the names, especially if they are derived from local people.

3 Examine the old school registers and try to recreate a history of the school – the people who founded it, built it, taught in it, acted as caretakers of it, attended it as pupils, served as managers, etc. If the school has buildings, rooms or houses named after specific people, examine the history of these people.

4 Examine some of the well-known surnames and see what they have to say about family origins, e.g.

a Cooper, Smith, Baker indicate a job of work.

b Williamson, Jackson indicate 'Son of'.

c Evans, O'Connor, McTavish indicate geographical regions.

c Saints and church fathers

Begin by talking about the people who have been well known throughout the church – the apostles, evangelists, saints, martyrs, church fathers, bishops, etc.

1 Examine the dedication of the local church and neighbouring churches. Find out something about the saints to which they have been dedicated. Make a list of local churches and their patron saints.

2 Look at the way in which the saints are represented in our church buildings and in religious art. Especially look at the stained glass windows. It is important not to let the children rest content with a 'stained glass' image of the saints. They were real men and women, wearing real clothes, at a real time in history – and they were not always good and seen to be carrying haloes! However, church art teaches us a lot by the idealised stained glass pictures of the saints. We need examples to look up to and to follow. Encourage the children to make their own stained glass windows from tissue paper and to decorate their room with them.

3 Find out something about the four evangelists. In Christian art they are represented by well established symbols. Encourage the children to produce large posters or models of them:

(a) Matthew is represented by a man.

(b) Mark is represented by a winged lion.

(c) Luke is represented by a winged ox.

(d) John is represented by a rising eagle.

4 Find out something about the twelve apostles, and about the emblems associated with them by the church. These emblems say something special about each of the apostles. Encourage the children to make banners depicting these signs and to write something about their meaning (for further details about the emblems see W. Ellwood Post, *Saints Signs and Symbols*, SPCK 1975).

St Andrew   A silver X shaped cross on a blue background. Andrew is said to have been crucified on this shape cross.

St Bartholomew   Three silver knives with gold handles on red background. Bartholomew is said to have been flayed.

St James the Great   Three gold shells on blue background. The shells are said to refer to pilgrimage.

St James the Less   A silver saw with gold handle on red background. James is said to have been sawn in two.

St John   A gold cup and silver serpent on blue background. John is said to have been offered a poisoned cup to drink.

St Jude   A gold ship with silver sails on red background. Jude is said to have travelled to many parts.

St Matthew   Three silver money bags on red background. Matthew used to be a tax collector.

St Matthias   An open book and a silver axe on red background. Matthias is said to have been beheaded.

St Philip   A gold cross and two silver circles on red background. The circles represent the two loaves Philip brought to Jesus to feed the five thousand.

St Peter   Crossed silver keys on red background. The keys represent the keys of the kingdom of heaven given to Peter.

St Simon   A gold book and silver fish on red background. Simon was a fisher of men.

St Thomas   Carpenter's square of silver blade and gold handle on red background. Thomas is said to have built a church in East India.

Judas Iscariot   Thirty pieces of silver with straw coloured rope on black background. Judas betrayed Jesus for thirty pieces of silver and subsequently hanged himself.

5 Look at one or two of the saints of the early church after the days of the apostles. Produce a project book on their lives.

d The symbol of light

The apostles, saints and fathers have been lights to the church in their different generations. Help the children to explore the symbol of light as a way of expressing the influence of the saints in the church. Make candles and display them in association with the other work produced in this unit. The candles can be lighted at a special service. Added meaning can be given to the whole work of this unit if the candles and display work are used during the feast of All Saints/All Souls, 1 and 2 November.

■ **ACTIVITIES**

a The natural cycle of life, death and rebirth

To enable the children to experience the feeling of resurrection begin by talking about the tortoise. Encourage them to act out the rhythm of hibernation and spring time awakening. The action can be aided by music carefully chosen to represent the act of hibernation, the winter slumber and the feeling of breaking out into the new life of Spring.

b Identity with the past

The children may like to act out some scenes from their local history and to dress up in period costume. For example, a pageant could be made about the life in their own school since the time that the school was founded – or the history of their own church could be re-enacted.

c Saints and church fathers

1 The children can enact episodes from the lives of the apostles, e.g.:

   a the call of James and John from being fishermen

   b the call of Matthew from being a tax collector

2 The banners can be processed at a special service.

3 Visit local churches to inspect the stained glass windows of saints, and to discover the patron saint of each church.

WRITING

1 The children can be encouraged to enter imaginatively into the experience of new life by writing about the tortoise's experience of spring time after the winter hibernation. 'I am Jerry the Tortoise and today I woke up to spring . . .'

2 Ask the children to write a history of the people who have been associated with their school or church, etc.

3 Study and write about the life of one of the saints.

DISPLAY HEADINGS

Useful headings for displaying with the work produced in this unit are

   1 The caterpillar dies in order to grow in a new way

   2 The seed dies in order to grow in a new way

   3 The tortoise hibernates during winter and comes up to a new life at spring time

   4 Spring is the time for new life

   5 The Beryff family were rich merchants in the sixteenth century

   6 Miss Cooper was headmistress of St Philips school in 1874

   7 We celebrate our communion with Jesus' twelve apostles

   8 The apostles, saints and Fathers have been lights to the church in their different ages

   9 We light candles to remember the saints

A short explanation might run like this, 'The prayer for the departed reminds us that after death we share in a new life in Christ. In the Eucharist the whole church of Christ, living and departed, is united.'

The Lord is Here or *At the Lord's Table* open at pages 30–1 can be displayed also.

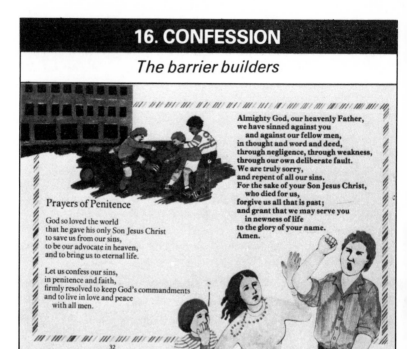

16. CONFESSION

The barrier builders

Prayers of Penitence

God so loved the world
that he gave his only Son Jesus Christ
to save us from our sins,
to be our advocate in heaven,
and to bring us to eternal life.

Let us confess our sins,
in penitence and faith,
firmly resolved to keep God's commandments
and to live in love and peace
with all men.

Almighty God, our heavenly Father,
we have sinned against you
    and against our fellow men,
in thought and word and deed,
through negligence, through weakness,
through our own deliberate fault.
We are truly sorry,
and repent of all our sins.
For the sake of your Son Jesus Christ,
    who died for us,
forgive us all that is past;
and grant that we may serve you
    in newness of life
to the glory of your name.
Amen.

32

| Background material |

☐ **TEXT**

This section contains two components, the priest's invitation to the people to confess their sins, and the people's confession.

The priest's invitation contains two ideas

1 Since God loves us and Jesus saves us, we should confess our sins confident in his mercy.
2 Our confession should be made in penitence and faith, and we should resolve to keep relationship with God and with our fellow men.

The confession is a very tightly packed statement

1 We confess that we sin against *God* and *our fellow men*.
2 We confess that our sin is a matter of what we *think*; *say*; *do*.
3 We confess that we sin as a result of *negligence* (i.e. when we don't know what is going on); *weakness* (i.e. when we are not strong enough to do what is right); *deliberate fault* (i.e. when we know what we are about).
4 We say that we are *truly sorry*; *repent of all our sins*.
5 We ask God, for Jesus' sake, to *forgive us what is past*; *help us in the future*.

PICTURE

Sin means the breakdown of the proper relationship between people, between man and God. The two pictures associated with this section of the text illustrate two different aspects of this break in relationship.

1 Three boys are playing football. The rules of football are clearly stated rules. The relationships between players are well-defined. One boy is breaking the rules of the game and the relationship between the players. He is ignoring the ball and kicking his fellow players.
2 Mother and child look on helplessly while father loses his temper. The relationships within the family are broken. It is important that sin and break in relationship should not be trivialized. Sin is not the prerogative of the 'naughty child': it permeates human society.

COMMENT

In this section comment is made on the difficult concepts of sin, repentance and penitence. Then John Gunstone looks at the position of prayers of penitence in the Communion service. In the New Testament reading Paul exhorts the Christians in Corinth to examine themselves before coming to the Eucharist. The Old Testament reading is a statement of the old law and the Gospel reading is an extract from the new law of the Sermon on the Mount. Joachim Jeremias comments on the distinctions between the old and new laws.

Sin, repentance and penitence

The word 'sin' is used to convey two different ideas. First, sin is the barrier between God and man. In this sense sin is what breaks the relationship between man and God. To be 'in sin' means to be out of relationship with God. Second, sins are the things which we do which are not in accordance with the will of God. To commit sins means to do wrong things. The word 'repent' literally means to change one's mind. The Shorter Oxford English Dictionary defines repentance at greater length as 'to change one's mind with regard to past action or conduct through dissatisfaction with it or its results'. Finally, the word 'penitence' implies both the sorrow for past failures and the desire and intention to do better in the future. For the Christian the sincere confession of sin involves both repentance and penitence.

The position of the Prayers of Penitence

In the Rite A service the Prayers of Penitence can be used either as printed in *The Lord is Here* after the intercessions and thanksgivings or at the beginning of the service immediately after the Collect for Purity. There is a long and widespread precedent for both of these positions. John Gunstone, 'The Act of Penitence', in *The Eucharist Today*, (SPCK 1974, pp. 80–81) writes

Both positions have much to commend them. An act of penitence at the beginning of the service prepares for the building up of the acts of intercessions, praise and thanksgiving which culminate in the eucharistic prayer and the Communion. On the other hand, communicants are sometimes not ready to participate in the eucharistic meal until their hearts and minds have been stirred by the Ministry of the Word. Furthermore, the logic of the position of the penitential rite (after the intercessions and thanksgivings) is that, after praying for the world and its needs, we go on to identify ourselves with the world and its shortcomings. We still prepare ourselves individually for Communion by a confession of our unworthiness, but we do this within the context of a general confession by the congregation on behalf of sinful mankind.

Furthermore, the latter position gives more exact liturgical expression to the biblical imperative in 1 Corinthians 11:28:

'a man must test himself before eating his share of the bread and drinking from the cup'.

Read Matthew 5:21–24 (An extract from the New Law)

One of the yardsticks that the Christian can use to measure his life against God's will for him is reflection upon the Law of God. We all fall short of the Law of God and need to confess our failure. But the implications of our failure are different under the New Law from what they were under the Old Law.

Under the Old Law our failure was reckoned to keep us distanced from God. Under the New Law our failure is just as great and our need for confession just as real, but God does not allow this to be an impermeable barrier. What, then is the New Law all about? Joachim Jeremias, *The Sermon on the Mount*, (Athlone Press 1961) argues that the New Law is a model for the Christian to follow when God is at his side, not an obstacle for the Christian to jump before God will come to his side. Jeremias writes that the Sermon on the Mount is not saying

'You must do all of this, in order that you may be blessed' . . . nor 'You ought actually to have done all this, see what poor creatures you are' . . . nor 'Now pull yourself together; the final victory is at hand' . . . They say 'I intend to show you through some examples what the new life is like, and what I show you through these examples, this you must apply to every aspect of life'. The result to which we have come is that the Sermon on the Mount is not Law, but Gospel. For this is indeed the difference between Law and Gospel: the Law leaves man to rely upon his own strength and challenges him to do his utmost. The Gospel, on the other hand, brings man before the gift of God and challenges him really to make the inexpressible gift of God the basis of his life. These are two different worlds.

WORSHIP

Merciful Father,
you sent your Son into the world
    to save us from our sins.
We pray you to absolve us from our sins,
    and to grant us your pardon and peace;
that we may serve you in newness of life,
    and to the glory of your name;
through Jesus Christ our Lord.   Amen.

First reading: Exodus 20:1–17
Second reading: 1 Corinthians 11:27–32
Gospel reading: Matthew 5:21–24

Teaching material

CONTEXT OF UNIT 16

The confession invites us to review the barriers which we build between ourselves and other people and between ourselves and God. These barriers break down the relationships which ought to exist. For the concept of confession to be meaningful to the child two things are necessary:

1 First, the child needs to understand the way in which people build barriers to keep others away. Barriers are built to break relationship.
2 Second, the child needs to become aware of the way in which his own behaviour builds barriers and breaks relationship both with other people and with God.

OBJECTIVES

1 To enable the child to explore the function of physical barriers and the reasons why people build them.
2 To enable the child to examine the way in which his own behaviour builds barriers between himself, his friends, his parents and God.
3 To enable the child to explore the standards of conduct which the Christian believes God expects of him.
4 To help the child to see the need for confession and forgiveness.

DISPLAY WORK

a Barriers and fortresses

1 Begin by inviting the children to think of all the barriers they know in their own neighbourhood. Talk about the job these barriers do. Make a list of them and ask the children to produce pictures or models, for example:

E

a The barrier outside the school gate prevents children from rushing into the road. It also makes crossing the road more difficult and it makes the distance from car to school door further on a rainy day.

b The barrier alongside the fast road makes the traffic safer. It also means that pedestrians have to go by a long way round.

c The barrier round the field keeps you safe from the bull. It also gets in the way of picnics.

d The level crossing gates protect you from the train. They also sometimes make you late.

e The less concrete barriers like 'no entry' signs and traffic lights regulate the traffic. They also sometimes make your journey take longer.

Explore the way in which such physical barriers are built to protect, but how at the same time they tend to be disruptive. In a similar manner people may build barriers by their behaviour or attitudes to protect themselves from others, and at the same time these barriers disrupt or destroy relationships.

2 Man builds his most powerful barriers in times of war. Talk about the medieval castle and fortress – the way in which walls, ramparts, moats and dykes were used as barriers to keep different groups of people apart. Encourage the children to make a large model castle including moat, exterior walls etc. Explore the ways in which these castle walls create suspicion, tension and anxiety between those inside and those outside.

b The Christian way of life

1 Begin by looking at the headlines in some newspapers. Then produce two large collages. On the first mount newspaper headlines and articles illustrating mankind's sinfulness – robberies, killings, etc. – possibly with the heading 'Dear God, please forgive'. On the second write out parts of the Ten Commandments and the Sermon on the Mount, together with newspaper cuttings of man's attempt to live in God's way – stories of kindness, generosity, etc. – possibly with the heading 'Dear God, please help us to live in your way'.

2 Help the children to explore different ways of behaving in situations that demand a moral choice. Help them to work out the consequences of moral choice, for example the way in which dishonesty leads to distrust, guilt and punishment. Begin by developing a short story and asking the children to talk about it and to complete it, e.g.

a Accidental damage. While playing with her ball Mary broke a window . . .

b Deliberate damage. David was cross with his brother, so he deliberately broke his brother's toy train.

c Sulking. John's parents wouldn't buy him the bike he wanted, so he went into a sulk and made life difficult for everyone.

d Cheating. Jane knew she could do better in the school test if she copied Peter's work, so she tried to sit next to Peter.

e Fighting. Brian wanted to play with the ball Peter was playing with, so he picked a fight with Peter.

f Carelessness. Ann was running along the street. She bumped into an old lady and knocked her shopping onto the ground. She kept on running.

g Insensitivity. Daniel was in a hurry. He saw a blind man trying to cross the road. 'I haven't time to help him' thought Daniel, 'because I am in a hurry'.

h Cruelty. The other girls didn't like Sally so they never played with her. Sally often felt very lonely.

i Stealing. Ruth went into a friend's home and saw a pound note on the table. No one was looking so she put it into her pocket.

When the children have written a number of these stories, compile a class project book called 'Right Choices'.

3 Encourage the children to think of the ways in which they put up barriers between themselves and other people. Confession is a time to look at the consequences of their own behaviour. Encourage them to seek God's forgiveness.

ACTIVITIES

1 Take a walk around the neighbourhood and spot the barriers.

2 Visit a medieval castle.

3 Act out the feeling of alienation produced by the walls of a castle, i.e. the suspicion and fear of those inside looking out and of those outside looking in.

4 Role play is a good way in which to work out the significance of situations which involve moral choice. For example help the children to develop the following scenes:

a Jane and Mary want to read the same book. There is a quarrel.

b Jack takes more than his fair share of lemonade. There is a row.

c Judith eats all the cake and there is none left for the others.

d Mother is sick in bed. The children make a noise and father is angry.

e John makes fun of Jeremy and there is a fight.

f No one remembers Ann's birthday. She is very upset.

g Adrian is not good to his grandmother when she comes to stay.

h Jim doesn't play games fairly.

i Pamela refuses to help set the table for dinner when mother is very busy.

j Jennifer takes a short cut through the flower bed and walks on the plants.

k Susan throws her banana skin on the floor and later Sally slips on it.

l Sam breaks the school tape recorder when he shouldn't have been using it.

m Daniel spills paint on a library book and puts the blame onto Carol.

■ WRITING

1 Ask the children to write about at least one of the situations explored in the role play.

2 Ask the children to write a story about barriers.

3 Read and write about the way in which Jesus dealt with temptation in Luke 4:1–13.

■ DISPLAY HEADINGS

Useful headings for displaying with the work produced in this unit are
1 Our sins are barriers
2 Men build barriers to keep others away
3 Barriers make life difficult
4 We build barriers whenever we fail to love other people
5 Dear God, please forgive the barriers we build

A short explanation might run like this: 'The confession invites us to examine the barriers we build between ourselves and our fellows and God. We say we are sorry about these barriers and we ask God to forgive us.'

The Lord is Here open at pages 32–3 (*At the Lord's Table*, pages 34–5) can be displayed also.

17. ABSOLUTION

The mender

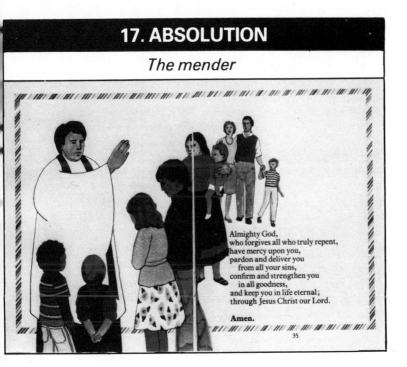

Almighty God,
who forgives all who truly repent,
have mercy upon you,
pardon and deliver you
    from all your sins,
confirm and strengthen you
    in all goodness,
and keep you in life eternal;
through Jesus Christ our Lord.

Amen.

35

Background material

TEXT

The Absolution is the church's formal act of pronouncing God's forgiveness of sins. To pronounce the forgiveness of sins is one of the sacramental privileges and responsibilities given to the priest at his ordination. After the confession, the absolution first reminds us of the relationship between forgiveness and repentance and then pronounces the words of pardon. It is customary, if a bishop is present, for the bishop to pronounce the absolution.

PICTURE

The picture focuses attention upon the sacramental sign of forgiveness. The priest is standing and has his right hand raised in readiness to make the sign of the cross over the penitents who have previously confessed their sins. The occasion is both solemn and happy.

☐ **COMMENT**

In this section Norman Snaith comments on the biblical relationship between forgiveness and repentance. Then the priest's commission to pronounce God's forgiveness of sins is quoted from the Ordination service. The Old Testament reading is a psalm of gratitude for the experience of God's forgiveness. The New Testament reading is a statement of faith in God's promise to forgive, and the Gospel reading is John's account of Jesus' commission to the disciples to continue his work of proclaiming forgiveness.

Forgiveness and Repentance

N. H. Snaith writing in Alan Richardson, *A Theological Word Book of the Bible*, (SCM 1950, p. 86) on the subject of forgiveness argues that in the bible

> forgiveness is throughout conditional upon repentance, a word which quite clearly in its OT and NT equivalents involves a change of mind and intention. Its result is a restoration of the original relationship of good favour with its accompanying blessings . . . The condition attached to forgiveness in the Lord's Prayer (Mt 6:12, Luke 11:4) is that unless we ourselves forgive, then we have no hope of forgiveness from God. This is enforced vividly by the parable of Mt 18:21–35 . . . where the servant who would not forgive his fellow-servant a trifling debt is delivered to the tormentors till he should have paid the enormous debt he was owing to his master. The moral is that he who does not forgive cannot repent. The modern attitude tends to suggest that the restoration to full relationship which is involved in the idea of forgiveness is a direct consequence of human repentance. This is part of that modern tendency which seeks to find rational and this-worldly reasons for the sequence of events, and so makes the restoration of fellowship automatic upon human action rather than upon the actual and personal immediate work of God. The Bible . . . regards God as actively busy in this matter in that he definitely and personally forgives every penitent, and this is a deliberate and separate act.

The priest's commission to forgive sins

At the service of Ordination of priests the Bishop reads the following declaration (*Alternative Service Book*, p. 356):

> A priest is called by God to work with the bishop and with his fellow-priests, as servant and shepherd among the people to whom he is sent. He is to proclaim the word of the Lord, to call his hearers to repentance, and in Christ's name to absolve, and to declare the forgiveness of sins . . .

Read Psalm 32:1–5 (The experience of forgiveness)

J. H. Eaton, *Psalms*, (SCM 1967, p. 96):

Addressing God, the singer tells of his own reconciliation in thankful acknowledgement. It is an experience that many have known. At first he would not face the truth about himself and make sincere confession. The resultant suffering probably had a physical aspect. He felt that the life-sap had dried up within him. Finding no way through, he was constrained to turn back from his course of self-deception. He made a true confession to the Lord, who lifted his burden from him.

Read John 20:19–23 (The disciples' commission)

William Temple, *Readings in St John's Gospel*, (Macmillan, paperback edn. 1961, pp. 368–70):

The body of disciples, being the Body of Christ, and being filled with that Holy Spirit which Christ has breathed into them, carries forward his work of pronouncing God's forgiveness of sin . . . In practice the Church must do this through appropriate organs, and the parallel charge to Peter included in the Matthean account of his confession at Caesarea Philippi (Mt 16:19) supports the practice of the Church in translating this commission from the plural to the singular in the Ordination of priests . . . Every Christian has a responsibility for drawing others to Christ and for declaring, if occasion so require, the forgiveness which the divine love offers to all who come in penitence. It is evidently appropriate that this, like other functions, should be representatively exercised by those appointed for the purpose; none the less the minister so appointed, when he pronounces absolution, does it, not in the name of his fellow-Christians, but in the name of Christ; for it is only in his name and by his commission that it can be pronounced at all.

WORSHIP

Almighty Father,
you give to your people the knowledge and joy of your forgiveness.
Give us grace freely to forgive others,
    as we have been freely forgiven.
Through Jesus Christ our Lord.   Amen.

First reading: Psalm 32:1–5
Second reading: 1 John 1:8–2:2
Gospel reading: John 20:19–23

Teaching material

■ CONTEXT OF UNIT 17

The absolution is the formal act of the forgiveness of sins and of the restoration of man's relationship with God. The priest is acting as God's authorised agent. The Christian believer accepts that as a result of the absolution things stand differently between himself and God, and he knows the feeling of liberation which comes with the assurance of forgiveness. Just as we frequently fail to keep our side of the relationship with God by acts of thoughtlessness or deliberate disobedience, so we need frequently to hear the words of forgiveness.

For this to be meaningful to the child three things are necessary:

1 The child needs to understand the priest as God's authorised agent who is uniquely commissioned to pronounce the words of forgiveness. As such the priest is the authorised 'mender' of the relationship between God and man.

2 The child needs to recognise the way in which the regular hearing of absolution is necessary.

3 The child needs to experience the joy and liberation of hearing the word of forgiveness.

■ OBJECTIVES

1 To encourage the child to think about a range of 'authorised agents' whose function it is to mend and to restore.

2 To enable the child to understand why frequent mending or 'servicing' is necessary for a variety of things.

3 To enable the child to understand the priest as God's authorised agent who is commissioned to pronounce the restoration of relationship between God and man.

4 To enable the child to appreciate the experience of forgiveness.

5 To enable the child to perceive the significance of the sign of the cross made by the priest which symbolizes the pronouncement of forgiveness.

6 To encourage the child to wish to forgive others and to wish to restore broken relationships.

■ DISPLAY WORK

a The mender

Begin by talking about the child's experience of *things* breaking and needing repair. Concentrate on the people who actually do the repair, for example:

the parent repairing a toy car or a doll
the shoe mender repairing worn shoes

the watchmaker repairing a clock
the AA or RAC patrol man repairing a car
the builder repairing a house (or church!)
the plumber repairing a burst pipe in winter
the GPO telephone engineer repairing overhead cables brought down in a
    storm
the roadman repairing a road – using pneumatic drills and road rollers

Next talk about the people who regularly 'service' mechanical things. Give
particular attention to the need for regular servicing, for example:
the garage mechanic servicing the private car
the mechanic servicing important vehicles, like buses, police cars, ambu-
    lances, fire engines, etc.
the heating engineer servicing the central heating installation at home,
    school or church
the electrician servicing the vacuum cleaner, washing machine, etc.

Most of these people have their own skills, tools, distinctive trade marks,
distinctive clothing, etc.

The child's understanding of these people can be sharpened by a number
of creative activities:

1 A class book can be produced on the theme of 'The Mender'. Sections can
be given to a number of different people like those listed above. Each section
can contain pictures and writing.

2 A sequence of murals can be produced about various 'menders'. For
example, the watchmaker is a good theme for this medium. A large collage
can be produced from pictures of clocks, watches, cog wheels, springs,
pendulums, etc.

3 The sequence of a) breakdown, b) calling the repairer, c) the arrival of the
repairer, d) the restoration can be well illustrated in a cartoon sequence of
pictures.

4 Some of the situations envisaged in the list of repairers can be represented
in the form of models. The AA or RAC patrol vehicle can be made – or a toy
car can be used – to set the scene for a motorway breakdown.

b Mending relationships

Begin by talking about the children's own experience of 'falling out of
relationship' with each other. Explore the reasons for the children breaking
relationship with each other. Encourage them to explore what it feels like to
break relationships. Explore the gestures, the facial expressions and pos-
tures they adopt in order to let each other know that relationship is broken.
Explore how they feel when their friends have broken relationship with
them – the feelings of isolation, loneliness, sadness, aggression, etc.

The next stage examines the child's own experiences of restoring broken relationships. Explore the gestures, actions and motives that initiate the mending of broken relationships. Suddenly one person who is part of the broken relationship smiles at the other, says 'sorry' or puts right the material damage: the other accepts the gesture and relationship is restored. In particular explore the signs and gestures that usually accompany the sealing of restored relationships – the handshake, the kiss, the smile, the hug – these are the gestures which are analogous to the sign of the cross made by the priest at the point of pronouncing the absolution.

Another way of developing the child's understanding of the breaking of relationship and restoration of relationship is to trace this pattern through the child's relationship with adults – the parent or the teacher. Care needs to be taken in examining this area. The point is that we can learn about God's relationship with man by watching some adults relate to children and to each other, but not by watching all adults! God does not break relationship by physically punishing or losing his temper. The sequence from which we can learn much about the meaning of God's forgiveness is this:

  a the child is naughty, or seems to the adult to be naughty.
  b the child feels that the adult withdraws approval from him and that his relationship with the adult is broken.

In effect the wise adult says, 'If you behave like that there can be nothing in common between you and me. That behaviour is so different from the way of life I expect that I cannot fit into the pattern you have adopted. You must change your ways or count me out of relationship with you.' In this way the adult mirrors God's response to man's foolishness.

Having discussed these situations the child's understanding of them can be furthered by creative activities:

1 A class book can be produced on the theme of 'Mending Relationships'. The book can include stories and accounts emerging from the class discussion and it can be illustrated.

2 A mural can be produced on the theme 'Friendship is restored'. The mural can be built up from scenes showing the restoration of relationship – the handshake, the smile, the hug, the priest making the sign of the cross.

c The sacrament of confession

This unit also provides an opportunity to introduce the child to the sacrament of confession. While different churches have different policies regarding the introduction of the young to the sacrament of confession, it is important for the child to know that this sacrament is practised in the Anglican Church, and how and why it is practised. Explore the significance of i) kneeling in the presence of the priest, ii) talking about the things that worry or oppress, and confessing them to God, iii) hearing the words of absolution. It is a good idea to invite to the school someone who practises this sacrament as a penitent to talk to the children about his or her reasons for doing so. A poster can be produced illustrating 'The Sacrament of

Penance'. Encourage the children to copy out and to associate with the poster John 20:22–3.

ACTIVITIES

1 Arrange a visit to see some repair work or servicing in progress, e.g.
   a visit the local garage and arrange to see the mechanic service the vicar's or teacher's car.
   b find out when the local builder is repairing the roof of a nearby house.

2 Invite the heating engineer or electrical engineer to talk about his work of regularly servicing the school's or church's heating system etc.

3 Encourage the children to act out some of the characteristic situations involving repair or servicing, for example
   a the AA patrol man visiting a car breakdown.
   b the routine visit of the heating engineer to service the heating installation.

4 Encourage the children to act out some situations of breaking and restoring relationships. Give particular attention to the gestures that accompany restoration and the feeling of well-being that ensues.

5 Ask the children to read the parable in Matthew 18:21–35 and then to produce a play about it.

WRITING

1 Ask the children to write a story beginning, 'The day we sent for the AA . . .'

2 Ask the children to write about an occasion when they needed something mended.

3 Read and write about Peter's denial of Jesus in Mark 14:66–72 and Jesus' subsequent forgiveness of Peter in John 21:15–17.

4 Read the healing story from Mark 2:1–12. Write about and illustrate the story – perhaps as a cartoon sequence.

DISPLAY HEADINGS

Useful headings for displaying with the work produced in the course of this unit are
   1 The priest acts as God's agent to pronounce the forgiveness of sins
   2 The priest pronounces the mending of relationship between God and man

3 When things are broken we need the proper mender to put them right
4 Many things require regular servicing by the authorised agent
5 When the car breaks down the AA patrol men are there to mend it
6 Often relationships break down and need mending
7 The priest is like the mender
8 The sacrament of Penance is available for all who seek it
9 The priest makes the sign of the cross when he pronounces the absolution

A short explanation might run like this, 'The absolution proclaims the forgiveness of sins. It says that the break in relationship between man and God is mended. The priest is commissioned by God to pronounce the absolution.'

The Lord is Here open at pages 32–3 (*At the Lord's Table*, pages 34–5) can be displayed also.

18. PRAYER OF HUMBLE ACCESS

The birthday invitation

We do not presume
to come to this your table, merciful Lord,
trusting in our own righteousness,
but in your manifold and great mercies.
We are not worthy
so much as to gather up the crumbs
under your table.
But you are the same Lord
whose nature is always to have mercy.
Grant us therefore, gracious Lord,
so to eat the flesh of your dear Son
Jesus Christ
and to drink his blood,
that we may evermore dwell in him,
and he in us.   Amen.

36

Background material

☐ **TEXT**

The Prayer of Humble Access was composed by Thomas Cranmer for the 1548 'Order of Communion', the first step towards the English Communion Service of the Church of England. It was designed to help the people to share in and to prepare themselves for fuller participation in the Eucharist. Now this prayer stands as part of the preparation of the people between the Absolution and the Preparation of the Bread and Wine. As we look forward to receiving the sacrament, we remind ourselves in the Prayer of Humble Access that we come to God's table, not because we are worthy to do so, but because God himself is kind enough to invite us.

☐ **PICTURE**

The picture focuses attention upon the meaning of sharing a family table. Three generations are sitting round the family table together. The family

joins hands to show awareness of its identity and to demonstrate its to-
getherness. The family dog, too, is at home there, waiting for crumbs or
tit-bits to come his way.

☐ **COMMENT**

In this section John Gunstone writes about the origin of the Prayer of
Humble Access, and Michael Perry comments on its use in Rite A. George
Herbert's poem meditates on man's approach to God's table. In the Old
Testament reading the psalmist approaches the temple sanctuary and in the
New Testament reading the author of the Epistle to the Hebrews states his
grounds for the Christian's confident approach to God. The Gospel reading
traces the source of Cranmer's image of gathering the crumbs from under the
table.

John Gunstone, *The Eucharist Today*, (SPCK 1974, pp. 78–9):

> What we call the Prayer of Humble Access was Cranmer's own composi-
> tion. It was intended to provide a prayer for worthy reception for the laity
> on the analogy of the prayers said by the priest in the Latin mass before
> communicating. It begins with a phrase from the priest's private prayer
> found in two missals printed before 1548. The rest of the prayer is made up
> from a wide range of sources including the Liturgies of St Basil and of St
> James, the Book of Daniel, the Gospels of St Mark and St John, the
> Hereford Missal, the Litany, Thomas Aquinas, Florus of Lyons, and
> Paschasius Radbert. With the exception of the gospel references, none is
> so literally reproduced as to be definitely identifiable as a source; but each,
> filtered through Cranmer's retentive memory, may have contributed
> something to the general sense, and a word or two of the actual phrases.

Michael Perry, *Sharing in one Bread*, (SPCK 1980, p. 45) writes that this
prayer

> hits exactly the right note as we pass from the Ministry of the Word to the
> most sacred part of the service, the Ministry of the Sacrament. In the prayer
> we acknowledge that we are so overwhelmed by the welcome which God
> extends to us that we can hardly credit it that people like ourselves could
> come to his most holy sacrament without presumptuousness. We go
> forward, then, trusting not in ourselves but in God, who will let us eat the
> flesh and drink the blood of Christ so that his indwelling of us and ours of
> him may be eternal.

George Herbert's poem, 'Love'

> Love bade me welcome: yet my soul drew back,
>   Guiltie of dust and sinne.
> But quick-ey'd Love, observing me grow slack
>   From my first entrance in,

Drew nearer to me, sweetly questioning,
   If I lack'd any thing.

A guest, I answer'd, worthy to be here:
   Love said, You shall be he.
I the unkinde, ungratefull? Ah my deare,
   I cannot look on thee.
Love took my hand, and smiling did reply,
   Who made the eyes but I?

Truth Lord, but I have marr'd them: let my shame
   Go where it doth deserve.
And know you not, sayes Love, who bore the blame?
   My deare, then I will serve.
You must sit down, sayes Love, and taste my meat:
   So I did sit and eat.

Read Psalm 24:3–6 (The ascent to the sanctuary)

J. H. Eaton, *Psalms*, (SCM 1967, pp. 79–81) argues that the questions and responses which constitute the greater part of this psalm accompanied a ceremony of ascent to the Temple and entrance through the sanctuary gates;

> we may suppose that as the column approaches the sanctuary gates, its spokesman engages in dialogue with the 'keepers of the threshold', priests of the highest rank . . . Verse 3 is the question from the procession: what are the requirements for admission to this sanctuary?

Read Mark 7:24–30 (The children's bread)

This story has to do with the extension of the salvation proclaimed by Jesus from the Jewish people to the rest of the world. The woman in question is a Jew neither by descent nor by religious conviction. And yet she comes to ask Jesus for his healing power. Jesus answers her that it is not right to take the children's bread and to give it to the dogs. The Gentiles were called 'dogs' by the Jews as an insult. The woman seems to accept this insult and to acknowledge that she has no right to demand anything from Jesus. Patiently she asks for the crumbs left from the Jewish table. William Barclay, *The Gospel of Mark*, (St Andrew Press 1954, p. 182–3) concludes,

> Her faith was tested and her faith was real, and her prayer was answered. Symbolically she stands for the Gentile world which so eagerly seized on the bread of heaven which the Jews had rejected and thrown away.

☐ WORSHIP

Most merciful Lord,
you invite us to your table,
   and your love compels us to accept.

We are not worthy to come,
   even to eat the crumbs.
But you share your bread with sinners.
So cleanse and feed us
   with the precious body and blood of your Son,
that we may sit and eat with him,
   in your eternal kingdom;
through Jesus Christ our Lord.   Amen.

First reading: Psalm 24:3–6
Second reading: Hebrews 10:19–23
Gospel reading: Mark 7:24–30

Teaching material

■ CONTEXT OF UNIT 18

The Prayer of Humble Access reminds us of two things:

1 We are coming to God's table because he invites us to do so. It is by his invitation and not by any right that we can claim.

2 God wishes us to feel at home around his table. We accept the fact that his invitation stands with all the generosity and kindness with which it is given. Therefore, we know that we can accept the invitation and feel comfortable as his invited guests.

For this to be meaningful to the child two things are necessary:

1 The child needs to understand the idea of invitation and feel that he or she is responding to God's special invitation.

2 The child needs to experience what it means to feel at home in God's house and around his table.

These two ideas can be developed around the theme of the invitation to a birthday party.

■ OBJECTIVES

1 To enable the child to understand the idea of an invitation to a birthday party, and to see the difference made by the giving and acceptance of invitations.

2 To enable the child to explore that idea of 'feeling at home' at a birthday party as a consequence of being invited.

3 To explore what it means to accept God's invitation and to feel at home around his table.

DISPLAY WORK

a The invitation to the party

Begin by talking about childrens' parties, parties held in school or at a parent's place of work. Think about holding a party in one's own house and inviting other children to it, or going to a party in someone else's house. You only go to a party when you have been invited. How are invitations given?

1 Encourage the children to prepare a large mural showing the setting for a children's party. Perhaps a huge table can be drawn and each child can contribute a picture of party food to stick onto the table. Then let the children draw a picture of themselves and add these pictures to the mural also. Each child's portrait can be named, perhaps by adding 'party hats' bearing their name. The mural can have the heading 'We have all been invited to the party'. In order to make the party more of a 'family affair' ask the children if they would wish to invite adults and pets as well. Add to the mural pictures of parents, grandparents and pets (suitably labelled). The new headings can be added 'No one is excluded from Class 4's party', and 'Rover is welcome to crumbs and tit-bits as well'.

2 Make party invitation cards. The theme can be elaborated to include the making of envelopes, stamps and post boxes. Finally, a display can be made of the different invitations, perhaps including a picture of the postman.

3 Prepare a sequence of pictures illustrating what is involved in the preparation for a party, including some of the following

the people who decide to have a party
the making of invitations
the distribution of invitations
the preparation of party food/decorations etc.
the arrival of guests
the party in progress

b Feeling at home at the party
Talk about the way in which both guests and host make an effort to make each other happy and at ease:

1 The host often provides a party hat so all the guests feel special and different. Make hats.

2 The guests often bring a present. Encourage the children to make something special and to display this as 'their present'.

3 Well known and favourite games are played. Ask the children to write about these games and to illustrate them.

4 The party really takes on its significance round a table. Prepare party food – either real food or play food. A convincing iced birthday cake can be made by coating a tin with polyfilla and later painting it.

The analogies between these four points and the Eucharist are for the adult to grasp in presenting the material: they are not to be consciously laboured for the children:
1 God invites us and makes us feel special (invitations and hats).
2 In return we give of our best (presents).
3 The familiarity of the liturgy makes us feel at home (games).
4 The heart of our worship comes around the table of bread and wine (birthday cake).

■ **ACTIVITIES**

The obvious activity is to seek an occasion on which to hold a special birthday party. Rather than celebrate a child's birthday, look for a special occasion in the life of the school or church – someone who is well loved (caretaker, verger or older member of the congregation) or an anniversary (the founding of the school or patronal festival). Make invitations and invite adults. Prepare food and make party hats, both for the children and for the adults.

WRITING

1 If a real birthday party is held, ask the children to write a diary account of how they prepared for it and what took place.

2 Ask the children to imagine their own next birthday celebration, and to write about it.

3 Look at St Mark's account of Jesus' conversation with the Gentile woman (Mark 7:24–30), and write about it.

▌ **DISPLAY HEADINGS**

Useful headings for displaying with the work produced in the course of this unit are
    1 We are sending out invitations to the party
    2 We have all been invited to the party
    3 We bring a special present to the party
    4 God invites us to his house and to his table
    5 We are here because God invites us.

A short explanation might run like this, 'The prayer of humble access reminds us that we come to the Eucharist because God himself invites us to share in his table. He wants us to feel at home in his house.'

A larger explanation might draw out the close parallels between the children's birthday party and the Eucharist, 'The children come to the party because they are invited. The host makes them feel at home by giving them the party hat. They respond by bringing a special present. Familiar party games break the ice and establish relationships. The climax of the party comes around the birthday cake. We attend God's Eucharist because he invites us. He makes us welcome. We respond by offering the best we can. Our relationship with God is established through the familiar words of the service. The climax of our worship comes around the bread and the wine.'

The Lord is Here open at pages 36–7 (*At the Lord's Table*, pages 32–3) can be displayed also.

19. PEACE

Say it with hands

The peace of the Lord be always with you

and also with you.

The Ministry of the Sacrament

The Peace

We are the Body of Christ.
In the one Spirit we were all baptized
into one body.
Let us then pursue
all that makes for peace
and builds up our common life.

38

| Background material |

☐ **TEXT**

The Peace brings to a climax the Ministry of the Word and initiates the Ministry of the Sacrament. In this way the Peace acts as a central hinge of the eucharistic rite. Now we stand and affirm our identity as the Body of Christ, the People of God moving forward into the Eucharist together. As the Body of Christ we acknowledge that we share a common life together. The keynote of this common life is the Peace of Christ. Just as the Confession and Absolution has proclaimed peace between God and man, so now the Peace proclaims restored relationship between the fellow members of the Body of Christ and symbolically includes the idea of our intended reconciliation with all men. The placing of the Peace immediately before the Offertory is influenced by Matthew 5:23–4. Quite often the words of the Peace are accompanied by some physical gesture as a sign of peace.

PICTURE

The picture focuses attention upon two ideas:

1 The family grouping illustrates the solidarity which we share in the Body of Christ. We are united and happy together.
2 The handclasp illustrates the way in which peace is extended from person to person. We stretch out our hands in order to receive another person into the community of peace.

COMMENT

In this section comment is made on the theology of Baptism into the Body of Christ, and on the significance of the words 'Peace' and 'common life'. Then attention is drawn to the ancient liturgical practice of the kiss of peace. The Old Testament reading looks forward to the establishment of the kingdom of the Prince of Peace. In the New Testament reading Paul salutes the Thessalonian Christians with the kiss of peace, and in the Gospel reading the Risen Christ greets his disciples with the message of peace.

Baptism into the Body of Christ The image of the Body of Christ, standing for the Church or the people of God, is given to us by St Paul. For Paul, the Body of Christ is the new creation made possible through the death and resurrection of Jesus. It is man standing in right relationship with God, as God intends him to be. The Body of Christ is in direct contrast to the Body of Adam. The Body of Adam is man fallen from right relationship with God. We are brought across from the Body of Adam into the Body of Christ in our baptism. For Paul, baptism is a real moment of change. At baptism we are raised up into the Body of Christ to share the new life of Christ's resurrection, life lived with God rather than life lived against or apart from God. We are no longer members of that fallen race represented by Adam. We are members of a restored human race represented by Christ. It is through our solidarity in the Body of Christ that we experience what it means to be Christians. We need, then, to learn to live out the quality of life which is expected of those who are in Christ rather than in Adam.

Peace Religiously speaking peace is that new quality of life which man only knows when God dwells with him. Its religious meaning comes from the Hebrew *shalom* which represents that ideal state of life in Israel when God is known to be among his people. Fundamental to the meaning of *shalom* is wholeness, well-being, harmony. In Old Testament imagery, peace is represented by material prosperity untrammelled by violence or misfortune.

Common Life The concept standing behind the phrase 'common life' is based on the Greek word *koinonia*. There is no simple way to translate *koinonia* into English. It contains all three of the ideas involved in sharing, fellowship and communion. It is the kind of life lived around the sharing of the Eucharist.

Kiss of Peace R. J. Halliburton, *The Eucharist Today*, (SPCK 1974, pp. 88–90):

> The President is then directed to give the Peace to the congregation, saying 'the Peace of the Lord be always with you'. By this rubric, an ancient and meaningful ceremony is rescued from centuries of oblivion . . . Its origins are to be found in the apostolic age; a number of references in the New Testament suggest that the kiss was used by the first Christians as a demonstration of their love for one another and of their peace and union with one another in the faith . . . The earliest evidence of its appearance in the ceremonies of the Christian Eucharist is to be found in the First *Apology* of Justin Martyr (who died 165 A.D.) . . . Clearly the Roman *osculum* or touching with the lips, which in the ancient world was a sign of reverence and affection, and which the early Christians may well have adopted, is out of place among the traditionally reserved social customs of the English. Some congregations have resorted to the simple handshake, others to the 'double handshake', whereby one either grasps both of one's neighbour's hands separately or else puts both one's hands together to be grasped between one's neighbour's hands, saying 'Peace be with you'. Each congregation and sometimes each individual must clearly choose his own way of giving and receiving the Peace. The point is that whether demonstrated by words in a physical gesture or simply conveyed from person to person by saying 'Peace be with you' without the gesture, the purpose of the Peace is to strengthen the congregation's sense of unity, to stress the fact that the Church's worship is not just a series of individuals but a corporate body, to break down the sense of isolation or strangeness of some (particularly newcomers) and to remind Christians of their duty to be reconciled to one another and to forgive one another as they too have been forgiven.

☐ WORSHIP

O God of Peace,
your Risen Son proclaimed the message of Peace to his disciples.
Give us your peace in our hearts,
that we may build up our common life,
 sharing with each other generously,
 forgiving each other lovingly,
 and serving you joyfully,
 now and always.
We make our prayer in Jesus' name.   Amen.

First reading: Isaiah 9:6–7
Second reading: 1 Thessalonians 5:23–28
Gospel reading: John 20:19–21

Teaching material

CONTEXT OF UNIT 19

The peace draws attention to the kind of relationships that should exist within the family of the church. It provides an opportunity for each individual in the congregation to exchange the sign of friendship and peace with one or several other people. The handclasp is a good outward sign for an inward intention to be at peace with all men. For this symbolic action to be meaningful to the child two things are necessary:

1 The child needs to experience the feeling of the 'common life' within the Christian community. He needs to feel himself part of a warm and accepting community.
2 The child needs to grasp the significance of the way in which hands can communicate and talk.

OBJECTIVES

1 To enable the child to appreciate the many things he does with his own hands.
2 To help the child to understand all the things that are done for him by other people's hands.
3 To draw attention to the way in which hands are creative and express our creative intentions.
4 To draw attention to the way in which hands express our feelings and communicate them to others.
5 To explore the significance of the handclasp in our worship.

DISPLAY WORK

1 Begin by asking the children to look at their hands. Ask them to draw round each other's hands, and to colour the drawings. They can be cut out and mounted together with the children's names. The theme can be extended by asking the children to bring drawings made round the hands of other members of their family. The pictures can be mounted in family groups. For those who like the idea of getting messy, the theme can be repeated by means of hand prints in paint or hand moulds in plaster or plasticine.

2 Ask the children to look at the 'hands' of animals, birds, etc. Look for paw prints in the ground and make casts of them. Discuss the greater usefulness of the human hand. Ask the children to write about the things they can do but other creatures cannot.

3 Ask the children to look at the episodes in the gospels which mention Jesus' hands. See how Jesus used his hands to express God's goodwill towards men and healing. Draw pictures of some of the following episodes.

Mark 1:16–18	Jesus beckons Simon and Andrew to follow him
Mark 1:29–31	Jesus takes Simon's mother-in-law by the hand and heals her
Matthew 19:13–15	Jesus laid his hands on the children
Mark 6:41–44	Jesus feeds the crowd
Mark 8:22–26	Jesus heals the blind man
John 13:5–9	Jesus washes the disciples' feet
Mark 14:22–23	Jesus breaks bread
Luke 24:50–51	Jesus blesses his disciples

4 Make a list of the things the children do with their hands everyday (dress, clean teeth, eat breakfast). Produce a long picture sequence, 'The things we do with our hands'.

5 Talk about the things our parents and teachers do with their hands to help us. These activities can become the subject of a mural 'Mummy uses her hands to clean the car'. 'Daddy uses his hands to wash the breakfast dishes'.

6 Talk about the jobs done for us by other people's hands – and collect pictures of
    the bus driver, lorry driver
    the postman, milkman
    the hairdresser
    the cashier in the shop, post office
    the person who stocks the shelves in the shop, weighs the vegetables
    the skilled craftsman, the potter
    the machine operator in the factory, the clerk in the office (i.e. people we
    do not often see at their work)

7 Let the children experiment with forms of creativity using their hands. Look for an activity of which they have not much experience, so they can discover the joy of developing new skills with their hands.

8 Examine the system of sign language used by the deaf in order to communicate.

9 Produce a poster or set of puppets showing how hand gestures can communicate feelings and intentions. For example, hands placed over the ears show that we are not listening; hands placed over the eyes show that we are not looking; hands placed over the mouth show that we are not telling. The clenched fist indicates anger, the wave indicates greeting or farewell, the hand clap indicates pleasure, holding hands indicates friendship. Display this work with a heading like 'Our hands say many things'.

10 Produce a poster showing the children or the whole congregation exchanging the sign of Peace in the Communion service: 'Our hands proclaim the Peace of Christ'.

ACTIVITIES

1 Arrange a visit to a zoo to look at the 'hands' of other creatures.

2 With younger children, play games that require hand holding like ring a ring of roses or the farmer's in his den.

3 Older children enjoy games that require greater dexterity and skill like pass the parcel or quoits.

4 Arrange a visit to see skilled craftsmen at work, a furniture restorer or potter.

5 Invite someone who is skilled with their hands to show their work off to the children, e.g. embroidery, origami, painting or the making of corn dollies.

6 Let the children explore the use of their hands for making shadow puppets.

7 Play panel games like 'What's my line?' when the children are allowed to communicate only through gestures with their hands.

8 Encourage the children to prepare short mimes in which the central theme is the making, ending and restoring of relationships with hand gestures, the wave goodbye, the handshake of welcome, the fist shake of anger, etc.

9 Devise games in which the children are not to use their hands (to emphasise our helplessness without hands) e.g., the egg and spoon race when the spoon is held in the mouth, balancing a matchbox on the nose or bob apple.

■ WRITING

1 If a visit has been arranged to see a skilled craftsman at work, or if such a person has visited the children, ask them to write about it.

2 Ask the children to write about what they have learned through their mime or 'what's my line'.

3 Write a story about being taken prisoner, being kept handcuffed and then somehow breaking free from the handcuffs and escaping.

4 Write about the hands of Jesus.

5 Write a letter to someone who has never been to the Communion service to explain what we do at the Peace and why.

■ DISPLAY HEADINGS

Useful headings for displaying with the work produced in the course of this unit are

1 Here are our hands
2 We use our hands to do many things
3 Other people's hands help us
4 Jesus used his hands in many ways
5 Often we can talk with our hands
6 The handclasp is a sign of friendship

A short explanation might run like this, 'At the peace we show our intention to build up the common life of the people of God. The outward sign of our inward intention is the handclasp.'

The Lord is Here or *At the Lord's Table* open at pages 38–9 can be displayed also.

20. PREPARATION OF THE GIFTS

The shopping spree

The Preparation of the Gifts

Blessed be God for ever.

**Yours, Lord, is the greatness,
the power, the glory,
the splendour, and the majesty;
for everything in heaven
and on earth is yours.
All things come from you,
and of your own do we give you.**

40   41

Background material

TEXT

In this section the gifts of the people are brought to the Holy Table. Two kinds of gifts can be presented at this point. These two kinds of gifts are different in their meaning and significance:

1 *The wine, water and bread* for the Eucharist itself are placed on the holy table. The theme here is that the Church must provide the gifts for the eucharistic meal. This theme is given more force if the gifts are actually seen to be brought by the people from the body of the congregation. The gifts are then presented to the President who, according to the rubric, may praise God for his gifts in appropriate words, to which the people respond 'Blessed be God for ever'.

2 *The offerings of the people* may be collected and presented. The theme here is that, especially at the Eucharist, Christian people should remember the needs of the Church and of the world – and joyously contribute to the work of Christ. The point made by the Offertory Sentence is that all things come from God and it is of God's own that we give to him. In the

preparation of the gifts we offer a token both of our dependence upon God and of our gratitude to him. This token should prompt us to adopt a different view both of our possessions and of our own obligation to God's world.

☐ PICTURE

The intention of the picture is to see the Offertory of bread and wine as part of something much greater. These are but symbols for the whole of what supports our life. The images of the supermarket and of the shopping trolley are intended to make a bridge between the stylized gifts of the Offertory and the whole sphere of the child's day to day experience of all that supports life. God is not just God of the bread specially made for the Eucharist, but of the supermarket packets and the processed food stuffs.

☐ COMMENT

First, the offertory prayers are quoted for the offering of the bread and wine. Then the close relationship between the offertory and the whole of life is explored. The Old Testament reading is David's prayer of thanksgiving after the whole people had contributed generously to the building of the House of God which his son Solomon was to complete. The New Testament reading gives Paul's instructions to the church at Corinth to raise a collection for the church in Jerusalem. The Gospel reading is Christ's command to sell one's possessions and to give in charity.

The Offertory Prayers

After the President has received the gifts of bread and wine Rite A prints the people's response 'Blessed be God for ever' and so hints that the Roman Catholic Offertory Prayers might be used by the President for the offering of the bread and the wine:

> Blessed are you, Lord, God of all creation.
> Through your goodness we have this bread to offer,
> which earth has given and human hands have made.
> It will become for us the bread of life.

> Blessed are you, Lord, God of all creation.
> Through your goodness we have this wine to offer,
> fruit of the vine and work of human hands.
> It will become our spiritual drink.

The Symbolism of the Offertory

The offering of the collection or the gifts of money represents the offering of the work of our hands and the gift of ourselves. Theodore Klauser, *A Short History of the Western Liturgy*, (OUP 1969, p. 109) argues that this close relationship between the offertory and our work and our very selves could be seen much more clearly in the early church when the offerings were made in kind (cheese, wine, oil, poultry, etc.) as well as in money:

> In the offering of these gifts, one could see how each member of the congregation expressed concretely his intentions of taking an active part in the sacrifice, and of making an offering of his very self. The fact that most of the oblations, in an age which was accustomed to trade in kind, were products of the labours of people's own hands served to enhance the symbolism of the offertory gift in the mind of the individual worshipper. For in his gift at the offertory, he gave something of his very own substance, something fundamental to his very existence and by doing this represented the giving of himself.

Speaking about the offertory today Hugh Montefiore, *Thinking about the Eucharist*, (SCM 1972, pp. 74–7), writes

> The money offered during the eucharist has also a symbolic aspect. Money shows that we mean business: it is a token of possessions, power and personal self-offering. The fact that it is associated in offering with the bread and wine to be consecrated, and that it is often placed upon the holy table, suggests that the rite is concerned with the sanctification of ordinary lives, which ordinary people offer to God for renewal.

Montefiore proceeds to argue that the bread and wine are themselves powerful symbols in the offertory. They constitute a kind of miniature harvest festival. Bread is a natural symbol for the satisfaction of need.

> Bread is ordinary food, a symbol of day-to-day sustenance . . . Wine is a natural symbol of feast and festival. Wine is the token of the special occasion. Men do not usually drink wine alone: the cup symbolises a party, a common meal, whether among friends or within the family.

Read 1 Corinthians 16:1–4 (The collection for the Jerusalem church)

John Ruef, *Paul's First Letter to Corinth*, (Penguin 1971, p. 180) writes about this collection for the church in Jerusalem that

> It is not altogether clear whether this collection was undertaken out of economic necessity or whether there were other motives as well. It is possible that the Christians in Jerusalem were boycotted by their fellow Jews . . . It is also possible that Paul had certain other motives, such as promoting the unity of the church . . . It is clear from the other references to this subject that it was most important to Paul . . . There is no evidence here that this putting-aside had anything to do with a worship service on Sunday. It sounds more like a practical means of making sure that some kind of contribution would be there when Paul arrived.

☐ **WORSHIP**

Almighty and everliving God,
we praise you and bless your name.
You have provided the resources of the world:
all things come from you.
Give us grace to use your gifts rightly,
　to your glory,
　for our own well-being,
　and for the relief of those in need;
through Jesus Christ our Lord.　Amen.

First reading: I Chronicles 29:6–14
Second reading: I Corinthians 16:1–4
Gospel reading: Luke 12:32–34

Teaching material

■ **CONTEXT OF UNIT 20**

In the symbolic actions of the Offertory, the Christian is acknowledging a number of the fundamental ideas of the faith

1 God is the origin of all there is.
2 We are dependent upon God for all that creates and supports life.
3 It is right that we should give thanks to God for what he has given to us.
4 We have a responsibility to God as stewards of his gifts to respond to the needs of others.
5 God's action in the eucharist gives to us the initiative of first bringing to him the gifts of bread and wine.

For these ideas to be developed for the child through the Offertory five things are necessary

1 The child needs to see the eucharistic gifts as symbolic of everything on which we depend for the support of life.
2 The child needs to experience the wonder and dependence that comes as a consequence of looking behind the supermarket and the packaging to the origin of our food and raw materials.
3 The child needs to experience the response of thankfulness to God for what he has given to us.
4 The child needs to be able to take an active part in the Offertory itself, in bringing to the eucharistic table the gifts which God uses.
5 The child needs to be aware that the plenty which he may experience is not shared by the whole world.

OBJECTIVES

1 To help the child become aware of his need for the material things which support life e.g. food, drink, clothing etc.

2 To help the child look behind what he sees in the shops and to appreciate the natural origin of the raw materials and basic food stuffs

3 To help the child become aware of his ultimate dependence upon God as the origin of everything

4 To give the child the opportunity of expressing his gratitude to God by offering him a token of his gifts to us

5 To help the child see the Offertory gifts of bread, wine and money as symbolising the totality of our material possessions

The Offertory both sums up and anticipates some of the themes which occur throughout the rest of the Communion service. In order not to overload this unit two of these themes are left for later units. First, the Offertory makes us aware of the needs of others and of our responsibility to share God's gifts. Units 27 and 31 examine this theme. Second, the Offertory draws attention to the specific gifts of bread and wine. Bread and wine are dealt with fully in Unit 24.

DISPLAY WORK

Begin by asking the children to talk about their experience of shopping. Draw out three separate issues and develop them in turn 1) food stuffs, 2) non-food stuffs, e.g. clothing, hardware, etc., 3) money.

a The supermarket

1 Ask the children to write a shopping list – and then to compare notes. These lists can become the basis of a display.

2 Prepare a map of the local shopping area, making a list of what is obtainable from each shop. Draw pictures of some of the local shops.

3 Conduct a price check among some local shops, producing a list comparing prices on certain well-known commodities.

4 Create a 'supermarket' in part of the church or classroom. Borrow a shopping trolley from a local store. Create shelving. Display empty food cartons. Certain food stuffs can be made from papier mâché, etc. Paint posters and adverts for the supermarket. A cash till can be used to create a check-out point.

5 Produce a collage using the advertising material produced for food stuffs.

6 Trace the processes involved in manufacturing some foods. Try to acquire some information from the manufacturers and create project books or wall charts on a few items. Draw out the natural origins of the food which children so often see only in the processed and packaged state. For example

a the process involved in making butter and cheese can be explored. This can be combined with visits to the museum to see the old-fashioned butter churns and to the farm to see the cows. Cheese can be made by the class from soured milk.

b a variety of home-made sweets can be produced, involving an examination of the raw ingredients.

b The other shops
Encourage the children to make a display of the non-food stuffs which they and their family need. Discuss the raw materials from which the things are made and see how these too have their origin in God's creation, for example woollen clothes, leather shoes, steel knives and the whole world of plastic products.

c Money
1 Encourage the children to see how money is a symbol for all their material possessions. Talk about the historical development of money and why it took the place of bartering. Ask the children to explore the history of money.

2 Arrange a display of foreign coins or pictures of money.

3 Encourage the children to make rubbings of coins, to draw pictures of bank notes etc.

4 Look at the signs associated with different banks and the Post Office. Make a display of them.

■ ACTIVITIES

a, b The supermarket and other shops
1 Arrange a visit to one or more shopping centres or markets.

2 Play shops. Using the supermarket created in the previous section, children can simulate all kinds of shopping situations.

3 During a special celebration of the eucharist, the supermarket can become the focus of attention and the full shopping trolley can become part of the offertory procession.

4 Arrange for a manager of a local shop or store to show the children around, or to visit the school and talk about his work.

5 Visit a factory which deals in food stuff – and give attention to the raw materials.

6 Let the children experiment with the making of some food stuffs.

7 Visit a factory which manufactures household goods from plastic or wood.

c Money

1 Visit a museum to see old coins.

2 Visit a bank and arrange for someone to talk about how a bank works.

3 Use toy money to play games which involve the concept of money and its worth.

4 Let the children take responsibility of planning and making some special expenditure on behalf of the school/church and ask them to write about their experience.

WRITING

1 Ask the children to write about the meaning of the Offertory.

2 Ask the children to write a story imagining that they lived in a pre-monetary society.

3 Ask the children to keep a diary for a few days listing all the things which they have eaten, used or possessed – and for which they should give thanks to God. These lists can be brought to church as part of their Offertory.

DISPLAY HEADINGS

Useful headings for displaying with the work produced in the course of this Unit are
  1 Class 6 goes shopping
  2 All things come from God
  3 Money symbolises all the things we can buy
  4 The Offertory shows our gratitude to God
  5 We bring to God what he has already given to us, so that he can use them for us

An explanation might run like this, 'In the Offertory we bring to God the gifts which he has given to us. The bread, the wine and the money are symbols for *all* God's gifts. They show our dependence upon God and our gratitude to him.'

The Lord is Here or *At the Lord's Table* open at pages 40–1 can be displayed also.

F

Bird watching

First Eucharistic Prayer

The Lord is here.
His Spirit is with us.
Lift up your hearts.
We lift them to the Lord.
Let us give thanks to the Lord our God.
It is right to give him thanks and praise.

It is indeed right,
it is our duty and our joy,
at all times and in all places
to give you thanks and praise,
holy Father, heavenly King,
almighty and eternal God,
through Jesus Christ your only Son
  our Lord.

For he is your living Word;
through him you have created all things
  from the beginning,
and formed us in your own image.

Through him you have freed us
  from the slavery of sin,
giving him to be born as man
  and to die upon the cross;

you raised him from the dead
and exalted him to your right hand on high.
Through him you have sent upon us
  your holy and
  life-giving Spirit;
  and made us a people
  for your own
  possession.

42

Background material

☐ **TEXT**

There are two parts to this section
1 the Opening Dialogue
2 the Preface

The President begins the Opening Dialogue by establishing his oneness with the congregation through the Greeting, and then he invites the people to lift up their hearts to God in worship. Thirdly, the President establishes the purpose of the Eucharistic Prayer as that of giving thanks. By their assent the people are associated with this thanksgiving from the very beginning.

The Preface is the foundation of all that follows in the whole of the Eucharistic Prayer, Sections 21–25. The word Preface comes from the Latin *Praefatio* and means not a foreword but a proclamation or a telling-out. In the Preface we give thanks for the work of God in creation, the love of God in redemption through Jesus Christ, and the power of God in establishing his people the Church. The five paragraphs of this section are

1 an ascription of praise
2 recollection of creation
3 recollection of redemption
4 recollection of the continued process of sanctification
5 a reminder that in our eucharistic thanksgiving we join ourselves to the whole company of heaven.

In the context of the Preface provision is made for the inclusion of Proper Thanksgivings for special seasons of the church's year.

PICTURE

The picture illustrates the way in which great theological themes can be expressed through the use of symbols and signs. This picture is a simple and stylized dove. The red of the dove is the colour which represents the Holy Spirit. The yellow aureole circling the dove's head represents holiness. The downward swoop of the dove symbolises the Spirit's presence among us. It focuses attention on the affirmation underlying the Preface, 'The Lord is here – His Spirit is with us', and becomes the basis for the teaching unit's project work.

COMMENT

In this section Colin Buchanan comments on the opening dialogue between President and people. The Old Testament reading speaks of God's work in creation. The Gospel reading speaks of God's work in redemption through Jesus Christ, and the New Testament reading speaks of God's work in calling into being his people, the Church.

The Opening Dialogue

Colin Buchanan in *Anglican Worship Today*, (Collins 1980, p. 139):

> The great action is the thanksgiving (eucharistic) prayer. The President and people greet each other in an opening dialogue which cements the relationship. Their words are not only a greeting but are also full of Christian teaching. An obvious – but delightful – feature is the assertion that we are in two places at once! For –
>
> 'The Lord is here'
> 'His Spirit is with us'
>
> – the assembly is the place where God the Holy Spirit who came to earth at Pentecost makes his home, and stirs us to worship.
>
> 'Lift up your hearts'
> 'We lift them to the Lord'
>
> – the people of God are to go into the heavenly places, to 'have confidence to enter the holy place' (Hebrews 10:19) to join 'with angels and arch-angels'. Then the dialogue gives a sense of purpose to this understanding

of ourselves as a people of God – there is a task to be done now:

'Let us give thanks to the Lord our God'

'It is right to give him thanks and praise'.

our task now is thanksgiving – thanksgiving for creation, for redemption, and for God making us his people. So the prayer continues with praise and thanks.

Read Genesis 1:1–8 (God at work in Creation)

Alan Richardson, *Genesis 1–11*, (SCM 1953, pp. 43–8) writes that the distinctive character of the creation story is displayed not only by the stylized phrases often repeated, but by the whole conception of the created world as the scene of the manifestation of the glorious majesty of God: everything in it reflects the glory of God, sun and moon and stars, day and night, trees and herbs and grass, beasts and birds and fishes. Finally man, as the crown of the whole created world, exercises dominion under God in this vast empire, in which everything that happens redounds to the glory of God. Then, commenting on the phrase that 'the Spirit of God moved' Alan Richardson writes

> *Ruach* is wind, breath or spirit; it denotes the vital element in man and when used of God it might refer to his life-giving power. But here the expression is hardly more than a Hebrew idiom meaning 'a very strong wind', and it can scarcely be used to support a doctrine of the Creator Spirit. Nevertheless, whatever the expression 'Spirit of God' might mean as a Hebrew idiom taken by itself, the sentence as a whole suggests a remarkable poetic image of God hovering or brooding like a mother bird over the new born world.

Read Matthew 3:13–17 (God at work in Redemption)

John Fenton, *Matthew*, (Penguin 1963, p. 59):

> The dove, to which the Spirit is likened, may refer to a rabbinic interpretation of Genesis 1:2. The Spirit of God was moving over the face of the waters like a dove which broods over her young but does not touch them. If this is the case, then the meaning of it may be that as at the creation of the world the Spirit of God was at work, bringing order out of chaos, so now, in the new creation, the Spirit of God is at work again, first on Jesus then on his disciples.

The rabbis denied the activity of the Spirit of God in their own age, but expected a great outpouring of the Spirit in the age of the Messiah: the coming of the Spirit of God upon Jesus indicates his endowment with power, wisdom and holiness for fulfilling the Messiah's Ministry.

WORSHIP

Almighty Father, heavenly King,
we worship you and praise you
   for your work in creating the world,
   for your work in restoring mankind,
   for your presence with us now.
By the power of your Holy Spirit,
grant that we who proclaim this faith
may live our lives to your Glory;
through Jesus Christ our Lord.   Amen.

First reading: Genesis 1:1–8
Second reading: Acts 2:1–4
Gospel reading: Matthew 3:13–17

Teaching material

CONTEXT OF UNIT 21

The Preface directs praise to God by reciting before him his great acts which both stand in history and transcend history, the creation of the world, the redemption of the world through Christ, and the continued sanctification of the world through the Holy Spirit. Second, it reminds the worshipping community very clearly that the God who is present in the Eucharist is none other than the supreme Creator, Redeemer and Sanctifier. For these sophisticated theological concepts to have significance for the child he needs to be aware of two things:

1 He needs to be aware of what the Christian means when he speaks about the presence of God and his Spirit.
2 He needs to be able to perceive a connection between the presence of God in the great acts recited in the Preface and in the Eucharist itself.

The child is best able to enter into the experience represented by the Preface through the use of symbols. The symbol offered by the illustration is the bird, a symbol which has been used in Christian art for the Holy Spirit and the presence of God throughout the centuries and has its roots in the New Testament.

OBJECTIVES

1 To enable the child to enjoy studying birds.
2 To enable the child to see the link between the symbol of birds and God the Holy Spirit.
3 To enable the child to associate by means of the symbols the presence of God in history and the presence of God in the Eucharist.

■ **DISPLAY WORK**

a Studying birds

1 Begin by encouraging the children to talk about birds. Develop lists of
the different kinds of birds found locally
pet birds owned by the children
birds found in the zoo, picture books, etc.

2 Produce a large mural background of trees, sky, a fence etc. Encourage the
children to paint pictures of birds, both in flight and resting. Alternatively,
pictures of birds can be made by building up layers of coloured paper to
represent the feathers, or a mosaic effect can be produced by using very small
pieces of paper. Cut out the children's pictures of the birds and fix them to
the background. Real feathers can be obtained from an old pillow.

3 Birds can be made from folded paper. At the simplest level a paper
aeroplane can be transformed by shaping the head and wings to look like a
bird. More adventurous paper models are suggested in many books on
origami. These models can be arranged on a table or suspended from the
ceiling. A bird table can be made to add interest to the scene.

4 Produce a mobile of birds. For example, the shape of a bird's body,
showing beak and tail, can be cut out of card. Make a number of cuts in the
tail to give the card a fan effect. Next fold a sheet of paper to make a
concertina. Make a vertical cut in the body of the bird and press the folded
paper through this cut. Now fan out the folded paper to make wings either
side of the card body.

5 Make a project book of birds. Find out as much as possible about some of
the local birds.

b The bird in Christian symbolism

Look at the story of the baptism of Jesus and develop the imagery of the bird
representing the Spirit. Draw out the analogies between the bird and the
Holy Spirit.

1 Encourage the children to produce posters and banners showing the
stylized bird as in *The Lord is Here* pages 42–3.

2 Make a life size picture of the baptism of Jesus – drawing round real
children to provide a model for the figures. Give prominence to the stylized
bird in this poster.

c God in history and Eucharist

When the symbol of the bird has been carefully established turn attention to
the idea of the Preface that the God who is present in the Eucharist is also
seen to have acted in and beyond history. Concentrate on the four themes
brought together by the Preface, the Spirit of God in creation, redemption,
sanctification, the eucharist. Give substance to each of these themes:

1 *Talk about the beginning of everything.* Invite the children to produce a mural of how they can see the world looking before civilization, i.e. the forest, the lake, the dinosaur, etc. Incorporate the stylized bird in the picture and the text 'Through him you have created all things from the beginning'.

2 *Talk about the time of Jesus.* Invite the children to produce a mural of how they can see Jesus. Incorporate the stylized bird in this picture and the text 'Through him you have freed us from the slavery of sin'.

3 *Talk about the presence of the Holy Spirit in the Church.* Invite the children to produce a mural of the scene on the day of Pentecost (Acts 2:1–4). Incorporate the stylized bird in the picture and the text 'Through him you have made us a people for your own possession'.

4 *Talk about the presence of God in the Eucharist.* Invite the children to produce a mural showing the holy table. Incorporate the stylized bird in the picture and the text 'The Lord is here. His Spirit is with us'.

Display these four posters in such a way that the symbol of the bird shows the consistent theme of the presence of God running through all four settings.

ACTIVITIES

a Studying birds

1 Make a bird table and take on a responsibility to provide food for the birds in the local area.

2 Make a visit to watch bird flight.

3 Listen to bird song and try to imitate it. Some music and songs imitate birds, like the hymn 'From out of the wood did the cuckoo fly'.

4 Bird flight suggests a number of different patterns for dance movement to appropriate music.

5 Encourage the children to speculate what it is like to be a bird, to be able to fly, to move about freely, to appear suddenly from nowhere. Ask them to produce a play on this theme.

6 Arrange a visit to an aviary or bird garden.

7 Arrange for the children to meet someone who is knowledgeable about birds and has photographs, slides, etc.

b The bird in Christian symbolism

1 Look out for the symbol of the bird in Christian art. Make a visit to a local art gallery, etc.

2 Explore the decoration of the local church (especially the font cover, stained glass, lectern, etc.) to see if the symbol of the bird appears there.

■ WRITING

1 Ask the children to imagine that they are a bird and write a story about a day in their life. Creative writing can be stimulated by extracts from Richard Bach, *Jonathan Livingstone Seagull*, (Turnstone Press, 1972).

2 Keep a diary of the birds seen locally over a certain period of time, e.g. around the church's or school's bird table.

■ DISPLAY HEADINGS

Useful headings for displaying with the work produced in the course of this unit are
1 The bird is a symbol for the Holy Spirit
2 The bird moves freely through the air
3 The bird reminds us of God's presence
4 The Spirit descended on Jesus as a dove
5 The Spirit is at work in creation
6 The Spirit is at work in Jesus
7 The Spirit is at work in Jesus' followers
8 The Spirit is at work in the Eucharist

A short explanation might run like this: 'The Preface reminds us that God's Spirit is present in the Eucharist. The same Spirit is at work in creation, in Jesus and in Jesus' followers. In Christian art and symbolism the Spirit of God is represented by the bird.'

The Lord is Here or *At the Lord's Table* open at pages 42–3 can be displayed also.

22. SANCTUS

Journey into space

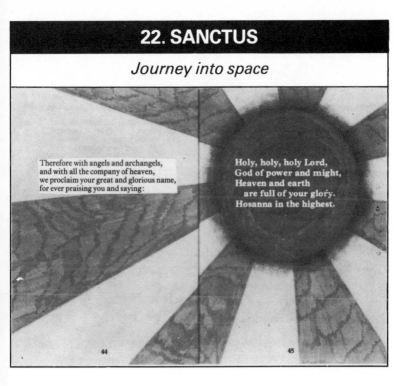

Therefore with angels and archangels,
and with all the company of heaven,
we proclaim your great and glorious name,
for ever praising you and saying:

Holy, holy, holy Lord,
God of power and might,
Heaven and earth
    are full of your glory.
Hosanna in the highest.

44   45

TEXT

The Preface reaches its climax with an invitation for the people to join with angels and archangels in a great shout or song of praise. The Rite A text presents two ancient hymns, which in the past have been used either separately or together:

The Sanctus (Holy, holy, holy Lord)

The Benedictus (Blessed is he who comes in the name of the Lord)

The Sanctus is dependent upon such passages of scripture as Revelation 4:8, and Isaiah 6:3. The Benedictus is dependent upon such passages of scripture as Psalm 118:26 and Mark 11:9–10.

Both the Sanctus and the Benedictus serve the same function in worship: they both emphasise the great majesty and otherness of God. Both excite in us the religious response of awe as we sense ourselves standing in relationship to God.

☐ PICTURE

The picture sets the text of the Sanctus in the middle of the radiant sun. The sun helps to convey three aspects of the Sanctus:

1 the warmth and happiness of the great hymn of praise
2 the majesty, the wonder, the power, the otherness of God
3 the sun evokes in us the awareness of something so much greater than ourselves. Similarly, the feeling of awe is aroused in us as we find ourselves confronted with the majesty of God. In this situation the only response is the recognition of God's holiness.

☐ COMMENT

In this section an ancient prayer attributed to St Francis meditates on the majesty of God. In the Old Testament reading the psalmist indicates that the heavens, and especially the sun, proclaim the glory of God. The New Testament reading reveals the elders chanting 'Holy, holy, holy is the Lord God Almighty', and the Gospel reading hails the Christ with shouts of 'Hosanna'.

A prayer commonly attributed to St Francis of Assisi (1181–1226)
You are holy, Lord, the only God,
    and your deeds are wonderful.
You are strong,
    You are great.
    You are the Most High,
    You are almighty,
    You, holy Father, are King of heaven and earth.
You are Three and One,
    Lord God, all good.
    You are good, all good, supreme good,
    Lord God, living and true.

Read Psalm 19:1–6 (The heavens proclaim the glory of God)
    Psalm 19 contains two independent songs: verses 1–6 constitute a song of nature, while verses 7–14 constitute a song about the Law of God. Commenting on verses 4 and 5 Artur Weiser, *The Psalms*, (SCM 1962, pp. 199–200) writes

In what the poet has to say about the sun, he forcefully joins his artistic impressions to a searching knowledge of his age and welds them into a unity under the religious aspect of the creative wisdom of God. The religious thought is once more prominent: it is *God* who has set a tent for the sun in the sea. In this way the author, deliberately alluding to the ancient mythical idea of the abode which the Sun-god has built for himself, discards the pagan character of that idea without destroying its poetic beauty. In like manner the comparison of the sun with the bridegroom, who comes forth from his chamber in the radiant splendour of his youthful strength and beauty, is based on the widespread mythological idea that the Sun-god rests during the night in the sea, lying in the arms of his beloved; and the image of the champion who delights in contests probably has its roots in mythology, too. The poet faces these mythological themes with remarkable freedom and ease. His faith in the one and only Creator of the universe guards him against any kind of pagan superstition.

Read Revelation 4:1–11 (Holy, holy, holy)

George Caird, *The Revelation of St John the Divine*, (A & C Black 1966, p. 63), writes that John makes no attempt to describe God himself:

> with evocative language he hints at what is beyond description, but that is all. Yet the whole chapter is numinous with the divine presence. John knows that to ordinary mortals the presence of God becomes real not through direct vision, even in the mind's eye but through the impact of those to whom God is the supreme reality. So he allows his readers to look on the Eternal Light through the mirror of the worshipping host of heaven.

The song 'Holy, holy, holy' was already part of the Jewish liturgy and almost certainly of the early Christian liturgy as well. The meaning of the word holy comes from the idea of separateness, of being set apart. When we call God holy we mean that he is completely different from ourselves – completely separate from all that is profane.

Read Mark 11:1–10 (Hosanna in the highest)

L. H. Brockington in Alan Richardson, *Theological Word Book of the Bible*, (SCM 1950, p. 105):

> When the people greeted Jesus on his way to Jerusalem with the words 'Hosanna in the highest' they were using a phrase which is capable of bringing together three things, the pious devotion of the OT, acclamation of Jesus as the Incarnate One, and God the Father who dwells in highest heaven. The word Hosanna comes from psalm 118:25, and is there addressed to God on behalf of the approaching pilgrims. It is an imperative form of the verb *y-sh-* 'to save', the same root as that from which the name of Jesus comes. God alone has the prerogative of salvation. The prayer is to be heard 'in the highest' – that is to say in the *highest* of the regions of heaven. Here in striking contrast to the strong belief in God's personal presence on earth, is the idea that God is above the earth, both greater than it and removed from it . . . The figure of height, loftiness, may be deemed one of the proper symbols to express a truth about God for which we shall reach no more exact definition. It conveys the idea of something superior, of something immeasurably greater, something that men can look up to.

☐ **WORSHIP**

Holy, holy, holy Lord,
you are Lord of earth and sea,
you are God of sun and moon.
Holy, holy, holy Lord,
you are Lord of stars and planets,
you are God of all there is.
Holy, holy, holy Lord. Amen.

First reading: Psalm 19:1–6
Second reading: Revelation 4:1–11
Gospel reading: Mark 11:1–10

Teaching material

■ **CONTEXT OF UNIT 22**

The Sanctus comes immediately after the Preface has recited our faith in the
Great Acts of God in creation, redemption and sanctification. The Sanctus is
our response as creature before the Creator. This response acknowledges
two things
1 that God is so much greater than man
2 that we hold God in awe.
   For the experience of the Sanctus to be meaningful to the child, two
things are necessary:
1 the child needs to be aware of the greatness and majesty of God,
2 the child needs to feel himself respond as creature before Creator.
   A way of exploring these feelings is through a growing awareness of one's
own smallness in relationship to the whole of God's universe.

■ **OBJECTIVES**

1 To give the child the opportunity to explore the greatness and wonder of
   the universe.
2 To encourage the child to discover that the ideas of space travel and the
   scientific study of the universe do not conflict with the Christian's faith,
   but make him even more aware of the greatness and wonder of God's
   creation.
3 To make a particular study of the sun as a symbol of God's majesty.
4 To give the child the opportunity to explore his response to God's
   greatness.

DISPLAY WORK

a The sun

1 Begin by talking about the Sun and its effect on us. Ask the children to make a list of the sun's influences, for example, it

gives light
gives heat
gives sun tan
gives growth
makes shadows
causes fruit to ripen.

Ask them to draw pairs of contrasting pictures: one with the sun and one without. Mount these pictures with the heading 'The sun makes the difference'.

2 Encourage the children to think about the movement of the earth around the sun and the way in which that influences

night and day
summer and winter
the warm and cold parts of the world

Help the children to explore the contrast suggested by these pairs of opposites and the transition period between them. Produce project books or wall charts on

a) the time of day
b) the seasons of the year
c) the climates of the world

3 Create a project book on the sun, looking at as many aspects as the children can consider.

4 Make sundials from cardboard and at regular intervals ask the children to note the place of the shadow. Or make a large shadow clock and mark the shadow with string and pegs on a field or chalk on a playground.

5 Explore the way in which early man was so overwhelmed by the power of the sun that he worshipped it like a God. Consider Stonehenge and the way it may have been associated with the study and worship of the sun. Make a model of Stonehenge.

b The sky

1 Talk about the great number of stars and planets, beginning from the earth, and moon. Learn some of the names and positions. Older children will enjoy producing maps of the solar system, etc. Younger ones will enjoy producing bold pictures of the sun and moon.

2 A model of the solar system can be made using balls of different size and wooden dowelling or wire.

c Space travel

Encourage the children to talk about the ideas of space travel – to discover what they would need and the dangers they might encounter.

1 Make space helmets which the children can wear.

2 Make a space ship control room, perhaps incorporating a disused and empty television cabinet and broken clock dials.

3 Make a large rocket, built up from boxes and painted.

4 Make a large model of life on another planet. Wire netting and papier mâché can produce an imaginative terrain. The terrain can be peopled by martians, spacemen, the visiting space ship, etc.

5 Develop a class book about the adventures of Dr Who or Dr Spock travelling through time and space.

■ ACTIVITIES

a The sun

1 Let the children experiment with photographic paper in order to learn about the effect of the sun on it.

2 Encourage the children to discover the properties of shadows. Ask them to draw round each other's shadow on the floor. Note the way in which the school/church casts a different shadow at different times of the day.

3 Compare the growth of plants, some exposed to the sun and others not exposed to it.

4 Visit a botanical garden, or a nursery, and note the properties of greenhouses.

5 Note the way in which moss, etc., tend to grow on the north side of churches, houses, trees, where there is a lack of sunlight.

b The sky

1 Ask the children to observe the sky at night and see if they can count the stars. It might be a good thing to make a winter evening outing into the countryside to experience the night sky uncluttered by the familiar or urban environment.

2 Arrange to visit a planetarium or exhibition where the sky is charted.

3 Arrange for the children to meet someone who has the equipment to study the stars and if possible to see his telescope etc.

c Space travel

1 The theme of space travel produces a number of ideas for drama, e.g. life at

the rocket landing station, in the space capsule or landing on the moon. Also such themes lend themselves well to creative dance in association with appropriate music, i.e. the launching of the rocket or the eerie exploration of an unknown planet.

2 See a film about space travel.

3 Visit a deserted area, say a beach out of season, and pretend it is a landscape on another planet.

◀ WRITING

1 Ask the children to write on the theme 'If there was no sun' or a story about the day when the sun was hidden from sight.

2 Ask the children to pretend that they are spacemen and to write about their journey into space.

3 Produce a cartoon sequence of a Dr Who adventure.

◀ DISPLAY HEADINGS

Useful headings for displaying with the work produced in the course of this unit are

1 The sun gives us night and day
2 The sun gives us summer and winter
3 The sun is so powerful that men used to worship it
4 God is so powerful that he made the sun
5 The sky at night reminds us of the vastness of God's universe
6 Space travel shows us how large the universe really is. God made it all
7 Heaven and earth are full of your glory

A short explanation might run, 'The Sanctus reminds us of the greatness and majesty of God. If we feel overwhelmed by the greatness of the universe, how much more are we overwhelmed by the God who made it. We are lost in awe and praise before him. Holy, holy, holy Lord. Heaven and earth are full of your glory.'

The Lord is Here or *At the Lord's Table* open at pages 44–5 can be displayed also.

23. INSTITUTION NARRATIVE

The wedding reception

Accept our praises, heavenly Father,
through your Son our Saviour Jesus Christ;
and as we follow his example
    and obey his command,
grant that by the power of your Holy Spirit
these gifts of bread and wine
may be to us his body and his blood;

Who in the same night that he was betrayed,
took bread and gave you thanks;
he broke it and gave it to his disciples,
    saying,
Take, eat; this is my body which is given
    for you;
do this in remembrance of me.
In the same way, after supper
he took the cup and gave you thanks;
he gave it to them, saying,
Drink this, all of you;
this is my blood of the new covenant,
which is shed for you and for many
    for the forgiveness of sins.
Do this, as often as you drink it,
in remembrance of me.

46   47

☐ **TEXT**

This is the third section on the Eucharistic Prayer. It consists of two parts

1 The first paragraph asks the Father to send the Holy Spirit upon the gifts of bread and wine that they may be to us Christ's body and blood. We call upon God to do this because we are following Christ's example and obeying his command.

2 The second paragraph relates the 'Institution Narrative'. That is to say, it gives the account of the origin of the Eucharist itself during Jesus' Last Supper with his twelve disciples. Two different views are held in the church about the function of the Institution Narrative in the Eucharistic Prayer. On both accounts, the narrative is of supreme importance. One view argues that the recitation of our Lord's words constitutes the consecration, that is to say the point after which the bread and the wine of the eucharist are no longer regarded as bread and wine. The other view argues that the whole Eucharistic Prayer constitutes the consecration. According to this view, the recitation of the words of Institution are

176

understood as the authority to proceed with the rest of the Eucharistic Prayer. Without this authority there can be no Eucharist.

☐ PICTURE

The intention of the picture is to focus attention upon three things:
    the table
    the special food
    the symbolic actions
A table is prepared and set out in a special way. The children are themselves preparing the table, placing the bread and pouring the wine. The priest has adopted one of the poses traditionally associated with the Eucharistic Prayer as he gives thanks over the bread and wine.

☐ COMMENT

In this section comment is made on the concept of covenant. Then comparison is made between the different accounts of the Last Supper presented in the New Testament.

The Old Testament reading relates the passover story from Exodus. The New Testament reading gives Paul's account of the Last Supper and the Gospel reading is Mark's account of the same event.

Covenant

The idea of covenant goes back to the heart of the Old Testament where it is the legal basis for a relationship between two people or groups of people, often two people of unequal status so that the more powerful person imposes an arrangement upon the less powerful. Von Rad, *OT Theology*, (Oliver and Boyd 1962, Vol. 1, p. 130):

> The covenant is . . . a legal relationship, and comprises the firmest guarantee of a relationship of human communion . . . The making of a covenant is intended to secure a state of intactness, orderliness, and rightness between two parties, in order to make possible, on the basis of this legal foundation, a relationship in matters affecting their common life.

The idea is that the blood of Christ seals a new and different kind of covenant relationship between God and man.

The Last Supper in the New Testament

An account of the Last Supper and the institution of the Eucharist is given in all three synoptic gospels and once in the letters of Paul (Matthew 26:26–29, Mark 14:22–25, Luke 22:17–20, 1 Corinthians 11:23–25). The institution of the Eucharist is not reported in John's Gospel. The four accounts which we have been given differ in some important ways regarding both the order in which the bread and wine are offered and the words spoken over them. It is difficult to establish what really lies behind these differences. The problem is made more difficult by the fact that the ancient manuscripts give two different versions of Luke's account. Four main questions are raised by these accounts.

1 *What is the common material?*
Vincent Taylor, *St Mark*, (Macmillan 1966, p. 543) writes that 'all the accounts agree that Jesus said: "This is my body" and that he looked forward to the perfected fellowship of the Kingdom of God.'

2 *Which is the earliest account?*
Paul's account is the earliest to have been actually written down in its present form, but this does not necessarily mean that it is the most reliable account of the words used by Jesus or that it is necessarily based on the earliest tradition. It is likely that a number of different accounts existed side by side in the oral tradition of the early church.

3 *When did the Last Supper happen?*
According to the synoptic Gospels the Last Supper was the passover meal. According to John's chronology this could not be the case since Jesus was crucified at the time when the lamb was slaughtered, i.e. before the supper. J. Jeremias, *The Eucharistic Words of Jesus*, (SCM 1966), argues that John deliberately changes the synoptic account in order to make his own argument that Jesus was the paschal lamb. On the other hand other scholars argue that both John and the synoptic Gospels can be chronologically unaltered. In the first century some Jewish sects followed an unofficial calendar in which the passover meal always occurred on Tuesday evening. If John's Friday passover represents the official calendar, the other Gospels indicate that Jesus celebrated the passover on the earlier unauthorised date.

4 *Which is Luke's original text?*
A. J. B. Higgins, *The Lord's Supper in the NT*, (SCM 1952, p. 40), argues that the longer text is original and that Luke himself combined two traditions 'one consisting of verses 15–19a, and the other of verses 19a–20. Luke (and those who left his account of the Last Supper unchanged) felt no difficulty in the presence of the two cups, because the first was not regarded as a eucharistic cup.' Later scribes who were not satisfied with this idea omitted part of the text.

☐ **WORSHIP**

Lord Jesus Christ,
at the Last Supper you took the bread and blessed it,
    you broke the bread and shared it,
    you said 'Do this in remembrance of me'.
May our celebration of this sacrament of your body and blood

help us to experience the salvation you won for us,
and the peace of your kingdom,
where you live and reign with the Father and the Holy Spirit,
now and for ever.   Amen.

First reading: Exodus 12:1–14
Second reading: 1 Corinthians 11:23–26
Gospel reading: Mark 14:12–26

Teaching material

CONTEXT OF UNIT 23

The recitation of the Institution Narrative emphasises three central aspects
of the Christian's understanding of the Eucharist

1 It traces the origin of the Eucharist back to the words and actions of Jesus
   at the Last Supper when he celebrated the Passover with his disciples.
2 It points to the way in which ordinary food takes on a new significance
   and, in a sacramental sense, points beyond itself.
3 It establishes the link between what is happening in the celebration of the
   Eucharist now and what happened at a specific point in history. In one
   sense the Eucharist is making present what happened in the past in such a
   way that we can share in it although separated both in time and space from
   its point of origin.

For these ideas to be explored by the child four things are necessary

1 The child needs to gain experience of the way in which meals take on
   special significance when people wish to celebrate something important
   to them. Often a particular item of food is of central concern. A good
   example of this is provided by the wedding reception. Here the cake and
   the champagne are treated as something special. After the bride and groom
   have ceremoniously cut the cake, the guests all share a small piece as a way
   of sharing in the celebration.
2 The child needs to see how those who are absent from the celebration
   meal are able to share in it by receiving something sent on to them from
   the table. This can be explored through the tradition of sending a piece of
   wedding cake to absent guests.
3 The child needs to know something about the background to the Last
   Supper in the tradition of the Passover meal.
4 The child needs to know the New Testament traditions about the Last
   Supper itself.

OBJECTIVES

1 To examine what happens at a wedding reception.
2 To explore ways in which guests who are unable to be present can be made

to feel that the reception has been extended to include them.

3 To study the way in which the Jewish people celebrate the feast of the Passover today.

4 To study the New Testament account of the Last Supper.

■ DISPLAY WORK

a The Wedding Reception

Begin by encouraging the children who have been to a marriage service and wedding reception to discuss what happens. Plan a 'reception' to take place in the class or church. Talk about the preparations that need to be made and plan the occasion.

1 Encourage the children to make appropriate decorations for the room in which the reception is to take place. For example, two dimensional horse-shoes and bells can be cut from card and covered with tinfoil. Three dimensional decorations can be made in paper sculpture. Paper flowers can be made for table decorations, etc.

2 Make wedding greeting cards to display at the reception.

3 Talk about the people who will be at the wedding and the kind of clothes they will wear; the bride, the groom, the bridesmaids, the best man, the clergyman. Invite the children to prepare a 'photograph album' of drawings showing various stages of the service and reception.

4 Prepare costumes for the children to wear at the reception, perhaps concentrating on the distinctive head-dress.

5 Talk about the preparation of food for the reception. Encourage the children to decide on what they will eat at the reception and how they will prepare it. All their menus may be different, but with a common core of the cake and the wine. Give special attention to the preparation of a wedding cake. Choose a simple recipe and let the children make it. Then hold a wedding party.

6 Encourage the children to discover how they can help people who are not present at their wedding reception to feel that they have a share in it. For example, concentrate on one or more of the following groups a) children absent from school that day, b) parents, c) the housebound. Explore the parts played by tape recorder, camera, verbal account and the slice of cake in establishing the link between those present at the reception and those who are unable to be present.

b The Passover

1 Look at the bible account of the Passover (see Exodus 12). Encourage the children to produce a wall chart showing Moses leading the way to freedom – use a heading 'The Passover celebrates the way God led us to freedom'.

Place the accent on God leading his people to freedom rather than the destruction of the enemy.

2 Study the way in which the Passover is celebrated today by Jews. Study the special food and the narrative associated with it. Produce a mural showing the table, the food and the family.

3 Produce a tape recorded 'radio programme' of the Passover as kept today by a Jewish family.

c The Last Supper

1 Look at the four accounts of the institution narrative in 1 Corinthians 11:23–25, Matthew 26:26–29, Mark 14:22–25, Luke 22:17–20. Write them out clearly and compare them. Discuss the way in which the children gave different accounts of the wedding reception and compare this with the phenomenon of the different accounts in the New Testament. Then examine the way in which the institution narrative is repeated in the Communion Service.

2 Discuss who was present at the Last Supper and produce a mural showing the table, the food and the disciples. Alternatively a model can be made using clay figures or paper sculpture.

ACTIVITIES

a The Wedding Reception

1 Invite someone to talk to the children about what happened at their marriage service and reception – and show the photographs of the occasion.

2 Hold a wedding reception with the children taking the part of bride and groom, etc.

3 Develop role play to explore what it feels like not to be able to be present at the wedding reception and then to be enabled to share in it through receiving a slice of cake.

4 Visit some people who were not able to be present at the reception. Tell them about it and present them with a slice of cake.

b The Passover

1 Invite a Jewish family to talk about the way in which they keep the Passover and what it means to them.

2 Help the children to prepare the food for the Passover meal. Make full use of the ritual and explanations.

c The Last Supper

1 Produce a play based on the Last Supper. This can also provide an op-

portunity to explore the context of the Last Supper before the betrayal and crucifixion.

2 Visit churches, museums and art galleries to look at pictures of the Last Supper.

■ WRITING

1 Look at the occasions when the Gospels describe the Kingdom of God in terms of a Wedding Reception and write about these stories (e.g. Matthew 22:1–14, Matthew 25:1–13, John 2:1–11).

2 Ask the children to imagine that they were unable to attend the Wedding Reception because they were ill, too old to travel, or living too far away. They have been sent a slice of wedding cake. They write a thank you letter to say what the slice of cake meant to them.

3 Write a letter to a friend describing the Passover supper.

4 Write a wedding telegram to be read out during the reception.

■ DISPLAY HEADINGS

Useful headings for displaying with the work produced in the course of this unit are

1 Special meals play an important part in celebrations like weddings
2 The bride and groom cut the cake together and then all the guests share in it
3 Guests who are not able to come to the reception can still share in the celebration when they are sent a piece of the cake
4 Jesus said the Kingdom of God is like a wedding reception
5 The Jewish people celebrate the Passover today
6 Jesus celebrated the Passover with his disciples at the 'Last Supper'. There he celebrated the Eucharist for the first time
7 Jesus invites us to share in the Last Supper when we celebrate the Eucharist

A short explanation might run like this, 'The Institution Narrative reminds us how Jesus first celebrated the Eucharist at the Last Supper. While celebrating the Passover with his disciples Jesus gave a new significance to the bread and the wine. Today we share in that meal with Jesus every time the Eucharist is celebrated. It is rather like the way guests who were not able to be at the wedding reception can share in the celebration when they receive their slice of wedding cake.'

The Lord is Here or *At the Lord's Table* open at pages 46–7 can be displayed also.

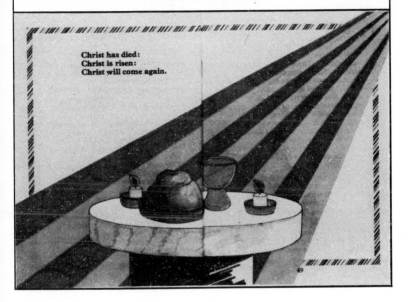

24. ACCLAMATION

Bread and wine

Christ has died:
Christ is risen:
Christ will come again.

Background material

☐ **TEXT**

The Acclamation, like the Sanctus earlier, is an ancient Christian hymn. Its place in the prayer of Thanksgiving provides an opportunity for the people to offer their assent to what has gone before. In some liturgies the priest invites the people to respond with the Acclamation by saying himself the invitation, 'Let us proclaim the mystery of faith'.

☐ **PICTURE**

The picture is closely related to the picture associated with the preceding section. The same table re-appears, but with a difference. Now the focus is upon the bread and the cup alone which are highlighted by beams of light. The picture concentrates the child's attention upon the bread which is for us the body of Christ, and the wine which is for us the blood of Christ.

☐ COMMENT

In this section Joseph Gelineau comments on the place of the Acclamation in the Eucharistic Prayer and Norman Habel meditates on the sounds of the Eucharist. The Old Testament reading comments on the meaning of the manna in the wilderness. The two Gospel readings comment on the meaning of Jesus as the Bread of Life and the True Vine. The New Testament reading shows the devotion of the early church to the regular breaking of the bread.

The Acclamation in the Eucharistic Prayer

Joseph Gelineau, 'The Commemorative Acclamation' in L. Sheppard, *The New Liturgy*, (DLT 1970, pp. 200–1):

> this acclamation forms an integral part of the prayer itself, just like the *Sanctus* or the concluding *Amen*. It is linked with our Lord's words, 'This is my body which will be given for you . . . my blood shed for you' . . . In form it is a profession of a commemorative character, that is, a *public* proclamation *recalling* (in the emphatic objective sense of making real, eschatologically) the paschal mystery as it is experienced in the sign of the Lord's Supper. The whole congregation is then called on to associate itself actively with what is fundamental in the eucharistic prayer.

'Sounds of the Eucharist', from Norman Habel, *Interrobang*, (Lutterworth 1970, p. 87):

> We acknowledge our God,
>   We summon our God,
> And we wait,
>   And we are silent.
> We wait for the sounds of God,
>   And the sounds of the sacrament,
> The breaking of bread,
>   And the gushing of wine . . .
> And we listen for the bursting of joy,
>   And the bubble of children's faces,
> The dancing of willows,
>   And the surprise of open lives,
> The shout of mountains,
>   And the laughter of a second birth . . .
> We will listen to God
>   And the celebration of God
> In the breaking of bread
>   And the gushing of wine.

Read Deuteronomy 8:1–6 (The manna from heaven)
  Gerhard von Rad, *Deuteronomy*, (SCM 1966, pp. 71–2):

In this context the giving of the manna receives an interpretation which distinguishes it from the older conception in Exodus 16 . . . Here it is bluntly stated that the direct purpose of the feeding was to teach Israel that man does not just live on earthly bread alone, but that he also depends on the word addressed to him by God.

Read John 6:26–35 (The Bread of Life)

The story of the feeding of the five thousand is one of the few traditions which has a place in all four Gospels – see Mark 6:35–44, Matthew 14:13–21, Luke 9:10–17. John's account adds to the synoptic tradition in two important ways. First, John records the reaction of the crowd. After the feeding the crowd is excited and wishes to proclaim Jesus as King. Second, in his usual manner John uses the episode as a spring-board for profound and enigmatic teaching on the theme of Jesus as the 'Bread of Life'. This teaching has played a very influential part in the church's teaching about the centrality of the Eucharist. Lightfoot, *St John's Gospel*, (OUP 1957, p. 162):

> We now learn that a condition of eternal life, and of being raised up at the last day by the Lord, is not only belief in him, but a partaking of his flesh and blood; by this means a mutual indwelling is set up between the believer and his Lord. Just as, through the fulfilment of the Father's will who sent him, the Lord lives in and because of the Father (the source of Life) and the Father in him, so he who partakes of the incarnate life of the Lord will live because of him, and that for ever.

Read John 15:1–10 (The True Vine)

John's Gospel does not include an account of the words of institution. Instead John presents this discourse on the significance of Jesus as 'The True Vine'. This discourse complements the discourse in chapter 6 on 'The Bread of Life'. C. H. Dodd, *The Interpretation of the Fourth Gospel*, (CUP 1953, p. 411–12):

> In the synoptic accounts of the Last Supper the contents of the cup are expressly described as the fruit of the vine . . . The thought is probably that of the church as the true people of God, his vine, now revealed through Jesus. John advances upon this: Jesus is the Vine, including in himself all members of the true people of God, as the branches of the vine . . . The organic union of the branches with the vine and so with one another provides a striking image for that idea of the mutual indwelling of Christ and his people which the author wishes to develop.

☐ **WORSHIP**

Lord Jesus Christ,
bread speaks to us of many things:
  the seed and the sower,
  the sun and the harvester,
  the flour and the miller,
  the oven and the baker,
  the store and the shopkeeper.
We thank you for the sign of this bread
  which speaks to us of all these things.
The same bread speaks to us of you;
  your life and your death,
  your resurrection and your presence with us.
We thank you for the sign of this bread
  which speaks to us of you.   Amen.

First reading: Deuteronomy 8:1–6
Second reading: Acts 2:42–47
Gospel reading: John 6:26–35 or John 15:1–10

Teaching material

■ **CONTEXT OF UNIT 24**

The Acclamation comes immediately after the Institution Narrative. It is the congregation's way of assenting to the significance seen in, and the meaning associated with, the bread and the wine. In Section 20 the bread and wine were seen as tokens of God's creation. In Section 23 they were seen as part of the celebration meal. Now in Section 24 they are seen as the body and blood of Christ. The elements which to the senses of sight, touch, taste and smell are obviously bread and wine, speak to the Christian believer clearly of the body and blood of Christ. This is the way in which a sacrament works. The outward sign focuses in a peculiar way the spiritual significance and reality to which it points.

For the notion of bread and wine as sacraments to be meaningful to the child three things are necessary:

1 The child needs to appreciate the way in which bread and wine can speak, at a purely natural level, about all that lies behind their manufacture. We see bread, and the bread can prompt us to think about the farmer, miller, baker, shopkeeper, etc.

2 The child needs to understand the way in which signs play such an important part in our day to day lives.

3 The child needs to know the importance of the concept of sacrament in the life of the church.

OBJECTIVES

1 to study the history of a loaf of bread.
2 to study the history of a bottle of wine.
3 to explore the way in which signs are used.
4 to appreciate the importance of the notion of sacrament within the Christian church.

DISPLAY WORK

a Bread

Begin by discussing all the different shapes and sizes in which bread is obtained.

1 Produce a mural showing the different kinds of bread loaves and rolls. Invite the children to draw a different kind of loaf each, e.g. white, brown, wholemeal, farmhouse, tin, cut and wrapped. Incorporate the wrappers from wrapped bread.

2 Make a list of all the different ways in which bread is eaten, e.g. cheese rolls, beans on toast, bread pudding, etc. Illustrate these ideas.

3 Produce a class book telling the history of a loaf of bread:
    the farmer orders the grain
    the grain is delivered by lorry
    the field is prepared
    the seed is sown
    the crops are sprayed
    the rain and the sun come
    the harvesting, threshing and storing of the corn
    the corn is transported to the mill
    the corn is ground into flour
    the flour is transported to the baker
    dough is prepared and baked into loaves
    the loaves are transported to the shops, delivery vans, etc.
    the bread is bought and we eat it

4 Compare the history of a loaf of bread today with what was involved in its manufacture in earlier times.

5 Make a model 'village' showing the corn growing farm, the mill, the baker, the shop, etc. Incorporate toy tractors etc.

B Wine

Begin by talking about how drinks are made from fruit.

1 Produce a collage from labels from different bottles and tins, e.g. lemon/orange juice, tomato juice, as well as wines.

2 Make a list of all the things from which 'home made wine' can be produced. Produce a mural showing these things, together with wine making equipment.

3 Produce a class book telling the history of a bottle of wine:
the planting of the vine
the tending of the vine
the rain and the sun
the picking of the fruit
the extraction of the juice
the fermentation process
the maturing in casks
the bottling
the distribution to shops
the wine is bought and we drink it

c Signs

Some aspects of signs have already been explored in Unit 7. It is appropriate to explore the theme of traffic signs, trade marks, etc., further in this section. A change of emphasis is to explore specifically the way in which signs are used to point to things we cannot see, and to make us aware of the presence of something. Produce a set of murals and prepare labels for them as follows

1 Make the kind of road signs which give us advanced notice of what we might meet e.g., signs which indicate bends, traffic lights, railway crossings, etc. 'These signs prepare us for meeting something.'

2 Discover the kind of signs that make us aware of something of which we would not otherwise be fully aware, e.g., high voltage electricity signs on the railway or the colouring of dangerous insects or plants. Produce a mural of these signs. 'These signs tell us that unseen danger is present.'

3 Look especially at the trade marks associated with the manufacturers of bread and wine. 'These signs tell us who made our bread and wine.'

4 Examine how people in special jobs wear symbols (uniforms) to let us know who they are – policemen, salvation army, etc. 'These signs tell us what is special about the people who wear them.'

5 Discuss the way in which the church uses the sacraments of bread and wine as external signs of God's activity and presence. 'These signs tell us that Jesus is present in the eucharist.'

ACTIVITIES

a Bread

1 Bake a loaf of bread and use some for a meal and use some in a special celebration of the Eucharist.

2 Visit a farm which grows corn, a flour mill or a baker.

3 Invite a local baker, corn grower, etc., to talk about his work.

4 The life story of a loaf of bread can be told by creative dance, to include the sowing of the seed, the growing of the grain, the cutting of the corn, the grinding of the flour, etc.

b Wine

1 Make some orange drink from real oranges.

2 Make some wine either from real fruit (e.g. blackberries, apples, dandelions or elder flowers) or from a tinned concentrate prepared for wine making.

3 If there is a local vineyard, arrange a visit to it.

4 Invite someone who is keen on wine making to talk about his hobby.

c Signs

1 Take a walk or outing to spot different signs (plants and insects as well as road signs).

2 Invite the local police to talk about their uniforms, and the signs used on their cars, etc.

■ WRITING

1 Ask the children to imagine that they are loaves of bread or bottles of wine and to write their life story.

2 Look at the stories in the gospels about bread, corn, wine, etc. and write about these stories (e.g. Mark 4:1–20, Mark 4:26–29, Mark 6:30–44, Mark 12:1–12).

■ DISPLAY HEADINGS

Useful headings for displaying with the work produced in the course of this unit are

1 A loaf of bread speaks to us of its whole history from the time the farmer sowed the seed until it is eaten
2 A bottle of wine speaks to us about its whole history from the time the vine was planted until it is drunk
3 Class 4 visited a flour mill
4 The bread and the wine are sacraments in the Communion service
5 Sacraments are like signs which point to things which you cannot see

A short explanation might run like this, 'In the Acclamation we say "yes" to what has gone before in the Prayer of Thanksgiving. We acknowledge the way in which the bread and the wine point beyond themselves to speak of the body and blood of Christ. The bread and the wine are sacraments.'

The Lord is Here or *At the Lord's Table* open at pages 48–9 can be displayed also.

25. THANKSGIVING AND DOXOLOGY

Carnival time

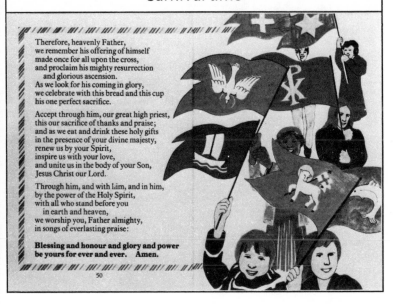

Therefore, heavenly Father,
we remember his offering of himself
made once for all upon the cross,
and proclaim his mighty resurrection
    and glorious ascension.
As we look for his coming in glory,
we celebrate with this bread and this cup
his one perfect sacrifice.

Accept through him, our great high priest,
this our sacrifice of thanks and praise;
and as we eat and drink these holy gifts
in the presence of your divine majesty,
renew us by your Spirit,
inspire us with your love,
and unite us in the body of your Son,
Jesus Christ our Lord.

Through him, and with him, and in him,
by the power of the Holy Spirit,
with all who stand before you
    in earth and heaven,
we worship you, Father almighty,
in songs of everlasting praise:

**Blessing and honour and glory and power
be yours for ever and ever.   Amen.**

50

Background material

☐ TEXT

This section concludes the Eucharistic Prayer. It is made up of four parts.

1. The first paragraph is the act of remembrance, which is known by the technical name of 'The Anamnesis'. It is the response by which the President verbalises what we do in the Eucharist with this bread and this cup to obey Christ's command 'Do this'.

2. The second paragraph is a prayer that God should enable us to receive the fruits of communion. This petition is closely linked with our prayer for God to accept through Christ, our great High Priest, our sacrifice of thanks and praise. We pray that we might be
   renewed by the Spirit
   inspired by God's love
   united in the Body of Christ.

3. The third paragraph is a Doxology which sums up our Eucharistic Prayer in the name of the Trinity and through a great upward sweep of praise.

4 The whole people join with the priest in bringing the Doxology to a climax with a final shout of praise. This shout of praise appears to be based on Revelation 5:12. All together are caught up into the heavenly places. All join together in the worship of the lamb.

☐ **PICTURE**

The picture reflects not the specific content but the overall mood of this final part of the Eucharistic Prayer. The mood is one of joy and of carnival – of thanksgiving in the presence of God. The children in the picture see the Thanksgiving and Doxology as an occasion to wave flags and to parade banners – for the Lord is present with them. The banners carry many of the signs and symbols of the Christian faith.

☐ **COMMENT**

In this section comment is made on the theological significance of the key phrase 'We remember his offering of himself'. The phrase is illuminated by quotations from Gregory Dix, J. D. Crichton and Max Thurian. The Old Testament reading is one of the great psalms of praise involving the whole creation in the worship of God. The New Testament reading is the heavenly song of praise from the Revelation of John. The Gospel reading is part of Zachariah's song of praise at the birth of his son, John the Baptist.

We remember

As used here the verb 'remember' conveys a very important theological idea. It translates a Greek word *anamnesis* and a Hebrew concept which is almost untranslatable into English. The English words 'memorial', 'commemoration', 'remembrance' all suggest that the person brought to mind is absent and belongs to the past. *Anamnesis* suggests exactly the opposite. *Anamnesis* is an objective act in which the person or action is actually made present and brought into the here and now. As the early Church understood it the Eucharist makes present the sacrifice of Christ.

Gregory Dix, *The Shape of the Liturgy*, (Dacre Press 1945, p. 243) writes that this is 'the "recalling" before God of the one sacrifice of Christ in all its accomplished fullness so that it is here and now operative by its effect in the souls of the redeemed'.

J. D. Crichton in Cheslyn Jones, *The Study of Liturgy*, (SPCK 1978, p. 14):

'By the liturgical mystery we are *actualizing* the past event, making it present so that the saving power of Christ can be made available to the worshipper in the here and now.'

Max Thurian, *The Eucharistic Memorial*, (Lutterworth 1960, vol. I, p. 17) argues that Christ's command to repeat the Eucharist can only be understood in the light of an understanding of the Passover.

The expression employed by Christ to enjoin the repetition of the Eucharist ('Do this in remembrance of me') was part of the current liturgical language of Judaism and was particularly used in the celebration of the Passover. It is found only in the accounts of Paul (1 Cor 11:24,25 and Luke 22:19). Its absence in Matthew and Mark is no reason for thinking that Jesus did not use it . . . 'Do this in remembrance of me' is not part of the liturgical text itself; it is a command to celebrate . . . and Mark and Matthew could have dispensed with it since the regular celebration of the Eucharist was the carrying out of this command . . . As they ate (the Passover) the Jews could re-live mystically, *sacramentally*, the events of the deliverance and Exodus from Egypt. They became contemporaries of their forefathers and were saved with them. There was in the mystery of the paschal meal a kind of telescoping of two periods of history, the present and the Exodus. The past event became present or rather each person became a contemporary of the past event. The unity of the redemptive act of the Lord was affirmed by this celebration. It is this mystery of the redemptive act accomplished once for all and yet ever renewed, present and applied, that the Church came to designate by the word *sacrament*.

Read Psalm 148:1–14 (A hymn of all creation)

J. H. Eaton, *Psalms* (SCM 1967, pp. 313–4) argues that in this psalm the universality of praise called forth is vividly suggested by the systematic listing of categories of creatures. First the call to praise is issued to the heavenly beings, not only the angelic hosts, but also such elements as sun, moon, stars, the vault above the heavens and the heavenly ocean. Then summons is directed to the terrestrial sphere, in which even sea monsters and deeps are not seen as enemies of life but as taking their place among God's servant-creatures.

Read Revelation 5:7–14 (the heavenly song of praise)

John Sweet, *Revelation*, (SCM 1979, pp. 126–7):

The hymns which John *hears* are again specifically connected with what he *sees* and convey its deepest meaning: the unification of the whole cosmos in the worship of God and Christ. They point us not to the victory of the cross or the opening of the scroll, but to the enthronement of the lamb . . . verse 13 speaks the same language as the hymn of Phil 2:5–11: 'therefore God has highly exalted him . . . that at the name of Jesus every knee should bow, in heaven and on earth and under the earth, and every tongue confess that Jesus is Lord, to the glory of God the Father'. This chapter is the most powerful statement of the divinity of Christ in the NT, and it receives its power from the praise of God the Creator which precedes it: that is the divinity which Christ has achieved, through suffering, and this divinity, so achieved, is the power behind all that follows.

☐ **WORSHIP**

Blessed Lord God,
heaven and earth proclaim your glory:
all creation blesses your name.
So renew us by your Spirit,
inspire us with your love,
and unite us in the body of your Son,
that we may join with all the company of heaven and earth in your eternal
    praise;
through Jesus Christ our Lord,
who is alive and reigns with you and the Holy Spirit,
one God now and for ever.   Amen.

First reading: Psalm 148:1–14
Second reading: Revelations 5:7–14
Gospel reading: Luke 1:67–75

Teaching material

■ **CONTEXT OF UNIT 25**

The Eucharistic Prayer concludes with a great shout of praise. Eucharist
itself means thanksgiving, and it is appropriate that the Eucharistic Prayer
should end on a high note or true climax. Remembrance of Christ's saving
actions in the past culminates in the joyful celebration of his saving presence. Solemnity and celebration merge.

A natural way in which man expresses his feelings of celebration is in the
carnival. The intention of this unit is to explore the child's natural expression of celebration in the carnival, and to link this experience with the
Eucharist.

For these experiences to be meaningful to the child three things are
necessary:

1 the child needs to experience being part of a celebration or carnival
2 the child needs to connect the idea of celebration with the recollection of
   important events
3 the child needs to experience the Eucharist as a time of celebration.

■ **OBJECTIVES**

1 To enable the child to enter into the joy of carnival time.
2 To enable the child to explore the role of specific Christian signs and
   symbols in the context of carnival processions.
3 To enable the child to recognise the reasons for celebration and the
   occasions on which people celebrate.
4 To associate the joy of carnival celebration with the Eucharist itself.

ACTIVITIES

a Carnival

Begin by encouraging the children to talk about their own experiences of carnival.

1 Produce a large mural of a carnival, asking each child to produce something for that mural. The mural might include such things as a band, drum majorettes, people in fancy dress, clowns, etc., decorated floats, a procession of vintage cars, traction engines, etc. The procession might be moving towards a fair ground, including stalls, side-shows, and amusements like dodgems and the big wheel.

2 Fair grounds are often closely associated with carnivals. Make a model of a fair ground.

3 Talk about the way in which other countries celebrate and hold carnivals. Like so much else of the modern world, carnivals have lost touch with the basic themes once celebrated. Therefore, it is helpful to concentrate some attention on primitive society in order to understand the motivation behind carnivals in such basic ideas as the welcoming of spring and the thanksgiving of harvest. Produce a book on 'Carnivals and Celebrations around the World'.

4 Talk about the famous carnivals and fairs that happen nowadays, like the Blackpool Illuminations, the midsummer fair in Cambridge, the St Giles fair in Oxford or the goose fair in Nottingham. Compare these with the medieval idea of fairs and celebrations. Give particular attention to the occasions on which and reasons for which the medieval world held its celebrations. Produce a class book on 'Fairs and Carnivals Today and Yesterday'.

b Banners

The illustration shows children demonstrating their celebration during the Prayer of Thanksgiving by waving flags and banners. A central aspect of this unit on carnival is the creation of such flags and banners which can be brought to the Eucharist and used by the children as an expression of their celebration. This unit provides an opportunity to explore Christian symbols and signs associated with our worship. Unit 15 has already explored some of the signs associated with the saints. Some of these banners can be reused, and the range of designs extended. A wealth of detail about Christian signs and symbols can be found in W. Ellwood Post, *Saints Signs and Symbols*, (SPCK 1975).

Begin by asking the children what they think ought to be on the banners and flags which they are to bring to the Eucharist. Three kinds of suggestions are helpful:

Straightforward text, e.g. Alleluia, Jesus is Lord, etc.

Pictures, e.g., the Easter tomb, Jesus talking to the crowd, etc.

The conventional signs and symbols of Christian art. A few suggestions for Christian symbols would include:

The cross   the major Christian symbol which can appear in a number of variations or designs.

The chalice   a symbol of Eucharist.

The ship   a symbol of the Church.

The triangle   a symbol of the Trinity.

The Lamb carrying a flag   a symbol of Christ as the Lamb of God.

The fish   the Greek word for fish spells the first letters of 'Jesus, Christ, Son of God, Saviour'.

The dove   a symbol of the Holy Spirit.

Chi Rho   the sacred monogram.

The lily   a symbol of St Mary.

■ ACTIVITIES

1 Invite someone who is familiar with carnival traditions in other parts of the world to talk about these traditions, and if possible to illustrate them with slides or pictures.

2 Plan a carnival for the church or school, or arrange for the children to take part as a group in a local carnival. This can include such ideas as decorated floats, fancy dress, etc.

3 Choose an occasion when the children's banners can be processed to the church for a special celebration of the Eucharist.

4 Encourage the children to make costumes and to devise drama about carnivals, involving some of the following contexts: a medieval fair; clowns; the military band; foreign carnivals.

5 Explore the theme of carnivals in dance and movement.

■ WRITING

1 Encourage the children to write a letter to a friend in a foreign country explaining and describing the work they have been doing on carnivals.

2 Ask the children to imagine that they live in the middle ages or in a foreign country and to describe the carnival in those distant times or places.

■ DISPLAY HEADINGS

Useful headings for displaying with the work produced in the course of this unit are

1 Carnival time is a time for celebration and happiness

2 Banners, flags and processions are an important part of our carnival celebration
3 Our banners are decorated with Christian signs and symbols
4 During the Doxology we wave our flags in Jesus' honour
5 St James' Church has arranged a carnival
6 Class 6 has built a model fair ground
7 In olden times carnivals were held to celebrate important occasions like the coming of spring and the gathering of the harvest

A short explanation might run like this, 'The Eucharistic Prayer concludes with a great shout of praise which is summed up in the Doxology. Eucharist itself means thanksgiving, so it is appropriate for the Thanksgiving to end on a high note. Our celebration can be expressed as a carnival held in honour of the presence of the Risen Christ.'

The Lord is Here or *At the Lord's Table*, open at pages 50–1 can be displayed also.

26. LORD'S PRAYER

Picnic time

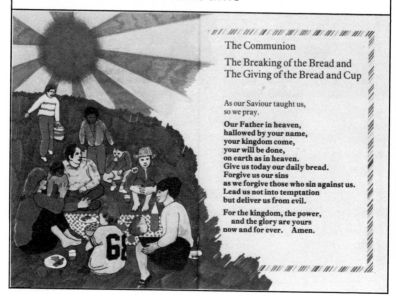

The Communion

The Breaking of the Bread and
The Giving of the Bread and Cup

As our Saviour taught us,
so we pray.

Our Father in heaven,
hallowed by your name,
your kingdom come,
your will be done,
on earth as in heaven.
Give us today our daily bread.
Forgive us our sins
as we forgive those who sin against us.
Lead us not into temptation
but deliver us from evil.

For the kingdom, the power,
and the glory are yours
now and for ever.   Amen.

Background material

□ TEXT

The Lord's Prayer seems to have occupied a place between the end of the
Eucharistic Prayer and the distribution of communion since the fourth
century, coming either before or after the Fraction and preparing the way for
receiving communion. A number of early Church Fathers saw this as an
appropriate place for the Lord's Prayer because of the petition 'Give us this
day our daily bread', which some of them interpreted as meaning the bread of
the Eucharist. St Ambrose, for example, advocates frequent communion on
the basis of this text.

□ PICTURE

The picture shows children and adults sitting on the grass covered slope of a
hill and enjoying a picnic together as a family group. The picture is chosen
for four reasons:

1 The family grouping emphasises that this is the 'Family Prayer' of the Church.
2 The sharing of the bread emphasises one of the petitions of the prayer.
3 It prepares us for sharing the bread of the Eucharist.
4 It draws a parallel between Jesus' feeding of the five thousand as they sat on the grass and the Eucharist.

COMMENT

In this section the phrases of the Lord's Prayer are commented on in turn. The Gospel reading relates Matthew's account of the giving of the Lord's Prayer to the disciples. In the Old Testament reading the prophet Isaiah looks to the days when God's name will be hallowed, and in the New Testament reading Paul draws out the implications of addressing God as Father.

The Lord's Prayer

The Lord's Prayer is given in only two of the gospels, Matthew and Luke. There are striking similarities and also striking differences between the two accounts which have puzzled the scholars who attempt to trace the way back to the earliest sources of the New Testament. A classic scholar of this movement, B. H. Streeter, *The Four Gospels*, (Macmillan 1924, p. 277) writes that 'the difference between the two versions is so great as to put a considerable strain on the theory that they were both derived from the same written source'. It is impossible to argue with any certainty which of the two versions more closely represents the words of Jesus. By way of tradition Matthew's form has always been the basis of liturgical use. For the present purposes it is more to the point to examine the text of the Lord's Prayer used in Rite A than to argue about what lies behind this text in the New Testament. Each phrase will be reviewed in turn.

Our Father in heaven   Section 7 has already drawn attention to Joachim Jeremias' comments on the distinctive aspect of Jesus' teaching which addressed God as 'Abba'. The word 'Abba' is Aramaic, the vernacular which Jesus spoke. It was a secular word, the intimate and familiar address of the child to its earthly father. Jeremias declares that in the whole field of Jewish literature he cannot find another incident of its use as an address to God. This bold, intimate form of address demonstrates the Christian's unique and close relationship with God.

Hallowed be your name   In Hebrew thought the name of a person distinguishes and expresses the nature and essence of the bearer, and can even be a substitute for the person himself. Here we are asking that God's name should be recognised to be holy. Holy means 'separate', 'distinct', 'other', the 'God-ness of God'. We are asking that God himself should be acknowledged for the God he is.

Your kingdom come   C. H. Dodd, *The Parables of the Kingdom*, (Fontana 1961, pp. 29–30) writes that behind the word 'kingdom' stands the Aramaic word *Malkuth*. *Malkuth* does not refer to territory but to 'kingship', 'kingly rule', 'reign' or 'sovereignty':

> In Jewish usage contemporary with the Gospels we may distinguish two main ways in which the Kingdom of God is spoken of. First, God is King of his people Israel, and his kingly rule is effective in so far as Israel is obedient to the divine will . . . In this sense 'The Kingdom of God' is a present fact. But in another sense 'The Kingdom of God' is something yet to be revealed. God is more than King of Israel; he is King of all the world. But the world does not recognise him as King . . . Israel, however, looks forward to the day when 'The saints of the most high shall take the kingdom', and so the kingship of God will become effective over the whole world . . . In this sense 'The Kingdom of God' is a hope for the future.

Your will . . . as in heaven   John Fenton, *St Matthew*, (Penguin 1963, p. 101) argues that 'these words are not in Luke's version of the Lord's Prayer; and they reflect Matthew's style: he has probably added them as a further explanation of the two previous petitions'.

Give us today our daily bread   The word 'daily' presents a lot of problems. It translates a Greek work which appears nowhere else in the New Testament. David Hill, *Gospel of Matthew*, (Oliphants 1972, p. 138) argues that a better translation is probably 'give us bread for the coming day' or 'give us bread for the morrow'. This would include the nourishment of the Messianic banquet, that is nourishment for life in the Kingdom of God. It embraces everything that Jesus' disciples need for body and soul.

Forgive us our sins . . . against us   Section 16 deals thoroughly with this theme of forgiveness.

Lead us not into temptation   The words of this petition cause considerable diversity of opinion among both scholars and worshippers. The 1971 version of Series Three has the translation 'do not bring us to the test'. The 1973 version of Series Three has the translation 'do not bring us to the time of trial'. On this petition C. F. Evans, *The Lord's Prayer*, (SPCK 1963, pp. 65–7) writes

> In the book of Daniel, and in the thought of others like him, temptation becomes the word for a trial which is of cosmic proportions, a 'tribulation' as it is called, of a final kind, when the whole force of Satan's power is to be hurled against God's saints to seduce them and break their allegiance . . . By it God brings to an issue the conflict between his own order and the disorder of evil . . . The disciple is simply to pray that God, in bringing matters to an issue, will preserve him immune.

But deliver us from evil   This may refer to deliverance from 'the evil one' whose activity would be increased in the 'time of trial'.

For the kingdom . . . Amen   This is a normal Jewish ending for a prayer. It does not occur in the most reliable manuscripts of the Gospel accounts, and is most probably a later addition.

⌋ WORSHIP

Father God,
your Son Jesus Christ
    showed us we belong to your family,
    and taught us to call you Father.
Feed us now as we celebrate
    the family meal of bread and wine,
    which you have prepared for us;
through Jesus Christ our Lord.   Amen.

First reading: Isaiah 29:22–24
Second reading: Romans 8:14–17
Gospel reading: Matthew 6:5–13

Teaching material

▌ CONTEXT OF UNIT 26

The Lord's Prayer is said before the Fraction and the Distribution of Communion. The family prayer of the church is said at the point when the Christian family prepares itself to eat the family meal. The illustration draws together the concept of the family prayer and the family meal by showing a family group having a picnic.

For the significance of the Lord's Prayer at this point of the service to be meaningful to the child three things are necessary:

1 The child needs to know the origin of the Lord's Prayer and the significance attached to it as the Family Prayer of the Church.
2 The child needs to be able to grasp the rich meanings that the church has derived from associating the Lord's Prayer with the distribution of communion.
3 The child needs to be able to relate the symbolism of the family meal and the family prayer to the sharing of the Eucharist.
These issues will be explored by developing the theme of the picnic.

■ **OBJECTIVES**

  1 To explore the theme of picnic as a way of drawing together the ideas of the Eucharist as the family meal and the Lord's Prayer as the family prayer.
  2 To study the Lord's Prayer.
  3 To encourage the children to use the Lord's Prayer as a regular part of their own prayer life.

■ **DISPLAY WORK**

Begin by encouraging the children to talk about their experiences of picnics. Encourage them to prepare a large Teddy Bears' picnic scene to be displayed in the school or the church.

1 Produce a list of all that is required for a picnic, the different foods, the drinks, the cups and plates. Models can be made of all these things.

2 Discuss the 'scene' in which the Teddy Bears' picnic is to take place. A large backcloth needs to be painted, showing trees, grass, flowers, toadstools, perhaps a castle or a house. The backcloth might also include the text 'Give us today our daily bread'. A foreground also needs to be made – perhaps a papier mâché surface or imitation grass. Trees, flowers, benches, toadstools, etc., can also be part of the foreground. A large and welcoming sun can be fixed in the sky. Perhaps signs can be arranged around the building pointing to the picnic area 'AA route, Teddy Bears' Picnic'.

3 Teddy Bears can be made in a number of ways – simple shapes can be knitted or cut from fabric and stuffed. Glove puppets can be made for the

children to use as puppets on their hand or to drape over bench ends, candle sticks and churchwarden's staves in the church!

4 A sequence of murals can be made to tell the story of the Teddy Bears' picnic from the time the Teddy Bears get up in the morning to the time they return home. This sequence can include the preparing of the picnic, the journey and the washing-up afterwards.

5 Encourage the children to make costumes so they can dress up as Teddy Bears.

6 Encourage the children to prepare the food for a real picnic. Let them decide what food will be needed and then to purchase and prepare it. The picnic might include biscuits baked to look like Teddy Bears.

7 Encourage the children to examine the traditions of the Feeding of the Five Thousand in the Gospels (Mark 6:32–44, Matthew 14:13–21, Luke 9:10–17, John 6:1–13). Discuss this narrative and draw out the relationship between what happened then and a picnic. Produce a class book 'Jesus feeds the crowd' of illustrations telling this story, giving just small portions of the text on each page. For example, give a separate page to each of the four actions of Jesus, the taking, blessing, breaking and sharing of the bread.

8 Examine the way in which Jesus taught his disciples the Lord's Prayer in Matthew 6:9–13 and Luke 11:1–4. Note the similarities and differences. Encourage the children to write the prayer carefully for the display board. Some may like to produce a richly illuminated text of the Lord's Prayer to be displayed in Church.

9 The Lord's Prayer repeats many of the ideas already expressed in the previous Teaching Units. It can be helpful to link these ideas together by looking at the clauses of the Lord's Prayer separately and illustrating them, for example:

i) God cares	Our Father	Kyrie
ii) God reigns	Your Kingdom come	Creed, God
iii) God provides	Give us today	Offertory
iv) God forgives	Forgive us	Confession
v) God protects	Do not bring us	Peace
vi) God is praised	For the Kingdom	Gloria

10 Look through the Alternative Service Book to see how the Lord's Prayer is part of so much of Christian worship. Produce a list of all the places where it is used.

ACTIVITIES

1 Arrange for the class to prepare a picnic and then go somewhere to share it together.

2 Encourage the children to arrange dance or drama on the theme of the Teddy Bears' picnic and to dress up as Teddy Bears. In this way encourage them to experience the significance of eating together, and the use of the four actions of taking food, saying grace, breaking it and sharing it.

3 Learn the song 'The Teddy Bears' Picnic'. Encourage the children to accompany this song with their own music.

4 Arrange for some simple food to be shared after the children have finally assembled the Teddy Bears' picnic scene.

5 Encourage the children to base a play on the tradition of the Feeding of the Five Thousand.

■ WRITING

1 Ask the children to write about a picnic they remember well.

2 Ask the children to imagine that they are teddy bears and to write about the day they had a picnic.

3 Read and write about Jesus' feeding of the five thousand.

■ DISPLAY HEADINGS

Useful headings for displaying with the work produced in the course of this unit are
   1 St James' church went for a picnic
   2 Jesus took the bread
     Jesus said thank you to God
     Jesus broke the bread
     Jesus shared it with the crowd·
     And five thousand people ate as they sat on the green grass
   3 Jesus taught his disciples to pray the Lord's Prayer
   4 The Lord's Prayer is the Family Prayer of the Church
   5 The Teddy Bears have their picnic
   6 'Give us today our daily bread'

A short explanation might run 'The Lord's Prayer is the family prayer of the Church. We pray it together as a family just before we share in the family meal in the Eucharist. We also remember how Jesus shared the bread with the five thousand people who made a picnic on the green grass.'

The Lord is Here or *At the Lord's Table* open at pages 52–3 can be displayed also.

27. FRACTION

Fair shares

We break this bread
to share in the body of Christ.

**Though we are many,
we are one body,
because we all share in one bread.**

■ **TEXT**

The Fraction, or the Breaking of the Bread, had a very practical aspect for the early church, which at this point of the service was faced with the basic task of dividing the small loaves into suitably sized pieces for distribution at the communion. The Fraction is also an important part of the symbolic action of the Eucharist. The primary symbolic significance associated with the Fraction in Rite A is indicated by the sentence printed in the text. This is derived from 1 Corinthians 10:17 where St Paul sees in this action a symbol of the unity of Christian people in Christ. At various times the Church has also seen other significances in the Fraction. First, it has been associated with Christ's own action of breaking the bread at the Last Supper. Second, 'The Breaking of the Bread' is the name used for the Eucharist in Acts 2:42, etc. Third, later piety saw the Fraction as symbolizing the death of Christ whose body was broken on the cross.

■ PICTURE

The picture shows the breaking of the bread. For the first time in the sequence of illustrations the bread is now represented in the stylized form of the communion wafer. The broken wafer is held up by the priest for the people to see. The many faces arrayed around the broken wafer portray the identity between the breaking of the bread and the unity of those who share that bread within the Body of Christ.

■ COMMENT

In this section comment is made on the concepts of sharing and the Body of Christ. Then two early interpretations of the Fraction are presented. The Old Testament reading shows the unity of the Israelite people around a fair distribution of the manna in the wilderness. The New Testament reading is Paul's teaching on sharing and unity in the Body of Christ. The Gospel reading shows Christ uniting the crowd by feeding them with the five loaves and two fishes.

To Share

The verb 'to share' used here is based on the Greek word *koinonia*. The problem is that *koinonia* cannot be easily translated into English. It means sharing, but it means much more as well. It contains all three of the ideas involved in the English concepts of sharing, fellowship and communion. It is the kind of life lived around the sharing of the Eucharist.

The Body of Christ

G. Johnston, 'The Doctrine of the Church in the New Testament', in *Peake's Commentary on the Bible*, (Nelson 1962, p. 722):

> Paul's supreme contribution to the idea of the Church is that of the Body of Christ. We cannot delineate precisely its origins, though it must be related to . . . the Semitic sense of solidarity (the High Priest on the day of Atonement represents all Israel before God and the sacral King too embodies his nation). Concepts of this sort, brought together with ideas of the world as a cosmic whole, of the Roman Empire as a body, and the people of God as one in the last Adam, Jesus Christ, may have led the apostle to formulate his metaphor. Some scholars would seek its beginning in the word of Jesus over the bread at the Last Supper 'This is my body', and this is plausible. What better concept than that of the body and its limbs? In Rom 12:3ff it seems to be merely a social analogy, but I Cor 12, taken in the light of the whole range of Pauline theology, proves that Paul has gone beyond mere metaphor. Christians were the limbs of the Messiah, and therefore his servants, expressing his mind and will (Col 1:24). It is as if the risen Lord actually lived in the churches to direct, teach and bless them.

The Pauline disciple who wrote Ephesians perceived the significance of this doctrine of the Body, and he displays profound understanding of its meaning. If we may say that the Creator is fulfilled by his creation, so may we say that Christ is completed by his Body, the church (Eph 1:22f). This body is not yet complete; it is growing and expanding, and its ultimate goal is the very fullness of God himself.

The Fraction

Some of the early eucharistic rites of the Church demonstrate how soon Christian worshippers began to attach symbolic interpretations to the Fraction. One of the earliest Eucharistic Prayers preserved is in the Didache. This prayer contains the following words:

> As this broken bread, once dispersed over the hills, was brought together and became one loaf, may thy Church be brought together from the ends of the earth into thy kingdom (from *Early Christian Writings*, Penguin 1968, p. 231).

Other early eucharistic prayers of the church placed on the lips of Jesus himself an interpretation of the fraction. For example, the Eucharistic Prayer attributed to St John Chrysostom makes a slight change in Christ's words spoken over the bread at the Last Supper:

> Take, eat of this: for this is indeed my body, which for you and for many is broken and given for the remission of sins and eternal life (from Arthur Linton, *Twenty-Five Consecration Prayers*, SPCK 1921, p. 47).

Read 1 Corinthians 10:14–17 (We all share in one bread)

C. K. Barrett, *The First Epistle to the Corinthians*, (A & C Black 1968, pp. 233–4):

> The sharing of the bread is taken to be a means of sharing in *the body of Christ*. It is very improbable that this is a reference to the human body of Christ in its physical aspect, since this is described by Paul in other terms (using the word *flesh*) whereas for him 'the Body of Christ' . . . refers to the Church. To eat the loaf means to share in that company of men which, through its union with Christ, has by anticipation entered upon the new age which lies beyond the resurrection . . . Paul argues from the fact that one loaf was broken and distributed to the consequence that those who partake of the one loaf are notwithstanding their plurality one body . . . Because Christ is sinless, they are ideally sinless, and must become so in practice. Because he is one, they are ideally one, and must become so in practice.

☐ WORSHIP

Eternal Father,
your Son Jesus Christ broke bread
  to give new life to your world,
    and to unite us in his body.
Every time we break the bread in your name,
help us to remember the needs of your world,
and our responsibility to care for others;
through Jesus Christ our Lord.   Amen.

First reading: Exodus 16:14–18
Second reading: 1 Corinthians 10:14–17
Gospel reading: Mark 6:35–44

Teaching material

■ CONTEXT OF UNIT 27

The Fraction concentrates our attention upon the idea of sharing. This is a rich idea in Christian tradition. The breaking and sharing of the loaf symbolises three distinct themes:

1 the unity of each individual worshipper with the whole church of Christ, both present around the one table and distant in time and space.

2 the life of sharing and mutual caring which ought to characterise the Christian family.

3 the responsibility of the Christian community for taking seriously the sharing of the world's resources.

These three large themes permeate much of the eucharistic rite. The first is examined in Unit 23 and the second in Unit 26. The present Unit concentrates on the third theme, the responsibility of the Christian community for taking seriously the sharing of the world's resources. In order for the child to begin to explore this theme four things are necessary:

1 The child needs to explore ways in which people in his own society depend upon each other.

2 The child needs to become aware of the needs of people in his own society which are not being taken seriously.

3 The child needs to explore the way in which the nations of the world depend upon each other. He needs to identify the nations on which his own life style depends – what is imported from these nations and the reward they receive.

4 The child needs to become aware of the poverty, hunger, and disease that holds sway in much of the world.

OBJECTIVES

1 To help the child to become aware of the way in which in our own day to day life we depend so much on other people.
2 To help the child to become aware of the people in his own society who are disadvantaged in one way or another.
3 To help the child to become aware of the ways in which his own country is dependent upon material imported from less advantaged nations.
4 To help the child to become aware of our need to conserve the world's resources.
5 To help the child to become aware of the extent to which so much of the world is afflicted by poverty, hunger and disease.
6 To give the child an opportunity to make some contribution to Christian work among deprived groups both at home and overseas.

DISPLAY WORK

Begin by encouraging the children to talk about all the different people that they and their families depend on – and perhaps take for granted.

1 Keep a class diary for a day, listing all the different people who have contributed to the class' life, from those who have a direct contact like the person who cooks the dinners, to those who have a less obvious influence like the people who cut down the tree that makes the paper.

2 Make a list and develop a wall chart or project book on the theme 'We share in each other's work'. Include, for example,
   public services; water, electricity, gas, sewerage, refuse collection, road repairs.
   public communications; post, telephone, buses, trains.
   health service; doctors, dentists, nurses.
   social services; welfare workers, job centres, schools, colleges.
   distribution services; lorry drivers, shopkeepers, milk delivery.
   food production; farmers, bakers, packaging and processing plant.
   consumer production; car manufacturers, furniture makers.

3 Collect information about the disadvantaged groups in our own society, and the charities organised to help them. Produce a wall chart or project book on the theme 'People who need our help'.

4 Make a list of the raw materials and goods we import from other countries. Try to discover something about the life style of the peoples who produce them. Produce another wall chart or project book on the theme 'Our share in the world's resources'. Include, for example, oil, coal, wheat, rice, coffee, iron ore, wood.

5 Examine the origin of the world's raw materials: the irreplaceable nature of oil, coal, etc., and the slow growth of trees, etc. Compare this with the

waste of our present society. Produce a mural or project book on the theme 'We need to use the world's resources responsibly'.

6 Make a study of one country or aspect of the Third World. A number of organisations like Christian Aid, Oxfam and the Missionary Societies are now producing useful curriculum material, which they are able to keep up to date. Follow one of these programmes.

▥ ACTIVITIES

1 Invite some of the people on whom we depend to talk to the class about their work.

2 Visit a factory that produces something the children regularly use and see what life is like inside that factory.

3 Explore through drama what it is like to belong to a disadvantaged group, to be blind, crippled, housebound.

4 Arrange a way in which the children can share their own work with a disadvantaged group. This can take a number of forms, e.g. they can make a mural for a children's hospital or arrange a concert for an old people's home.

5 Arrange a money raising event so that the children contribute directly to a body like Christian Aid.

6 Encourage the children to collect those waste materials which our society is willing to recycle or redeem.

7 Use films on life in the Third World and visual aids produced by Oxfam, Christian Aid and the Missionary Societies.

▥ WRITING

1 Invite the children to imagine that they belong to a disadvantaged group in their own country or overseas and to write about themselves.

2 Ask the children to write a letter to a friend explaining why they support a specific missionary society or charity concerned with the disadvantaged.

3 Ask the children to write about the sort of job they could do when they grow up if they wished to serve others.

▥ DISPLAY HEADINGS

Useful headings for displaying with the work produced in the course of this unit are

   1 We share in each other's work

2 Many people still go neglected in our own society
3 We depend on resources imported from all over the world
4 Many parts of the world are poor, hungry and sick
5 We must share and conserve the world's resources responsibly
6 St James' Church is helping Christian Aid to help the Third World
7 St James' is helping USPG/CMS
8 Class 4 is helping Help the Aged

A short explanation might run like this, 'The Fraction reminds us of the basic Christian idea of *Sharing*. Because we live in God's world we have a responsibility to see that the resources of his world are fairly shared.'

The Lord is Here or *At the Lord's Table* open at pages 54–5 can be displayed also.

28. INVITATION AND ADMINISTRATION

The pilgrim way

Draw near with faith.
Receive the body of our Lord Jesus Christ
which he gave for you,
and his blood which he shed for you.

Eat and drink
in remembrance that he died for you,
and feed on him in your hearts by faith
with thanksgiving.

The Body of Christ keep you
in eternal life.
Amen.

The Blood of Christ keep you
in eternal life.
Amen.

56   57

Background material

☐ **TEXT**

This section contains two things
  the words of Invitation
  the words of Administration.

The words of Invitation are addressed to the whole people at once. The words of Administration are addressed to each communicant in turn, who responds by saying 'Amen'. It is customary in many churches for those who are not yet admitted to communion to come to the altar rail to receive a blessing.

☐ **PICTURE**

The picture portrays a row of people kneeling at the altar rail. Adults and children are side by side. Those who are not communicants are shown holding their hands at their side to indicate to the priest that they do not intend to receive communion. The picture focuses attention on the solemnity and reverence of this part of the service.

⏋ COMMENT

In this section comment is made on the practice of the Church of England regarding admission to communion. Then Denis Taylor comments on the use of silence at this point in the communion service and one of Michel Quoist's *Prayers of Life* illustrates Christian devotion before the presence of God. The Old Testament reading is a classic illustration of man's attitude of reverence in God's presence. In the New Testament reading Paul admonishes the Corinthian church to approach the communion with reverence. The Gospel reading is a passage which has given rise to Christian devotion before receiving communion.

Admission to Communion

The established custom of the Church of England has been to admit to communion only those who have previously received the sacrament of confirmation. One modification of this tradition is now in current practice and a second modification is the subject of discussion.

1 According to Canon B15A of the Church of England promulged by the General Synod on 9 July 1972, the Church of England is able to welcome to its altar 'Baptised persons who are communicant members of other churches which subscribe to the doctrine of the Holy Trinity, and who are in good standing in their own church'.

2 The report *Christian Initiation* (CIO 1971, paragraph 119) sees advantages in changing the relationship between confirmation and communion:

> We believe that it should be permissible to admit baptised Christians to communion after preparation without using confirmation as some kind of a preliminary spiritual or educational qualification. As the rite of confirmation ceases to be no more than a conventional gateway to communion, so its significance will be enhanced, as it becomes an act of personal commitment and commissioning at an age when such an act becomes truly meaningful.

The silences at holy communion

Denis Taylor, *In His Presence*, (REP, Series 3 Edn, 1973, pp. 60–2):

> The third silence is just before the people go to the altar to receive the consecrated bread and wine. In this silence *adore* him. Try to realise that he is there with you in the church . . . Kneel, yes, and tremble before him.
>   Thee we adore, O hidden Saviour, thee,
>   Who in thy Sacrament dost deign to be;
>   Both Flesh and Spirit at thy Presence fail,
>   Yet here thy Presence we devoutly hail.

Pour out your love, your worship. Now is the time to pray about your special intention, the people or matters you made ready at your preparation for this moment. You go and kneel at the altar rail. Worship and adore your Saviour. Bring him again all that you decided in your preparation . . . In the silence while the other people are making their communion, continue to pray about these matters.

'Before you, Lord' (from Michael Quoist, *Prayers of Life*, Gill 1963, pp. 113–4):

To be there before you, Lord, that's all.
To shut the eyes of my body,
To shut the eyes of my soul,
And be still and silent,
To expose myself to you who are there, exposed to me.
To be there before you, the Eternal Presence.
I am willing to feel nothing, Lord,
    to see nothing,
    to hear nothing.
Empty of all ideas,
   of all images,
In the darkness.
Here I am, simply,
To meet you without obstacles,
In the silence of faith,
Before you, Lord.

But, Lord, I am not alone
I can no longer be alone.
I am a crowd, Lord,
For men live within me.
I have met them.
They have come in,
They have settled down,
They have worried me,
They have tormented me,
They have devoured me.
And I have allowed it, Lord, that they might be nourished and refreshed.
I bring them to you, too, as I come before you.
I expose them to you in exposing myself to you.
Here I am,
Here they are,
Before you, Lord.

Read 1 Corinthians 11:17–22 (The Corinthian's Eucharist)
 In the early Church the Eucharist was offered as part of a common meal. At

Corinth this seems to have led to a lack of reverence. This may well be one of the reasons why the church separated the Eucharist from a common meal.

Read St Matthew 8:5–13 (The Centurion's boy)

Generations of communicants have echoed the Centurion's words of humility as they have approached the altar rail: 'Lord I am not worthy that you should come under my roof, but speak the word only and I shall be healed'.

WORSHIP

Lord Jesus Christ,
as you stand among us in the bread and the wine
   you invite us to draw near to your presence.
As we respond to you now,
come and live in us,
come and stay with us,
come Jesus come.   Amen.

First reading: Exodus 3:1–6
Second reading: 1 Corinthians 11:17–22
Gospel reading: Matthew 8:5–13

Teaching material

CONTEXT OF UNIT 28

The Invitation invites each person in the worshipping community to 'draw near with faith'. Generally this involves the worshipper in two things:

1 He moves from his seat and journeys to the point at which the Administration is taking place.
2 He recognises the Administration as a special focus for his encounter with and response to Christ.

The way in which the progression to the altar rail takes place itself becomes a symbol of the special significance attached to the bread and the wine.

For the Invitation and Administration to be meaningful to the child three things are necessary:

1 The child needs to understand the place of journeys and pilgrimages in religious tradition.
2 The child needs to experience the administration as a particular point of encounter with the Christ. In churches where children are not admitted to communion at a young age, the blessing can function as an equally meaningful point of encounter.

3 The child needs to be taught how to develop his spiritual response to the period of time surrounding the Administration.

This Unit explores these themes through the idea of pilgrimage. A pilgrimage is a journey undertaken with a special religious intention. The concept of pilgrimage can be given its meaning within the Judaeo-Christian tradition by studying such topics as

1 Abraham in the Old Testament
2 The medieval pilgrimages to the Holy Land.
3 The medieval pilgrimage shrines.
4 The Pilgrim Fathers.
5 Contemporary Christian Pilgrimages.

■ OBJECTIVES

1 To study the part played by pilgrimages in Christian tradition.
2 To relate the concept of pilgrimage to the administration of communion.
3 To develop the child's spiritual response to the administration.

■ DISPLAY WORK

Begin by talking about pilgrimages and the ideas which the children have about the pilgrims.

1 Discuss Abraham who responded to God's call, set out from his home and risked the unknown to seek for a new place in which to serve God. Produce a large collage of Abraham, his family and servants, his tents and his flocks of sheep.

2 Discuss the Pilgrim Fathers who risked their lives sailing to a strange land in order to find a new place in which to serve God. Produce a mural or model of their ship and figures of the pilgrim fathers in their characteristic dress.

3 Discuss the crusaders who made pilgrimage to the Holy Land to protect the Holy Places. Produce a mural of the crusaders on horseback carrying colourful shields and flags.

4 Talk about present day pilgrimages to the Holy Land. Collect travel material about the Holy Land and pilgrimage advertisements from church newspapers to produce a mural.

5 Talk about the medieval pilgrimage shrines. Collect information about one particular shrine like Canterbury and conduct a project on that place. For example, produce a class book on 'What the Pilgrim found in Medieval Canterbury'.

6 Produce a series of costumes or headdresses for the children to dress up as 'Pilgrims throughout the ages', including Abraham, the Crusaders, the

medieval pilgrims to Canterbury, the Pilgrim Fathers and contemporary pilgrims.

7 Produce a class book about pilgrimages, including pictures and stories of famous pilgrims and places of pilgrimage.

8 Study one contemporary place to which pilgrimages are made. Collect information and photographs about that place for a project book 'Pilgrimages Today'.

9 Talk about the purpose of the pilgrimage to the altar rail and the way that period of time can be employed in prayer. Produce a mural of the congregation during the period of the Administration – some receiving communion or being blessed at the altar, some sitting or kneeling in their seats before or after coming to the altar, and others walking from their seats 'The Pilgrimage to Communion'.

10 Make a collection of prayers which Christians have used as they prepare to receive the Sacrament 'Our Pilgrimage Prayers'. For example, the Rite A service book includes two versions of the Agnus Dei (Lamb of God). Devotional books include other material like Matthew 8:8. Encourage the children to add to this collection their own prayers.

ACTIVITIES

1 Invite someone who has made a pilgrimage to the Holy Land to tell the children about his or her visit and to show pictures of the Holy Land.

2 Make a visit to a medieval place of pilgrimage like Canterbury Cathedral or Durham Cathedral.

3 Discover whether any local churches have memorials to or associations with any pilgrims, for example the Pilgrim Fathers or the crusaders.

4 Conduct a pilgrimage to a contemporary place of pilgrimage like Walsingham. See if it is possible to arrange for the children to talk with other people who have made pilgrimage there about their reasons for going.

5 Produce a play about a medieval pilgrimage, 'The Canterbury Tales', and dress up in costumes of that period.

WRITING

1 Invite the children to imagine that they lived in medieval England and went to the Holy Land with the Crusaders: write a story of their adventures.

2 Describe a modern pilgrimage.

3 Write a story about the history of one of the ancient pilgrimage shrines.

■ **DISPLAY HEADINGS**

Useful headings for displaying with the work produced in the course of this unit are

1 Abraham was a pilgrim who set out to serve God in a new land
2 The Crusaders made pilgrimage to the Holy Land to protect the Holy Places
3 The Pilgrim Fathers set out to serve God in a new land
4 Throughout Christian history pilgrimages have been conducted to places made holy by the saints
5 Pilgrimages have been made to the shrines of St Cuthbert in Durham Cathedral and St Thomas A Beckett in Canterbury Cathedral
6 Walsingham is a pilgrimage shrine in modern England
7 Pilgrimage Prayers

A short explanation might run 'The Invitation invites us to draw near with faith and to receive the sacrament. We respond by making a pilgrimage to the altar rail. There we meet with Christ in a special way.'

The Lord is Here or *At the Lord's Table* open at pages 56–7 can be displayed also.

29. PRAYER AFTER COMMUNION

Come dancing

After Communion

Almighty God,
we thank you for feeding us
with the body and blood of your Son
    Jesus Christ.
Through him we offer you
    our souls and bodies
to be a living sacrifice.
Send us out
in the power of your Spirit
to live and work
to your praise and glory.   Amen.

59

Background material

☐ **TEXT**

This short Prayer after communion sums up in a very succinct way the communicant's response to the nourishment which God has offered to him in the holy sacrament. The prayer expresses the three ideas of thanking, offering and asking:

1 we thank God for feeding us in the holy Eucharist
2 we offer our whole selves to God – souls and bodies
3 we ask God to send us out in the power of His Spirit.

These three ideas point to the qualities of life which ought to follow from receiving holy communion.

☐ **PICTURE**

The picture shows priest and people with arms outstretched. The intention of the picture is to portray an attitude of thankfulness, happiness and openness to God. Priest and people are joining in a dance of thanksgiving.

☐ **COMMENT**

In this section J. D. Crichton and Carla de Sola and Arthur Easton comment on the place of gesture and dance in liturgy. In the Old Testament reading the psalmist invites us to praise the Lord in the dance. In the New Testament reading the healed cripple enters the temple leaping and praising God. The Gospel reading is Mary's song of praise, the Magnificat.

Dance in Liturgy

J. D. Crichton in Cheslyn Jones, *The Study of Liturgy*, (SPCK 1978, p. 10):

> Man is a unity . . . when he acts he acts in the wholeness of his personality. He lays hold of the faith with the whole of his being . . . When in worship he responds to God in faith, in praise and thanksgiving as well as with love, he does so with his whole being and feels the need to express his worship, his outgoing from self to God, in words and song and gesture.

Carla de Sola and Arthur Easton in Gloria Durka, *Aesthetic Dimensions of Religious Education*, (Paulist Press 1979, pp. 69–73) write that the author of the epistle to the Hebrews

> declared that we will come to Mt Zion, to 'innumerable angels in festal gathering' (Heb 12:22); but instead we come to Sunday service, to sit, and kneel, and hear words. We do not hear the song, only words; we do not dance the festal dance, only sit. And the living water becomes stagnant, and the ineffable murmur is lost. There is not festal dance to awaken the soul and lift the heart. 'Singers and dancers alike say "All my springs are in you" ' (Psalm 87). We have taken this to mean that we dance and sing out of the well-spring of God's life within us. We sing and dance when we love and are loved. But how many times is it true that *until* we move or speak we do not even know what we feel, or where we are in relation to the world? . . . Ten years of giving workshops on dance and its connection to liturgy and prayer have made it overwhelmingly clear to us that dance opens a pathway to a more personal and vivid experience of God . . . Religious dance can be assumed to be the result of a personal, meditative experience of God; the movement's source comes from the heart's response, in an overflowing of gratitude or speech *to God*. In Christian terms, one could speak of Christ as the partner in an ever-new dance which is inspired by the Holy Spirit and offered to the Father. The highest level, point, or state would be a contemplative absorption, moving in a reality filled with God's love, realising the words of scripture: 'In him we move and live and have our being'.

Read Psalm 149:1–5 (Praise his name in the dance)

> A. F. Kirkpatrick, *The Book of Psalms*, (CUP 1903, p. 830):

> Dancing was a natural expression of joy among the Jews as among other

nations of antiquity, in all periods of their history, on occasions of religious as well as secular festivities. Even the leading men of the city and famous teachers joined in it, and it was a current proverb that he who had not seen this joy had not seen any joy in his life.

Read Luke 1:46–55 (Mary's song of praise)
George Caird, *Saint Luke*, (Penguin 1963, p. 55):

Mary's song is called the Magnificat, and like the Benedictus and the Nunc Dimittis which follow gets its name from the first word of the vulgate version. All three are a mosaic of Old Testament texts, and the Magnificat is based largely on the Song of Hannah in 1 Sam 2:1–10. As in many of the Old Testament psalms the psalmist passes quite naturally from his individual concerns to those of the nation for which he is spokesman, so here Mary sings of her own exaltation from lowliness to greatness as typical of the new order which is to open out for the whole people of God through the coming of her son. She uses the past tense not to describe God's past care for the down-trodden, but because God has already taken decisive action in the promised sending of his Son, and she foresees as an accomplished fact the results that will follow in his mission.

□ WORSHIP

Lord Jesus Christ,
We shout your praise:
  accept our words.
Lord Jesus Christ,
We sing your praise:
  accept our music.
Lord Jesus Christ,
We dance your praise:
  accept our movement.
Lord Jesus Christ,
We offer you our souls and bodies:
  to be a living sacrifice of praise.   Amen.

First reading: Psalm 149:1–5
Second reading: Acts 3:1–10
Gospel reading: Luke 1:46–55

███ **Teaching material**

■ **CONTEXT OF UNIT 29**

The prayer after communion is a prayer of thanks. We say thank you to God for the Eucharist, and we do so by offering our whole selves to his service. The words are, however, empty unless they are matched by feelings of gratitude and joy. These are the feelings that need to be cultivated and given expression in our worship.

It is not sufficient to rely upon words alone as the only means of expressing our thanks to God in worship. Many of the other expressive arts have a contribution to make as well. This Unit explores dance as an expression of praise and thanks. Dance often comes more naturally to children than words.

For the prayer after communion to be meaningful to the child two things are necessary:

1 the child needs to understand why we are saying thank you at this point of the service.

2 the child needs to be able to express his feelings of gratitude in ways that are natural and meaningful to him, and then to associate these feelings with the formal prayer itself.

■ **OBJECTIVES**

1 To express our gratitude to God.
2 To explore different ways of saying thanks.
3 To explore different forms of dancing.
4 To explore the place of dance in our prayer of praise and thanksgiving.

■ **DISPLAY WORK**

Begin by encouraging the children to talk about dancing – their own experience of dancing, what they have seen on television, etc.

1 Develop the child's understanding of different forms of dancing. Discuss the different styles of dress associated with each: and the different kinds of environment in which they generally take place. For example

   a) Music and movement in the schools' broadcasts
   b) Country dancing in the old style barn
   c) Scottish Dancing by the loch side
   d) Morris dancing in the village market place
   e) Disco dancing in the church hall amid colourful lights
   f) Ballroom dancing in the grand style ballroom

Produce collages of these different forms of dancing. For example each child could produce one figure or pair of figures in the appropriate clothing.

The backgrounds can be very enjoyable creations – from the chandeliers of the ballroom to the multi coloured patchwork of the disco lighting.

2 Produce a display of dolls dressed for different styles of dancing. Either make dresses to fit the children's dolls, or make dolls or even simple wire frames on which the clothes can be displayed.

3 Produce costumes so that the children themselves can take on the role of dancers and transform part of the school or church into a disco, ballroom or barn. A lot of enjoyable work can be invested in transforming the environment in this way.

4 Look at the history of some forms of dancing and produce a class book on 'Dancing through the ages'.

5 Talk about ballet as a special form of dance communication. Listen to some ballet music, and better still watch some ballet. Produce a model stage together with some silhouette figures.

6 Talk about the different ways of saying 'thank you'. Encourage the children to write thank you prayers.

7 Keep a class diary of the things for which we should say thank you. 'Class 4's Book of Thanks.' Illustrate the different ideas suggested in the diary.

8 Produce a collage of things for which we should thank God and place at the centre of the collage the bread and the wine of the Eucharist – use the heading 'Thank you God'.

■ ACTIVITIES

1 Invite a local group of dancers to talk about their dancing and to give a display.

2 Hold a real dance/disco in the school/church hall and let the children help to make the preparation.

3 Make a visit to see a ballroom.

4 Invite one of the children's parents to teach the group a few dance steps.

5 Learn and perform some country dances. Dress up for these dances. Let the children, with the help of adults, provide their own music and rhythm.

6 Let the children experiment with different forms of dance movement as a way of expressing their feelings. Select a range of expressive music.

7 Let the children create their own dance movement as a hymn of praise. Choose an appropriate piece of joyful music that will encourage free expression. Employ this creative dance during the celebration of the Eucharist before saying the Post Communion Prayer.

8 If living in a multi-faith area, arrange for the children to witness the place of dance in Hindu worship and festivals.

■ WRITING

1 Write a letter of thanks to some of the people who have helped to prepare for the Unit, for example, those who visited to talk about their dancing and to give a display, or those who gave admittance to the ballroom.

2 Write a letter to someone who was not able to see the display and attend the final Eucharist to describe it all to them.

3 Read and write about the life of a famous dancer.

■ DISPLAY HEADINGS

Useful headings for displaying with the work produced in the course of this unit are
1 Praise his name in the dance (Psalm 149:3)
2 We dance for joy
3 We offer you our souls and bodies
4 Words alone cannot express our thanks
5 Ways of saying thank you
6 Class 4 says thank you
7 Thank you God

A short explanation might run, 'In the Prayer after Communion we thank God for feeding us in the Eucharist. We offer him our souls and bodies – our words and our dance.'

The Lord is Here or *At the Lord's Table* open at pages 58–9 can be displayed also.

30. BLESSING

After the flood

The Dismissal

The peace of God,
which passes all understanding,
keep your hearts and minds
in the knowledge and love of God,
and of his Son Jesus Christ our Lord;
And the blessing of God almighty,
the Father, the Son,
    and the Holy Spirit,
be among you,
    and remain with you always.

Amen.

Background material

□ **TEXT**

The last but one action of the Rite A Communion Service is the Blessing.
The Blessing contains two parts:

1 The first part (The peace of God . . . Jesus Christ our Lord) has its origin
   in Philippians 4:7. Rite A also provides, in one of the appendices, a range
   of alternatives for this part of the Blessing designed for particular seasons
   of the church's year.

2 The second part had a long history in the usage of the church. According to
   Procter and Frere, *The Book of Common Prayer*, (Macmillan 1901, p. 497)
   it derives from the bishop's blessing during the middle ages.

□ **PICTURE**

The picture employs imagery from the Genesis tradition about Noah and the
flood. Because of this narrative (Gen 8:11) the white dove and the olive

branch have become the symbols of peace and of good relationships between God and man. According to the same narrative (Gen 9:14–16) the rainbow is placed in the sky by God as a sign of his covenant with man. The picture focuses these three images of peace – the dove, the olive branch and the rainbow.

COMMENT

In this section comment is made on the concept of blessing in the bible and on the place of the blessing in the communion service. In the Old Testament reading the author of Genesis establishes the rainbow as a sign of God's goodwill towards his people. In the New Testament reading Paul prays that the peace of God might be with the church in Philippi, and in the Gospel reading Jesus bequeaths peace to his disciples.

The biblical concept of blessing
Tracing the concept of blessing through the bible, Alan Richardson, *A Theological Word Book of the Bible*, (SCM 1950, p. 33) writes,

> In the Bible blessing means primarily the active outgoing of the divine goodwill or grace which results in prosperity and happiness amongst men. In the OT this prosperity or blessedness is usually measured in material things – long life, increase in family, crops and herds, peace, wealth (Gen 1:22, Deut 33:11, 2 Sam 6:11 etc.); but in the Wisdom writers wisdom itself is the chief result of the divine blessing (Proverbs); righteousness and peace are held to be the marks of the coming Messianic blessedness on the part of the later apocalyptic writers. Jesus gives a much more profound and spiritual connotation to the idea of blessedness in the Beatitudes (Matthew 5:2–12) and elsewhere. Even when blessing is pronounced by men it is to be understood that it is a divine blessing that is imparted, because such men stand near to God, as in the case of the priestly orders (Lev 9:22) or in that of saintly individuals (Gen 48:14ff).

The blessing after communion
In Rite A the blessing is optional, although the following section, the dismissal is mandatory. Colin Buchanan in *Anglican Worship Today*, (Collins 1980, p. 143) argues that the movement of the communion service is not towards 'a great verbal climax with a solemn blessing but, if anything, is moving away from the high point of communion to a simple departure into the everyday world'. It is this departure which the dismissal emphasises.

Read Genesis 9:8–17 (The flood subsides)
    Genesis 9 is God's blessing of the new age which follows on after the Flood and after destruction. God promises to bless the world and to establish a new covenant between himself and mankind. This Old Testament concept

of covenant is probably derived from the political arrangements made between neighbouring groups of people. Usually it is an arrangement devised by the stronger to establish the behaviour of the weaker tribe. In Old Testament theology the covenant is the formal relationship between God and his people based on the notion that God expects certain things from his people in return for his favour, protection and blessing. The rainbow is to be a sign of this covenant. S. R. Driver, *The Book of Genesis*, (Methuen 1911, p. 99) writes,

> As the rainbow appears, when a storm is passing by . . . it is interpreted as an emblem, to a religious mind, of God's returning friendliness and grace, and made a symbol of the mercy with which he regards all mankind. The marvel of the phenomenon, to people ignorant of the optical laws by which it was produced, led many ancient nations to seek imaginative or symbolical explanations of it. Thus, with the Indians, it is the war-bow of Indra, which he has laid aside after finishing his contest with the demons.

In the poetry of ancient Greece 'it is the bright and swift messenger of the gods'. In the myths of Iceland 'it is the bridge, built by the gods, connecting heaven and earth'. The distinctive point about the use of the rainbow in Genesis 9 is the way in which the OT takes a natural phenomenon and makes it speak about God's relationship with men.

Read John 14:23–27 (The peace which Jesus gives)

William Temple, *Readings in St John's Gospel*, (Macmillan paperback 1961, p. 238) writes that peace

> was the ordinary term of greeting or farewell. But on the lips of Jesus it meant something special. That special gift is his bequest; *peace I leave with you, the peace that is mine I give to you*. He is in the toils of a traitor; his enemies are gathering to destroy him; and he speaks of *the peace that is mine*. It is an inward peace, independent of circumstances, springing from his union with the Father. That it is which he bequeathes, and which can be ours by his gift if we will receive it. *Not as the world giveth do I give to you*. How does the world give? The immediate reference is to the words of salutation, 'I give you peace', which can be no more than a good wish. Christ's bequest of peace is effectual, and actually bestows a permanent possession.

☐ **WORSHIP**

Lord God,
you gave to your servant Noah
   the sign of the rainbow
   as an assurance of your blessing.

Give to your servants now
the gift of your blessing
   in the sign of your peace
   and the assurance of your presence;
through Jesus Christ our Lord.   Amen.

First reading: Genesis 9:8–17
Second reading: Philippians 4:6–9
Gospel reading: John 14:23–27

Teaching material

CONTEXT OF UNIT 30

The Blessing pronounces God's continued favour towards mankind and reminds us of the covenant relationship which he has established with his people. In the Old Testament the story of Noah provides an archetypal model of God's covenant and blessing. The emphasis in the story is not on the destruction of the bad but on the way in which God calls out the faithful and enables them to respond effectively and creatively to his call to establish the kind of life he envisages for his creation.

For this to be meaningful to the child three things are necessary

1 The child needs to be familiar with the biblical tradition of the covenant with Noah. He needs to be able to see this story as portraying God's relationship with mankind, not necessarily as conveying historical information.
2 The child needs to be able to recognise in his own world the continued signs of God's presence and goodwill.
3 The child needs to experience the blessing in the service as a reaffirmation of God's continuing favour.

OBJECTIVES

1 To enable the child to understand the covenant with Noah as a model of God's relationship with man.
2 To concentrate the child's attention specifically upon the symbols of the dove, the olive branch and the rainbow as symbols of peace and God's covenant.
3 To study the progression of the seasons as a symbol of God's goodwill (Genesis 8:22).
4 To examine the seasonal blessings provided by Rite A and to distinguish their individual contributions.

■ **DISPLAY WORK**

Begin by encouraging the children to talk about the story of Noah.

1 Create a large model of the Ark, Noah's family and the animals. Animals can be made in a great number of ways, including cardboard shapes, paper origami, plaster and clay, fabric and knitted work, wood, straw, etc.

2 Produce a series of murals relating the progression of the story of the flood and the establishment of the covenant.

3 Make a large rainbow and fix it high on the wall, or across the chancel arch.

4 Make mobiles of the dove and olive branch.

5 Make costumes/head-dresses to represent Noah's family and the animals. For example, animal faces can be painted or cut out from cardboard to be worn with a headband by the children.

6 Study the use made of the rainbow in myths and stories. Study the way in which light is refracted to produce the rainbow. Make a careful note of the order of the colours. Produce a project book on 'The rainbow' including both the scientific and the mythological aspects. Help the children to see that the mythological and the scientific interpretations are not contradictory alternatives, but complementary to each other.

7 Begin by talking about the seasons. Make sets of murals showing the different seasons and incorporating a rainbow in each. Link the pictures with the text from Genesis 8:22. There are two different ways in which this could be achieved. The same scene can be produced as it looks at different times of the year. This might be easier for children living in country areas where the seasons are much more obvious, but even the city centre changes with the seasons. Alternatively, four different scenes can be taken to show how the child thinks differently about the four seasons,
   a) winter scene of snow around the supermarket and Christmas tree
   b) spring scene of trees and flowers
   c) a summer scene at the seaside
   d) an autumn scene of falling leaves

8 Encourage the children to look at the alternative blessings in the ASB. Talk about the occasions for which each of these blessings are designed. Plan a series of murals to accompany each alternative blessing and incorporate the actual text; for example, appropriate pictures might be

Advent	John the Baptist
Christmas	Stable, the Manger, shepherds, etc.
Epiphany	The wise men
Holy Week	The three crosses
Easter	The empty tomb
Ascension	The disciples waiting with Jesus on the mountain
Pentecost	The disciples in the Upper Room

Once again these murals can be linked with the common symbol of the dove or rainbow.

ACTIVITIES

1 Experiment with light and glass to see how the rainbow is produced.

2 Produce a play or dance about the Noah story. Encourage the children to enter into the experience of being caught in a flood and waiting for the waters to go down: then the experience of rescue and safety.

3 Listen to at least part of Benjamin Britten's 'Noye's Fludde' – or perhaps even produce the cantata itself.

4 Visit a zoo to take a closer look at some of the animals of which models are being made for the Ark.

WRITING

1 Encourage the children to write a story about the day they were rescued from a flood.

2 Write to someone explaining the picture on pages 60–1 of the children's book.

3 Write a story about the four seasons of the year.

DISPLAY HEADINGS

Useful headings for displaying with the work produced in the course of this unit are

1 God makes a covenant with Noah
2 When we see the rainbow we remember God's covenant
3 The dove and the olive branch are symbols of peace and of God's good-will
4 The Seasonal Blessings are for special times in the Church's year
5 God is faithful to the covenant he makes with us
6 God's Blessing is with us always

A short explanation might run, 'The Blessing pronounces God's favour and goodwill. We are reminded of the covenant he made with Noah and his promise to bless his people.'

The Lord is Here or *At the Lord's Table* open at pages 60–1 can be displayed also.

31. DISMISSAL

A helping hand

Go in peace to love and
serve the Lord.

**In the name of Christ.
Amen.**

Background material

☐ **TEXT**

The Rite A Holy Communion Service ends with the Dismissal. The Dismissal is made up of two parts:

1 The president commissions the people to 'Go in peace to love and serve the Lord'.
2 The people respond that they will do so in the name of Christ.

The Dismissal emphasises that worship leads on naturally to the Christian's daily life in the world. Worship is not something isolated from the rest of life, but something that determines the way in which the whole of life is lived.

☐ **PICTURE**

The picture echoes the words of the Dismissal. People are coming out of the church. The Eucharist complete, they come out into the world with a new sense of joy – for they come in the name of the Lord. Some are seen to be lingering to talk with each other. Others are making their way home. In the background children are playing and flying kites. Against the background of Unit 9, kites remind us of the presence of God the Holy Spirit active in his church in the world.

COMMENT

In this section David Head comments on Christian service. Then Mother Teresa of Calcutta and St Teresa of Avila speak about seeing Christ in today's world. In the Old Testament and the New Testament readings the point is made that genuine religion is characterised by acts of benevolence. In the Gospel reading Jesus sends his twelve disciples out to continue his work of teaching and healing.

Christian Service

David Head, *Seek a City Saint*, (Epworth 1965, p. 73) argues that to serve the Christ is to serve him in the world. The Christian of today needs to be aware of the way in which his Christian faith can distinctively change his attitude to the world. Our faith needs to inform our attitude to our job and leisure:

> Many of the services once begun and carried out by the churches have been taken over by government and secular service agencies. Certainly in health and education, social welfare and youth work, Christians have great possibilities and obligations in our day. They can, because of their faith and outlook, turn what might be impersonal service into truly personal service through a consciousness of the saving presence of Christ. The city saint is also involved in the needs of the community through leisure-time activity. Unless he and many like him are prepared to make themselves available to people in special need, many in the city will be neglected and the wide needs of people throughout the world unmet. He may do this within voluntary organisations, or in less formal ways. With increased leisure, and the promise of much more to come, people have a growing responsibility for one another . . . Do you sometimes go to bed remembering someone who would really have welcomed a visit and now must wait?

Christ in today's world

In Malcolm Muggeridge's study *Something Beautiful for God*, (Collins 1971, p. 99) Mother Teresa of Calcutta uses these words to describe her work:

> This is what we are aiming at, to bring to the people the willing hands to serve and the hearts to go on loving them, and to look at them as Christ.

St Teresa of Avila wrote:

> Christ has
> no body now on earth but yours;
> no hands but yours;
> no feet but yours;
> yours are the eyes
> through which is to look out Christ's compassion to the world;
> yours are the feet
> with which he is to go about doing good;
> yours are the hands
> with which he is to bless men now.

Read James 1:22–27 (True religion)

R. R. Williams, *The Letters of John and James*, (CUP 1965, p. 108) writes that according to James

> the pure religion that is acceptable with God is marked by practical kindness – going *to the help of orphans and widows in their distress* (verse 27) – and personal purity – *keeping oneself untarnished by the world* (verse 27). The first of these two features is in line with the prophets' teaching that the unprotected members of the community are a special responsibility to those who wish to obey God's commands. In this book *the world* is used much as it is in the Johannine letters (e.g. 1 John 2:15: 'Anyone who loves the world is a stranger to the Father's love'). It means human society in so far as it is alien to God's will and purpose.

Read Mark 6:7–13) (The mission of the twelve)

The dismissal identifies us with the twelve disciples when Jesus sent them out to heal and to preach. Denis Nineham, *St Mark*, (Penguin 1963, pp. 167–8):

> No doubt Mark understood the incident as the foundation event on which all subsequent Christian missionary activity was based. The twelve were appointed in chapter 3 *to be with Jesus* (3:14) and also *to be sent out to preach and have authority to cast out demons*. They have now spent their period of preparation with Jesus, hearing his words (4:1–34) and witnessing his mighty works (4:35—6:6), and the time has come for them to take an active ministry, both by words and works . . . The instructions belong essentially to Palestine and presuppose the conditions to be found there. In the missionary circumstances of St Mark's time and place they have lost a great deal of their relevance, and even their practicability; St Paul, for example, could never have carried through his immense missionary journeys had he remained faithful to the letter of these commandments.

WORSHIP

Lord Jesus Christ,
you teach us to serve you by helping others.
Make us more aware of the needs of others,
    and less aware of our own needs.
Make us willing to do more for others,
    and not to expect something in return.
We make our prayer in your name.   Amen.

First reading: Isaiah 58:6–7
Second reading: James 1:22–27
Gospel reading: Mark 6:7–13

Teaching material

CONTEXT OF UNIT 31

The Dismissal brings the service to an end. It commissions the worshippers to set their faith to work, to put their religion into practice and to serve Christ in the world. It is necessary for every Christian to work out what this means in practice for him or herself. The implications of the Dismissal stretch into every aspect of life. They influence both what the Christian decides to do, and the attitude with which he or she does everything.

In order for the child to be able to see how the claims of Christ extend into the whole of his or her life five things are necessary:

1 The child needs to be familiar with the teaching of the Gospels regarding the life style expected by Christ.

2 The child needs to explore the way in which the claims of Christ have influenced other people.

3 The child needs to experience contact with a community in which the claims of Christ are taken seriously.

4 The child needs to be aware of the opportunity within his own community for expressing his own commitment to Christ.

5 The child needs to explore the relationship between doing things for others and praying for others.

OBJECTIVES

1 To help the child to become familiar both with the Gospel's examples of Jesus himself helping others and the Gospel's teaching regarding the claims of Jesus on his followers.

2 To enable the child to study the lives of some famous people who have served Christ in the world.

3 To help the child to see how members of his own church have served the needs of others in the past, and how they continue to do so today.

4 To help the child to identify the needs in his own community regarding which he can make some contribution in the name of Christ.

5 To help the child to see the relationship between doing things for other people and praying for them.

6 To help the child to think about the influence the claims of Christ have on people choosing the kind of job they do, etc.

■ DISPLAY WORK

1 Begin by talking about the voluntary organisations in the child's own community, and why people give their time to these groups, e.g. the Womens' Royal Voluntary Service, St John's Ambulance, Red Cross, meals on wheels, prison visiting, youth clubs, scouts/guides. If some of the children belong to a local scout or guide group begin by exploring that particular group and the people who give their time to run it – for example, produce a mural or a model of a scout camp. From this basis develop murals or models of other helping groups and link them with the title 'Helping Hands in Ambridge'.

2 Study one or two voluntary organisations in depth, for example examine what is involved in the local meals on wheels service. Discuss who organises it locally, the people who work it, where the meals are cooked, how people are able to benefit from the service, etc.

3 Encourage the children to talk about the way they help others. It is necessary to avoid the danger of letting it seem that serving Jesus can become synonymous with helping mummy. Develop the child's own experience of spotting the needs of others and responding to them. Develop the idea of praying for the people whom we also help. The work can be organised under the title 'Helping Hands in Class 4'.

4 Make available to the children information about some famous people who have served Christ in different ways. Encourage them to produce a class book 'Helping Hands of Famous People' each contributing pictures and words about one famous life.

5 Discover whether there are any well-known people in local history who are remembered for their services to others – for example, by founding a charity or alms house, establishing a school or hospital or fire service, by caring for those in need or risking their lives to save others. Develop a project around this person. For example, if he founded a school make a model of it.

6 Discover the way in which in the Gospels Jesus helps others. Invite the children to select one story and to prepare it for a project book 'Jesus' Helping Hands'. The book might include the healing miracles from St Mark:

1:30–31	healing Simon's mother in law
1:40–42	healing the leper
2:6–12	healing the paralysed man
3:1–6	healing a man with a withered arm
5:1–17	healing Legion
5:21–24,35–43	healing Jairus' daughter
5:25–34	healing the woman with haemorrhage
7:32–37	healing a deaf and dumb person
8:22–26	healing a blind man

7 Look at passages in the Gospels which present teaching about Christian service and invite the children to copy a few texts for the display board:

Luke 3:10–14	the teaching of John the Baptist
Matthew 5:1—7:29	the Sermon on the Mount
Matthew 25:34–40 and Mark 9:33–37	serving Christ in others
Mark 12:28–34	the great commandments

8 Talk about the people in the local community who might need help. Encourage the children to care for them and to pray for them (perhaps writing about them on the intercession board).

ACTIVITIES

1 Invite to talk to the children one or two local people whose faith in Christ has influenced
   a) their choice of job or the way they do their job
   b) their contribution to voluntary organisations.

2 Encourage the children to develop short plays about famous Christian people.

3 Encourage the children to help with the meals on wheels service and to talk with the people to whom the meals are taken.

4 Encourage the children to see ways in which they can help the community in which they live. For example, perhaps the elderly are given cards to place in their windows if they need help. Help to establish links between the children and the elderly who cannot come to church, perhaps simply to tell them what is happening in their church.

5 Visit a place associated with a famous person noted for Christian service and study that person.

■ **WRITING**

1 Ask the children to write the life story of a famous Christian who served Christ by helping others.

2 Ask the children to write a letter to a friend in another country explaining how people in their own church serve Christ in the local community.

■ **DISPLAY HEADINGS**

Useful headings for displaying with the work produced in the course of this Unit are

1 Jesus taught his followers to serve him by helping others
2 We have studied a few of the many people who have served Christ by helping others
3 Many people need our help every day
4 Helping hands in Ambridge
5 Helping hands in Class 4

A short explanation might run like this, 'The Communion Service ends with the Dismissal. The Dismissal tells us to go into the world and to set our faith to work.'

The Lord is Here or *At the Lord's Table* open at pages 62–3 can be displayed also.